The Natural Healing Handbook

Natural Treatments for Pain, Stress Sleep & Hormone Health

ISBN: 978-2-8447-3840-0

Table of Contents

Introduction

Welcome to "The Lost Book of Natural Herbal Remedies," an immersive journey into the rich and often forgotten world of healing plants and natural remedies. In our modern age, dominated by pharmaceuticals and synthetic solutions, it is easy to overlook the wisdom and power inherent in nature's own apothecary. This book aims to reconnect you with the healing properties of plants, trees, mushrooms, and other natural resources that have been used for centuries to promote health and well-being.

We begin with the fundamental principles of identifying, harvesting, and preparing plants for medicinal use, ensuring that you capture their maximum therapeutic benefits while respecting and preserving nature. You'll discover that many of these powerful remedies can be found right in your own backyard, where common plants such as dandelions, mint, and other everyday greenery hold a treasure trove of healing properties.

As we venture further, we explore the diverse flora of forests, scrublands, and woodlands, uncovering the unique medicinal properties of plants that thrive in these wild environments. From the soothing balm of forest herbs to the invigorating essence of scrubland shrubs, these natural resources offer potent solutions for a variety of ailments.

Trees and shrubs, often seen as merely part of the landscape, reveal their medicinal secrets in the next section. You will learn about the healing powers of various species, such as the pain-relieving bark of the willow tree and the immune-boosting berries of the elder. These perennial plants are a robust source of natural remedies that have been used for generations.

The fascinating world of mushrooms and lichens is next, where we delve into the potent healing properties of these often-overlooked organisms. With insights into their medicinal uses, you will learn how to safely incorporate them into your health regimen, benefiting from their unique bioactive compounds.

Water-loving plants, with their distinctive growing environments, offer a different spectrum of healing properties. This section explores the benefits of aquatic plants, revealing how they can be utilized to address various health concerns, from skin conditions to digestive issues.

Finally, the book concludes with practical applications, focusing on how to create effective household remedies. This section empowers you to use the knowledge gained from the previous chapters to treat common ailments and enhance your overall well-being with natural solutions. You'll learn to craft salves, teas, tinctures, and other remedies that harness the healing power of nature.

Throughout "The Lost Book of Natural Herbal Remedies," you will find a wealth of knowledge that bridges ancient traditions with modern understanding. By the end of this book, you will not only have a deeper appreciation for the natural world but also a comprehensive guide to harnessing its healing power. Embrace the journey and rediscover the natural remedies that lie all around us, reconnecting with the time-honored practices that have sustained human health for millennia.

How to Harness the Healing Properties of Plants

When compared to the timeline of human history, modern medicine hasn't been around that long. Medicine has a much longer history than the modern pharmaceutical industry. Humankind has used medicines for thousands of years. But the medicines used before our modern knowledge of science were natural medicines, making use of the medicinal qualities of what nature provides for us.

The herbal medicines that have always existed still work today, just as they have throughout history. What was once our sole medicine still exists, even though the number of people who have knowledge of these natural remedies has dwindled. It is our hope that this book will help you relearn and pass on this lost knowledge.

Herbal medicine is often scoffed at by the pharmaceutical industry and yet it is the grandparent of much of that same modern medicine. Many of today's pharmaceuticals try to replicate what nature provides. Most of what we call "medicines" are artificial creations that have been slightly chemically altered from nature. This is necessary, as patent laws don't permit filing a patent on something that exists naturally. Thus, the large pharmaceutical labs have to come up with a suitable alternative and many of their products have serious side effects. This isn't to say that modern-day medicine and herbal medicine can't coexist. They can. But many new medicines can be easily replaced by herbs at a fraction of the cost and risk – to both our wallets and our bodies.

In a post-apocalyptic world, these herbal medicines may be the only thing available to us. If modern manufacturing and distribution methods become unavailable, we will have to rely on what can be grown locally.

One of the advantages of growing and using your own herbs, as opposed to buying herbal supplements at the local health food store, is that you know how fresh they are and how they've been grown. The sooner you can prepare and store your herbs for use, often the more potent they are. At the same time, you will know exactly what is in any herbal mixture that you create, giving you the peace of mind that there are no additives or fillers, and only the herbs you want and need.

How to Harvest Herbs

All herbal medicines start as living beings. They are not always what most people traditionally think of as herbs. Medicines come from trees, flowers, roots, mushrooms, lichens, and more. While those who are interested in herbal medicines tend to grow an herb garden, some are harvested from plants that grow in the wild. It is a useful skill to learn how to identify medicine in the wild.

When looking at pictures for plant identification, be sure to look at pictures that depict plants in the various stages of their life cycle. A good plant identification guide for your area is essential.

Many people know flower identification; but when the plants are not in flower, they can't identify them. Considering how short the flowering season is for most plants, that severely limits the amount of time for harvest.

Before even thinking about harvesting herbs, it is necessary to understand how the herb will be used; specifically, what part of the plant will be used for medicinal purposes. Never assume that the whole plant carries the same chemical compounds. Often, only the leaves or the flower will provide what you need; but in some cases, it will be the bark of a tree or a piece of root that you will need to harvest.

It is best to harvest herbs early in the day, after the dew has gone, but before the hot sun can dry out the essential oils. Whenever possible, avoid harvesting the whole plant, unless it is a plant that needs to be collected whole. If you are harvesting leaves you will usually cut off small branches, making it easier to dry them. For flowers, wait until they develop fully and harvest them as soon as possible after they have fully opened. If you are harvesting only the seeds, you'll need to wait until the seeds mature and the seed pod dries on the stem before harvesting. We give harvesting instructions for almost every herb in this book.

How to Dry Herbs

Traditionally, herbs are air-dried without the use of any additional heat source. Bundle them together by tying the stems with string or a rubber band and hang in a warm, dry place. It is usually easiest to hang them upside-down by the bundled stems to dry.

Drying racks may be used for individuals who are drying a lot of herbs or doing so regularly. But you can accomplish the same thing by hanging them from a coat hanger, a nail in the wall or on a curtain rod over the window. I often spread flowers or leaves on a cookie sheet or pizza pan and let them dry.

If you are collecting the seeds, tie a paper bag over the bundled stems and hang them. The bag will catch the seeds as the seed pods dry and they fall out.

Drying in this manner can take as long as three weeks (though is often accomplished much faster) depending on the plant and its moisture content.

If you are drying something that dries extremely slowly, like rosemary, it is easier to strip the leaves off of the stems and spread them on a drying rack, as the coating of the leaves will hold in the moisture. They need to be fully dry before storing.

It is possible to dry herbs with a dehydrator if you have one of the better ones that has temperature control. Ideally, it should have a fan to circulate the warm air, allowing the entire batch to dry evenly. To avoid singing or burning the herbs you are drying, you'll need to use the lowest possible temperature. I have used this method successfully many times. If using a dehydrator, it is very important to keep a close eye on your herbs so that you don't leave them to dry too long.

Once dried, remove the leaves from the stems. In the case of smaller leaves, you can strip them from the stem by lightly pinching the stem between your thumb and forefinger and running it down the stem, from top to bottom.

However, in the case of larger leaves with thicker stems, you will need to cut or pinch them off individually, cutting the stems as near the leaf as possible.

Store your dried herbs in sealed glass jars until you are ready to use them.

Encapsulating Powdered Herbs

If you go to the health food store to buy herbs, you'll often find them offered in powdered form, encapsulated. This is a convenient way to store and use herbs, especially if you are using them with people who are unaccustomed to taking herbal remedies.

There are two ways of encapsulating your herbs, but to start you need to turn the herbs into powder. This is most easily done by grinding them in a food processor or electric coffee mill. If you want to go for a more traditional method or are trying to encapsulate them during a time when there is no electrical power, use a mortar and pestle. If you are going to make any sort of herbal mix, you'll need a scale to measure out your various herbs. Be sure to mix the powdered herbs well, so that your capsules all have the same herbal concentration.

Capsules come in three sizes; "0," "00" and "000." They can be filled by hand or with the aid of a simple filling machine.

The least expensive method is to fill them by hand. To start, put the powder in an oversized bowl. Open the capsules individually by hand, and scoop up the powder in both sides of the capsule, trying to get them reasonably full. Then push the sides of the capsule together. The powder will compress as the capsule slides closed.

This is a very boring and time-consuming operation, although effective. You might want some company or some assistance while doing this task.

Capsule Filling Machines

For a slightly more efficient operation, you can buy a simple capsule-filling machine. These are available in 50 or 100 capsule sizes and must be bought to match the size capsules you are using. The machine consists of several plates, which have holes to hold the capsule halves and a base.

Separate the capsules, putting the two parts into separate bowls. The thinner, longer part goes into the base plate on the machine. There is a funnel-like device used to fill this plate. Simply place the funnel over the base plate and pour a quantity of the capsule halves onto it. Shake the machine, until the capsule halves fall into the holes in the plate, ready to be filled. The same basic operation is done with the top plate.

The part of the capsules that is in the bottom plate is the part being filled. Pour a quantity of the powdered herbs onto this plate and move it around with the supplied scraper, allowing it to fill the capsules. Once filled, remove any extra powder by scraping it off.

To close the now-filled capsules, place the top plate over the bottom one. The machine will have aligning pins to ensure that the two halves of the capsules are aligned. Then push down on the plates, several times, seating the capsules. Remove your finished capsules and put them in a jar for storage.

Herbal Water Infusions: Cold and Hot Methods

Tea and coffee are both infusions; usually hot infusions. Cold versions of these drinks are often still infused hot, and then chilled in the refrigerator or with ice; however it is possible to make cold infused coffee and tea; the process is just slower. This cold-infusion process takes time.

The properties of the herbs are simply extracted from the leaves or beans into the water. This same process can be used with just about any herb.

The typical means of hot infusing herbs is to make a tea out of it. Herbal teas can be made from individual herbs, but it is more common to use a mixture of herbs that work well to treat the condition you are seeking to heal.

The advantage of hot infusion over cold is that it often extracts more of the essential ingredients from the plant tissue. The heat breaks down cell walls, creating a stronger infusion. On the other hand, a hot infusion may also extract ingredients that are not desirable, such as those that give the infusion a bitter flavor. In that case, a cold infusion may be better. Mucilaginous herbs tend to extract better cold, leaving the mucilage intact. Some common herbs we do cold infusions with are lemon balm, marshmallow, slippery elm, and comfrey.

Sun tea is probably the most common "cold" infusion made. Leave the herbs loose (and strain later) or put the crushed leaves in a cheesecloth or muslin bag (you can find these sold as reusable tea bags) and tie it to the top of your jar or cup. For tea, most people simply use 1 to 2 teaspoons of dried herb to 8 ounces (250ml) of water. Moisten dried herbs before putting them in the cold infusion – this is not necessary for fresh herbs.

Leave the cold infusion for at least 48 hours to fully extract the beneficial compounds from the herbs.

Teas

Herbal tea is a very common way that herbs are used for medicinal purposes. As mentioned above, an herbal tea is a "hot infusion," which works extremely well to extract the beneficial components from many herbs. Hot infusions can be made in a matter of minutes, unlike cold infusions, which take longer.

Teas can be made from either fresh or dried herbs, producing different results. Each particular herb will react differently whether it is dry or fresh, so you will want to know what is recommended for that herb or for that herbal mixture.

Decoctions

A decoction is a concentrated form of a hot infusion or tea. This can be an extremely useful method for herbs that don't give up their beneficial chemicals easily or for woody parts or roots. It is also a great way of creating a more concentrated form of an herbal supplement, and for use with children, animals, or anyone else who it is unlikely to drink enough of a hot infusion to do them any good.

To make a decoction, start with cold distilled or purified water. Cold water is important, to help ensure you extract the maximum amount of beneficial nutrients from the herbs. It is best to make your decoction in an earthenware, glass, or glazed ceramic cooking pot, so that you don't end up with the metal pots reacting to the astringent herbs, affecting the final flavor.

Use a ratio of 1 oz.(28g) of dried herbs per 16 ounces (500ml) of water. Decoctions are normally made in a quantity that can be used within a couple of days, as they don't keep well in the refrigerator for more than three days. If you do need to keep one for more than three days, keep it in a tightly sealed container or freeze them (ice cube trays work well). You may also add two tablespoons of alcohol (like vodka, rum, or brandy) per cup (8oz) for better preservation.

1. Crush, chop or grind the herbs, as appropriate, into small pieces and place them in the cold water in your cooking pot.
2. Allow the herbs to cold soak for a few hours.
3. Cover the pot and bring to a slow boil. Once the water is boiling, reduce the heat to a simmer.
4. Keep simmering until the volume of liquid has been reduced to ½ of what you started with (about 15-20 minutes).
5. Strain (cheesecloth works well). Once cooled, squeeze the herbs left behind, to ensure that you have removed all the liquid from them.
6. Pour the decoction into a jar with a lid for storage. Use within 48 hours or freeze.

Decoctions contain four times more medicine than a tea. Adults in good health can take up to 1 cup of a decoction, three times per day, depending on the herb. Children's dosages should be cut, based upon their weight.

Double Decoctions: Double Decoctions are the same as decoctions, with the exception that they are simmered until the final volume equals ¼ of the original volume of liquid, increasing your final medicinal concentration. Adults should only take 1 TB of a double decoction and children up to ½ tsp for most herbs.

Double decoctions are especially useful when decocting shredded bark and dried roots, where the useful compounds come out of the herbs slowly. When working with these herbs, allow them to soak for 12 hours in cold water before bringing it to a boil and simmering.

Oil Infusions

The hot and cold infusion methods outlined below are used to infuse herbs into oil. For cold extractions in oil, cold actually means at room temperature. This method takes time. It takes 6 to 8 weeks to infuse herbs into a carrier oil using only time. The "hot" method is actually a "warm" method of extracting herbs into a carrier oil. Some herbs need the heat to extract and this method also shortens the amount of time needed if you need the remedy sooner. Be careful not to boil or overheat the oil, as this alters the chemical compounds of the herbal properties you are extracting.

Carrier Oils and "Cold" & "Hot" Infusions: To cold-infuse oil use only dried herbs to start (with a few exceptions), as moisture can make your oil turn rancid or mold. Many carrier oils will work. I prefer organic olive oil as it is temperature stable, well-priced, and works well for salve-making. It is important to purchase organic oils from somewhere with strict labeling laws (like California). Other good carrier oils are sweet almond oil, coconut oil (although it changes consistency with temperature), jojoba oil, baobab oil, tamanu oil, castor oil, grapeseed oil, argan oil, avocado oil, apricot kernel oil, emu oil, and many more. Rendered fat or tallow, like bear fat, can also be used.

"Cold" Oil Infusion:

1. Tear or crush the dried herbs then lightly pack into a clean, sterilized glass jar. Fill a glass jar 1/3rd full with dried herb (for some herbs, like cottonwood buds, I fill it well over half-full).
2. Pour your high-quality organic olive oil (or other natural plant oil) over the herbs. Fill to within ½ inch (1.25 cm) of the top with your carrier oil. Mix well, removing all air bubbles. Cap and label with herb and date.
3. Store your jar for 6 to 8 weeks. Make sure you don't go longer than 8 to 10 weeks or your oil may go rancid (cottonwood buds are an exception to this). I often kickstart certain herbs with a little heat by placing my glass jars in a water bath on low for a day or two and then storing for 6 to 8 weeks.
4. After 6 to 8 weeks strain out the herbs using cheesecloth or a tincture press. Squeeze the cheesecloth to get all of the herbal oil out. Pour into a clean, sterile bottle or jar. This oil can be used directly for medicine or for making salves. Lasts about 1 to 2 years.

"Hot" Oil Infusion: To infuse oils using heat use a crock pot that has a "warm" or very low setting or use a water bath on low on the stovetop. This works well for infusing several oils at once.

1. Tear or crush the dried herbs then lightly pack into a clean, sterilized glass jar. Fill a glass jar 1/3rd full with dried herb (for some herbs, like cottonwood buds or *Usnea*, I fill it over half-full).

2. Pour your high-quality organic olive oil (or other natural plant oil) over the herbs. Fill to within ½ inch (1.25 cm) of the top with your carrier oil. Mix well, removing all air bubbles. Cap and label with herb and date.
3. Place your glass jars in the crock pot and cook on low for 4 to 7 days, depending on the herb, making sure the water in your water bath/crock pot stays full. If you are using fresh herbs leave the caps off the jars letting the moisture evaporate out and make sure no water gets in from your water bath.
4. Once cooled, strain herbs using cheesecloth or a tincture press. Pour into a clean, sterile bottle or jar. This oil can be used directly for medicine or for making salves. Lasts about 1 to 2 years.

Salve-making

Salves are a useful way of applying herbs to the skin. They are useful for treating burns, rashes, skin irritations, bites, wounds, eczema, sore muscles, arthritis, nerve pain, and more. Turning herbal oil infusions into salves provides a good way to apply herbs and to take them with you when not at home.

In order to make a salve, you have to already have turned the herbs into an infused oil . You may also use the "fast method" below:

The quickest method for making herbal salves com-bines the infusion and salve-mixing steps into one. It uses a lot of dried herb. Combine your herbs and enough oil to cover the herbs in the top of a double-boiler being sure there is water in the bottom half of your double boiler. Simmer for a few hours (don't over-heat – about 100 degrees). Stir, cool slightly, and strain through cheesecloth. Pour back into your double-boiler and add melted beeswax (about 1/4 cup to 1/5 cup per cup of oil) to the oil. Then add 15 to 20 drops or more of each of your essential oils for every 8 oz of oil. Vitamin E can be added to help rancidity. Mix well, pour into containers, and let set.

To make a simple salve out of your infused oil and beeswax:

1. Measure and pour your infused oil(s) into the top part of a double boiler.
2. Add beeswax and melt. I usually use a 1 part bees-wax to 4 parts infused oil mixture and common us-age is 1/4 cup to 1/5 cup per cup of oil. For 8 oz (250ml) of oil I use 2 oz (48g) of beeswax.
3. Mix together thoroughly until the beeswax has melted.
4. Add 15 to 20 drops or more of each of your essential oils for every 8 oz (250ml) of infused oil. Vitamin E can be added to help rancidity (1/2 tsp for 16 oz (250ml) oil). Add essential oils just before pouring.
5. Before you pour into your containers (jars/tins) to set you may add just a few drops to your container to test the consistency. If it's too hard add more oil and if it's too soft add more beeswax. Then complete pouring, label, and date.

Tinctures/Extracts

Tinctures are medicinal extracts of any herb or herbal concoction in an alcohol, vinegar, or glycerin base. Because alcohol is a universal solvent, it is usually able to extract the essential oils from herbs, as well as extract most of the other chemical compounds that water is able to extract (note that some herbs need a double-extraction in water and alcohol to access all of the medicinal compounds).

But alcoholic tinctures have another, much more important attribute. They absorb into the body faster than any other means of using herbal medicines. This is due to the alcohol base, which starts absorbing through the stomach wall and even through the mouth upon taking the tincture. Rather than being digested, like other things that are eaten and drunk, the herbs are absorbed right into the bloodstream.

Another benefit of tinctures is that they last virtually forever, as long as they are stored in a well-sealed container. The alcohol is uniformly fatal to any microorganisms might that come into contact with it, so there is no possibility of the tincture decomposing. The big-gest risk is evaporation.

To make a tincture you will need some sort of consumable alcohol that is at least 80 proof (40% alcohol). Vodka is the preferred alcohol to use, because it has no flavor, but rum, gin, brandy, and whiskey will work as well. You can also use apple cider vinegar or food grade vegetable glycerin, although these often don't work as well for many herbs and they don't last as long.

1. Fill a glass jar 1/3 to 1/2 full of the dried herbs you are using for your tincture, but don't pack it down (amount of the herb used depends on the surface area and extractability of the herb). You can also use fresh herbs – use 2x the amount of dried herbs.
2. Fill the jar with the alcohol, leaving ½ inch (1.25 cm) of headspace. Stir well.
3. Close the lid on the jar, label and date, and store in a cool, dry place. Tinctures can take anywhere from 4 weeks up to 6 months to fully extract, depending on the herbs you are using. 2 months works well for most herbs. Shake the jar once a day if possible.
4. Once your tincture is complete, usually around 8 weeks, strain out the herbs and rebottle the finished product. The alcohol renders it very shelf-stable and tinctures can last up to 7 years. Many people put tinctures in dropper bottles for ease of use, but any small glass bottle will work. ½ to 1 teaspoon is a normal dose for adults. For children dosage is about 1/4 to 1/3 of the adult dose, depending on weight.

Double Extractions

A double extraction is a combination of a tincture and a decoction, often used for mushrooms and lichens. In recent years, the medicinal value of various types of mushrooms has been researched heavily. If only a water-based decoction is used with Reishi Mushroom, for example, it extracts the beneficial polysaccharides (including the betaglucans) and the glycoproteins but not the triterpenes (like ganoderic acid in Reishi), as they are not soluble in water. Both water and alcohol are needed to extract all of the medicinal compounds.
For this tincture, alcohol and water are required. There are two methods. Both are below and different herbalists prefer different methods. Final alcohol percentage should be 25% to 30% or higher. The recipes below give you that percentage but you may also start with a higher proof alcohol. If you see cloudiness in your final product that is OK - it is just the polysaccharides coming out of solution. Simply shake before use.

Method #1: Starting with the alcohol ex-traction Feel free to scale down this recipe. You'll need: 8 ounces (224g) or more of dried mushroom or lichen, 24 ounces (750ml) of 80 to 100 proof alcohol (40 to 50 % alcohol), 15 ounces (500ml) distilled water.

1. Fill a quart-sized (1 liter) canning jar half-full with diced dried mushrooms, then fill it to about ½ inch (1.25 cm) of the top with alcohol. Stir and cap it, shaking it every day for 2 months. Then strain out the alcohol and set it aside.
2. Make the decoction. Put 16 ounces (500ml) of water into a ceramic or glass pot with a lid and put the mushrooms into it. Cover and simmer the mixture until half of the water has boiled off. This will take a few hours. If the water level drops too quickly, add more so that you can continue simmering your mushrooms. The end result should be 8 ounces (250ml) of your decoction.
3. Allow the water to cool, and then strain out the mushrooms. Mix the water and alcohol (you should have about 24 oz (710ml) of alcohol tincture) together to create the finished double-extraction. It has a high enough alcohol content (30%) that it should be shelf-stable for many years, as long as it is stored in a sealed container.

Method #2 Starting with the water extraction I like to use a small crockpot for this recipe. You may also place the herbs and water into a jar, which is then covered and placed into a crockpot of water on low or a pot of water on low on the stove. Feel free to scale down this recipe. You'll need: 8 ounces (230g) or more of dried mushroom or lichen, 24 ounces (710ml) of 80 to 100 proof alcohol, 16 ounces (500ml) distilled water.

1. Cut up the herbs into very small pieces. Place the distilled water and the dried herbs into the crock-pot and stir well. Cover and cook on the lowest possible setting for 3 days. It will cook down to about 8 oz (250ml) of medicinal decoction (water).
2. Allow the herb and water mixture to cool and pour it into a large glass jar. Add the alcohol while the mixture is still quite warm, but not hot. Make sure the jar is large enough that you are adding 24 ounces (710ml) of alcohol or split everything evenly between 2 jars.
3. Cap the jar tightly, label and date the jar and allow it to macerate for 6 to 8 weeks, shaking the jar daily.
4. Strain out the herb (cheesecloth works well for this) or carefully decant the tincture off. Store it in tightly capped glass jar. Label and date.

Distillation

Distillation is a process used for extracting essential oils from herbs or other plants. Not all plants provide essential oils; but for those that do, this is one of the surer methods of extracting the essential oil.
Distillation is something that should only be under-taken by someone who wants to make a lot of essential oils, due to the equipment investment and the amount of plant matter you need. The amount of essential oil that is distilled out of plants is very small and it takes a pretty good size still to get enough oil to make the effort worthwhile. You may want to simply purchase organic essential oils from a reputable source to have on hand.

There are three basic types of distillation, requiring mi-nor differences in the still:

- **Water distillation** – The herbs are immersed in water and the water is boiled. This works best for herbs that don't break down easily.
- **Water and steam distillation** – The only difference in the equipment for this and water distillation is the insertion of a rack inside the still, which holds the herbs up out of the water and only allows the steam to have contact with it. This method produces essential oils much more quickly than water distillation.
- **Direct Steam Distillation** – A different sort of still is needed for this method, so that the steam can be created in a separate chamber. The steam is then injected into the retort/still that is holding the herbs, below a rack holding the herbs. This allows a lower temperature to be used, reducing the potential for heat damage to the essential oil. This is the most common method used commercially, especially for essential oils like rosemary and lavender.

Much expertise is needed for distillation as the amount of plant material, distillation times, and temperatures are specific to the still and the herb from which you are trying to extract the essential oil.

Medicinal Syrups

Herbal syrups are a great way of getting children to take herbal medicines and supplements. Made with raw honey, they store extremely well, taste good, and can also soothe a sore throat. Making a medicinal honey syrup for treating colds, sore throats, or the flu will have the added benefit that the raw honey brings.

Before starting, decide how sweet you want your syrup. Some people like a sweeter syrup, using a 1:1 ratio of honey to decoction, while others use a 1:2 ratio, using less honey. The 1:1 ratio will store longer, as honey doesn't spoil easily. You can add glycerin in place of some of the honey to extend shelf-life.

To make any medicinal syrup, start out by making a decoction. You want to end up with a known amount of decoction, so that you'll know how much honey to add. This is easy, as you will need to strain out the herbs before adding the honey. When you do this, measure using a Pyrex glass measuring cup.

Typically, these syrups will last about six months in the refrigerator if you use a 1:2 ratio. You can also extend the life by adding a tincture to the mixture, as the alcohol in the tincture will act as a preservative, or by adding glycerin.

Poultices

Poultices may be one of the oldest ways in which herbal medicines are used. They provide an excellent way of applying healing herbs directly to the afflicted area. Usually used for first-aid field situations, such as dealing with burns, bee stings, cuts, and infections, they are also useful for deeper problems, like joint problems and bruises. They can even be applied to the chest to aid with congestion.

Normally, poultices are made of fresh herbs, picked on the spot. This means that they are at their most potent, able to provide the maximum possible benefit. They are also able to help draw out splinters, bee stingers, and other infection-causing foreign matter that has embedded itself into the skin.

One of the great things about poultices is that they are made on the spot to deal with a specific need. There is little preparation and they are not stored. Rather, they are often made of whatever herbs are readily available at the time. Of course, that requires the ability to recognize those herbs growing in the wild so that they can be harvested and put to use immediately.

How to Make a Poultice: To make a poultice, select the necessary fresh herbs and tear or cut them finely. If you don't have the ability to cut them, crushing them between the fingers will work too. Doctors carried a mortar and pestle in ancient times for this purpose. The idea is to have the leaves broken, so that the sap of the plant can come out, contacting the skin. Chewing also works but make sure the herbs are safe to chew.

A generous quantity of the poultice is applied to the afflicted area of the skin and bound in place with a bandage. Gauze is normally used for this, but an elastic bandage or a large leaf are other options. The poultice must be kept damp to work, so it is usually changed out a couple of times per day.

Poultices can be made from dried herbs as well. In that case, the crushed or chopped herbs are soaked in warm water, softening them so that they won't irritate the skin and to draw out their medicine.

A little fine-tuning can be applied by using either hot or cold water with it. A hot poultice (not hot enough to burn) helps to increase the circulation in the area where it is applied. This can help get the medicinal properties of the herbs to the cells needing it more quickly. Using cold water, on the other hand, reduces circulation, while also reducing swelling.

How to Make a Field Poultice

Poultices have been used as field bandages and dressings for countless generations. In wartime, poultices helped manage many serious traumatic wounds and prevented as well as treated infection.

I have used poultices on both others and myself many times in the field. My most common go-to poultice herbs are Plantain, Yarrow, Mullein, and Usnea. I al-ways carry dried Yarrow and Plantain with me in the winter when these plants are not readily available.

These herbs are all in this book, so rest assured you'll have no problem identifying them. You can use these as single-herb poultices or mix them together. One of my favorites is a plant growing in many back yards and probably yours as well: Plantain (Plantago spp.).

Plantain has a powerful antibacterial effect. It also contains allantoin, which is a phytochemical (a chemical found in plants) that speeds up wound healing and stimulates the growth of new skin cells. Plantain stops bleeding and helps relieve pain and itching. We use it for immediate relief for bites and stings.

Another common poultice herb is the plant known as "The Cowboy's Toilet Paper": Mullein. Mullein works in two different ways to enhance the effects of the plantain already in the poultice.

Mullein is an analgesic and thus lessens the pain, and it works as an astringent as well. That means it will contract your skin and, in doing so, will help close the wound. This plant has the added benefit of being used as, well, toilet paper if you ever run out. It's very soft. Another plant you can use alone or mix into your field poultice is Yarrow. Yarrow is a very strong anti-bacterial and is also a blood coagulant and thus helps stop bleeding.

Usnea Lichen is my other fantastic go-to for applying to a wound. It is very absorbent and has anti-microbial, anti-bacterial, antiviral and anti-fungal properties. It is ready to go as is!

A strong herbal field poultice:

1. Gather plantain, mullein, and yarrow in equal quantities.
2. Grind the leaves together until you get a paste-like mixture. Add clean water if needed.
3. Apply it to your wound or cut.
4. Leave it on for one to two hours; then reapply as needed.
5. Keep the paste in place by using a non-toxic plant that has big leaves and high flexibility or normal bandages if you have some around. Burdock leaves are perfect for this if you don't have normal bandages.

Garden Vegetation

Agrimony, Agrimonia eupatoria

Agrimony, also called sticklewort, cocklebur, or church steeples, is native to Europe and is now found across North America. It is a pretty plant with spikes of tiny yellow flowers. It is in the Rosaceae (Rose) Family.

Identification: This dark green perennial has a rough stem. It is covered with soft hairs that help it spread its seeds. It grows to a height of 2 feet (0.6meters). The leaves are serrated and pinnate. They are large (7 inches) (17.5 cm) at the base and get smaller at the top of the stem. Its roots are deep woody rhizomes. The short-stemmed flowers have a sweet, apricot-like scent. They bloom from June to September on long terminal spikes. Each flower is a cup with rows of hook-shaped bristles on the upper edge. Flowers have five sepals and five yellow, rounded petals, each with 5 to 20 stamens.

The fruit has hooked bristles called cockleburs that attach to animals, thus spreading the seeds.

Edible Use: The leaves are used for tea, and the fresh flowers are often added to home-brewed beer or wine to enhance flavor.

Medicinal Use: Both the leaves and seeds are used in medicinal preparations. It is astringent, anti-inflammatory, and antibacterial.

To Induce Sleep: While lying in bed, place a few of this plant's leaves under your head to induce sleep.

Anti-inflammatory, Wound and Skin Care: Agrimony is effective for wound care. It stops excessive bleeding by promoting the formation of clots. It contains tannins and is an astringent. It also has antibacterial and anti-inflammatory properties. Agrimony tea can be used as a wash for wounds and all types of skin diseases or the fresh leaves can be pounded and applied directly to a wound as a poultice.

Digestive Problems and Diarrhea: Agrimony Tea is used for digestive problems. The tea acts as a tonic to the digestive system and heals underlying problems.

Migraines: An herbal poultice made from fresh agrimony leaves and applied to the head is a good topical treatment for migraines. Use it at night as it may also induce deep sleep.

Conjunctivitis and Eye Infections: For application as an eye wash, mix equal parts of Agrimony Tea with boiled and cooled water.

Harvesting: Harvest agrimony in the late spring to early summer when the herb is in full bloom. Pick the leaves, flowers, and stems. Use the herbs fresh or dry them for later use.

Warning: Some people develop an allergic rash with sun exposure while using agrimony. Do not use if taking anti-coagulant therapy or taking blood-pressure medications. Avoid using agrimony if pregnant or nursing.

Recipes: Agrimony Tea. 1 to 2 teaspoons of powdered agrimony leaves or 3 teaspoons of crushed fresh leaves, 1 cup boiling water, raw honey, to taste, if desired. Steep the agrimony leaves in boiling water for 5 to 10 minutes. Cool and strain. Take one cup, three times daily.

Aloe Vera

Aloe Vera is edible and is incredibly effective for many afflictions. It's not native to North America, but it's been naturalized in many places. I find it readily in the southwest where the weather is warm and it is easy to grow in pots around the house. It is in the Asphodelaceae (Aloe) Family.

Identification: Aloe Vera plants have succulent leaves that grow to 2 to 3 feet (0.6 meters to 0.9 meters) tall. The plant is stemless or has very short stems. Aloe Vera leaves are thick, fleshy, and filled with gelatinous sap. The leaves grow in clumps, and are green to grey-green and may have white flecks on the leaf surfaces. The leaf margins are serrated with small white teeth. Flowers appear in the summer on a tall spike growing from the center of the plant. Flowers range in color from white and yellow to orange and red.

Edible Use: Eat aloe vera leaves raw or cooked. The outer green skin can also be eaten, but is bitter and tough. Removing the skin with a sharp knife leaves the meat and gel inside the plant; both are edible. Aloe is good poached or otherwise gently cooked. Fully cooked, it loses its slimy texture. Some people enjoy raw aloe as juice or by putting a chunk in their water.

Medicinal Use: Aloe Vera gel, the gelatinous substance inside the leaf, is used as a relief for sunburn, wounds, and other minor skin irritations. It also has internal uses.

How to Use Aloe Vera: For external use, split the leaf long ways with a knife and scrape the gel from the leaf's interior. I most often use it as a soothing salve directly on the skin. For internal use, try 1 to 3 ounces (28-85g) of the gel added to juice, since the gel can be unpleasant and bitter when taken alone.

Heartburn Relief and Irritable Bowel Syndrome: Consuming 1 to 3 ounces (28g to 85g) of aloe vera gel with each meal reduces the severity of acid reflux and the associated heartburn. It also helps the cramping, abdominal pain, flatulence, and bloating caused by irritable bowel syndrome. However, there are some safety concerns and it may cause irritation, so use internally with care for these conditions.

Bleeding or Swollen Gums: Aloe Vera extract makes a safe and effective mouthwash that reduces swelling, soothes, and provides relief from bleeding or swollen gums. Try adding the gel to the final rinse water and swishing it around, holding it in the mouth for a minute, then spitting it out.

Lowering Blood Sugar in Diabetics: If you suffer from type 2 diabetes, you can regulate your blood sugar levels by simply ingesting two tablespoons of Aloe Vera juice or pulp extract daily.

Laxative: Aloe Vera gel relieves constipation but should be used sparingly.

Skin Care, Sunburn, Eczema: Aloe gel is soothing on the skin and an excellent remedy for sunburn, skin abrasions, eczema, and other mild skin irritations. It also keeps skin clear and hydrated. Excellent as a moisturizer and pain reliever.

Warning: Long term internal use of Aloe Vera is not recommended due to the latex found in Aloe Vera. Do not use internally while pregnant. Do not use if you have hemorrhoids or kidney issues.

Anise Hyssop, Agastache foeniculum

Anise Hyssop is also known as blue giant hyssop, lavender giant hyssop, elk mint, and licorice mint. It belongs to the Lamiaceae (Mint) Family. It is native to northern and central North America.

Identification: Anise hyssop grows from 2 to 5 feet (0.6 to 1.5m) tall, with bright green leaves that are notched at the edge and covered with fine white hairs on the underside. New growth has a purple tint. The plant has an aroma suggestive of mint and anise. The herb is partially woody with branched and usually hairless stems. The fibrous roots are also branching. Clusters of small lilac-blue flowers appear on elongated flower spikes from July through September.

Edible Use: Anise hyssop can be used as a sweetener and to make tea. It can be used as a flavoring or seasoning. The leaves and flowers can be eaten fresh, cooked, or dried. Medicinal Use. Heart Healthy, Angina Pain: An infusion of anise hyssop is a tonic for the heart and a quick remedy for angina pain.

Sores, Wounds, and Burns: For skin infections, wounds, and burned skin, use a poultice of anise hyssop leaves. Soak dried leaves or bruise fresh leaves and flowers and apply them directly on the affected area. Cover with a clean cloth. Anise hyssop leaves have anti-bacterial and anti-viral properties.

Facilitates Digestion: Drinking Anise Hyssop Tea with meals eases digestion and prevents excessive gas and bloating.

Diarrhea: Anise hyssop tea is helpful in relieving diarrhea. The tea works best if continued throughout the day even after the diarrhea has been successfully eliminated. Continuing to sip occasionally prevents the return of diarrhea.

Sore Muscles and Anxiety: Try gathering 3 to 4 tablespoons of anise hyssop leaves in a square of cheesecloth and hang it from the faucet while drawing a bath. The scent released as the water flows calms the spirit. When the bath is ready, drop the herbs into the bathwater and soak your sore muscles in the bath.

Colds, Flu, Bronchial Congestion: Anise hyssop tea helps expel mucus from the lungs, making it a good choice for treating colds, flu, and congestion.

Herpes: Try Anise Hyssop Essential Oil externally as an antiviral treatment for Herpes Simplex I and II and drink the tea to treat the virus internally.

Poison Ivy: Wash the skin in Anise Hyssop Infusion to help relieve the itchiness of poison ivy.

Athlete's Foot, Fungal Skin Infections, Yeast Overgrowth: Soak the foot or infected area in a bath with a strong infusion of Anise Hyssop. Soak daily until the infection is cured.

Recipes: Anise Hyssop Tea or Infusion. You'll need one cup of boiling water and raw honey to your liking. Add one teaspoon of dried leaves and flowers or one tablespoon of fresh leaves and flowers. Add them to the boiling water and cover tightly. Allow the leaves to steep for 15 minutes. Strain the tea through a fine sieve. Add raw honey to sweeten, if desired.

Ashwagandha, Withania somnifera

Ashwagandha, Withania somnifera, is a member of the nightshade family. It is sometimes called Winter Cherry or Indian Ginseng, due to its importance in Ayurvedic medicine. Ashwagandha is considered a rejuvenating adaptogenic herb, useful for treating many debilitating conditions.

Identification: Ashwagandha is native to India but can be grown in herb gardens across the United States. It is a perennial in warm climates with no frost. Ashwagandha likes sandy or rocky soil, full or partial sunlight, and moderately dry conditions. The bush grows to a height of 2 to 3 or more feet (0.6m 0.9m), with dull green leaves. Light green, bell-shaped flowers appear in midsummer and orange to red berries in the fall. Branches grow radially from a center stem.

Edible Use: The plant is not generally eaten, but its seeds are used in the production of vegetarian cheeses. The leaves are used to make Ashwagandha Tea.

Other Uses: The fruits are rich in saponins are can be used as a substitute for soap. The leaves repel insects.

Medicinal Uses: Ashwagandha is an adaptogenic herb that has been in use for thousands of years. It is highly valued for its ability to strengthen the immune system, balance hormone levels, and for its antianxiety, anti-depressant, and anti-inflammatory properties.

Roots and leaves of the ashwagandha plant are used for their medicinal properties. Root extracts in powdered or capsule forms are effective as are leaf extracts and tinctures. Powders can be added to food or drinks thought they have a strong taste. Ashwagandha tea made from the leaves is also used. Adding a little honey improves the flavor.

Expect it to take two weeks or more to begin to notice the benefits of ashwagandha. Long-term use has not been studied and may not be safe, but many patients do well taking the herb long-term.

"Adrenal Fatigue" (= HPA Axis Dysregulation – HPA-D): Ashwagandha supports adrenal function and overcoming "adrenal fatigue", though this term is really a summary of stress response symptoms that are often caused by a hypothalamic–pituitary–adrenal (HPA) axis dysfunction. Essentially, HPA-D is our stress response system and a more accurate term for adrenal fatigue. Ashwagandha helps balance this.

Combats Stress, Fight or Flight, Anxiety, and Depression: Ashwagandha has long been used to relieve anxiety, improve mental health, concentration, vitality, and overall improve the quality of life. It also acts as a mood stabilizer and relieves symptoms of depression. It provides benefits similar to anti-anxiety and anti-depressant drugs without drowsiness, insomnia, or other side effects.

Reduces Cortisol Levels: Cortisol is a stress hormone implicated in controlling blood sugar levels and fat storage in the abdomen. Studies show that ashwagandha helps significantly reduce cortisol levels in chronically stressed adults.

Balances Blood Glucose Levels: Ashwagandha is particularly beneficial to diabetic patients in reducing blood glucose levels. It may help improve insulin sensitivity and reduce inflammation.

Cancer: Research shows that ashwagandha has antitumor effects. It reduces cancerous tumors by preventing cell growth and killing cancerous cells. Ashwagandha is useful in treating breast, lung, stomach, ovarian, and colon cancer cells. These benefits are due to its antioxidant abilities and their effects in helping the immune system.

In addition to reducing the growth of cancer cells, it can also help the body deal with the side effects of conventional anti-cancer drugs in boosting immunity and improving the quality of life. Ashwagandha stimulates the production of white blood cells and helps cancer patients fight infections.

Memory and Brain Cell Degeneration: Research suggests that ashwagandha protects the brain from the damaging effects of emotional, physical, and chemical stress. It protects the brain from cell degeneration, which may help in treating neurodegenerative diseases like Alzheimer's and Parkinson's disease.

Ashwagandha contains naturally occurring steroids and antioxidants that protect the brain and improve cognitive function. Patients notice an improvement in attention, processing speed, and mental acuity.

Stamina, Endurance, and Muscle Performance: Studies suggest that ashwagandha boosts endurance and reduces muscle pain. It calms stress, energizes the brain, and enhances cardiorespiratory endurance in athletes. It increases muscle mass and strength in athletes engaging in resistance training and strenuous exercise when taken for 8-weeks or longer.

Anti-inflammatory: Joint Pain and Arthritis: Patients taking ashwagandha for eight weeks or longer experience improvement in joint function and a reduction in joint pain related to rheumatoid arthritis.

Sexual Function and Fertility: Ashwagandha helps improve sexual function. It boosts testosterone levels and improves male fertility. When used for a period of 3 months, ashwagandha increases sperm count, sperm volume, and sperm motility. In women, it improves arousal, lubrication, and orgasm.

Immune Function: Ashwagandha helps regulate immune function by reducing the body's stress hormones, reducing inflammation, increasing the white blood cell count, and increasing immunoglobulin production.

Harvesting: Pick berries in the fall when red and fully ripe, then dry them for planting in the spring. For medicinal use, dig up the roots in the fall and clean thoroughly. Slice, dry, and powder for future use. Leaves are used fresh or can be dried to use in tea.

Warning: The herb is generally believed to be safe and has an extensive history of use. However, there are no long-term studies on the safety and long-term use may make it more likely that side effects will be experienced. Consult your doctor and watch for side-effects when using ashwagandha over the long term.

Black-Eyed Susan, Rudbeckia hirta

Black-eyed Susan is a member of the Aster/Sunflower Family, and is found throughout eastern and central North America. It is also called brown-eyed Susan, hairy coneflower, gloriosa daisy brown betty, yellow daisy, yellow ox-eye daisy coneflower, poor-land daisy, and golden Jerusalem. It prefers full sun and moist to moderately-dry soil.

Identification: Black-eyed Susan is usually an annual; but sometimes a perennial, growing up to 3 feet (0.9m) tall and up to 1 ½ feet (0.5m) wide.

The leaves are alternate, 4 to 7 inches (10 cm to 20 cm) long, and covered by coarse hair. The branched stems grow from a single taproot. There is no rhizome and reproduction is by seed only. Be on the lookout for these flowers during late summer and early autumn. They are about 4 inches (10 cm) in diameter, with a brownish black dome in the middle, circled by yellow petals.

Medicinal Use: Black-eyed Susan is a traditional herb used for colds, flu, infection, swelling, and snake bite. The roots and sometimes the leaves are used to boost immunity and fight colds, flu, and infections.

Colds and Flu: A root infusion treats colds and the flu. Common usage is to drink the root infusion daily until all symptoms are gone. **Parasites:** The Chippewa people have traditionally used Black-eyed Susan Root Tea to treat worms in children.

Poultice for Snake Bites: A poultice of blackeyed Susan is said to treat snakebites. Moisten the hopped leaves or ground root and place over the affected area as a poultice. Wrap with a cloth and keep it on the wound until the swelling is reduced.

Skin Irritations: Black-eyed Susan root infusions are soothing on irritated skin including sores, cuts, scrapes, and swelling. Use a warm root infusion to wash the irritated skin.

Earaches: If you have fresh roots, use the sap or juice as drops to treat earaches. One or two drops in the affected ear treat the infection and relieves pain. Place the drops in the ear morning and night until the infection is completely cleared up.

Stimulates the Immune System: Like Echinacea, Black-eyed Susan roots have immune-stimulant activity and boost the immune system to treat colds, flu, and other minor illness. Those with autoimmune issues should be careful using this herb internally due to its immune-stimulating properties.

Tuberculosis: Black-eyed Susan contains compounds that act against the bacterium that causes tuberculosis.

Harvesting: To harvest the taproot, wait until the plant has produced seeds, then dig the plant up by the root. Black-eyed Susan has one central taproot with hairs, but no other rhizomes. Dig deeply to get the entire root. Use it fresh in season and also dry some root for future use.

Warning: Black-eyed Susan plants are toxic to cats and are reported to be poisonous to cattle, sheep, and pigs. The seeds are poisonous. Those with autoimmune conditions should be careful with internal use of this herb due to its immune-stimulating properties.

Boneset, Eupatorium perfoliatum

This herb supposedly got the name boneset due to its use treating dengue fever, also known as break-bone fever. It is excellent for treating fevers and is a great choice for chest colds and flu. The herb is a perennial native to North America. It is a member of the Aster/Sunflower family. It is also known as feverwort.

Identification: Boneset has erect, hairy stems that grow 2 to 4 feet (0.6m to 1.2m) high and branch at the top. The leaves are large, opposite, and united at the base. They are lance-shaped, finely toothed and have prominent veins. Leaves are 4 to 8 inches (10 cm to 20 cm) long with the lower ones larger than the upper ones. The blades are rough on the top and downy, resinous, and dotted on the underside. The leaves of boneset are easily distinguished. They are either perforated by the stem or connate; two opposite leaves joined at the base. The numerous large flower heads of boneset are terminal and slightly convex, with 10 to 20 white florets, and have bristly hairs arranged in a single row. The fragrance is slightly aromatic, while the taste is astringent and strongly bitter. Flowering from July to September, this plant's size, hairiness and other aspects can vary greatly.

Medicinal Use: The flowers and leaves are used. Best to let dry rather than use fresh due to some degree of toxicity. The major medicinal properties of boneset include use as an antispasmodic, sweat inducer, bileproducer, emetic, fever-reducer, laxative, purgative, stimulant, and as a vasodilator.

Colds, Flu, Bronchitis, Congestion and Excess Mucus: Boneset is an excellent choice for the treatment of the common cold, flu, and respiratory infections. It discourages the production of mucus, loosens phlegm and helps eliminate it from the body, fights off both viral and bacterial infections, and encourages sweating, which helps reduce the associated fever. People given boneset early in the disease process have milder symptoms and get well faster. A tincture is the easiest form to use.

Dengue Fever, AKA Break Bone Fever: Dengue fever thrives in tropical environments, and while it is not yet a problem here in the United States, it is probably only a matter of time before it arrives. Boneset is the herb of choice for fighting dengue, a painful mosquito-borne disease that results in high fevers and terrible muscle and bone pain. It reduces the fevers and fights the underlying causes of the disease. It also gives the patient some relief from the "bonebreaking" pain.

Malaria: Native Americans have commonly used boneset to treat malaria. It promotes sweating, which helps relieve the fever associated with malaria and lessens the severity of the disease.

Yellow Fever and Typhoid: Boneset is helpful in the treatment of yellow fever and typhoid, although it is not as effective as it is for treating dengue fever and malaria. Its main use here is its ability to reduce the accompanying fevers.

Harvesting: Harvest the leaves and flowering stems of boneset during the summer, just before the buds have opened. Dry them for later use. Seeds of boneset ripen about a month after flowering and are collected when the heads are dry, split, and the fluffy seed begins to float away. If seeds are collected earlier, dry the seed heads for 1 to 2 weeks in open paper bags.

Warning: Do not use boneset for pregnant or nursing mothers or for young children. Not for long-term use.

Recipes: Boneset Infusion. Take Boneset Infusion hot to relieve fevers and treat colds, flu, and similar diseases. Use it cold as a tonic or tincture.

Ingredients: 1-ounce dried boneset leaf, 1-quart (1 Liter) boiling water, 1-quart (1 Liter) jar with a tightfitting lid.

Instructions: Put the dried boneset leaves into the jar and pour the boiling water over it to fill the jar. Tightly cap the jar and shake it gently to distribute the herb. Let the infusion steep for 4 hours. Strain through a coffee filter or a fine sieve. Warm it before drinking. It is very bitter, but warming it helps.

Borage, Borago officinalis

Common Borage is an annual frequently found in gardens. Bees are attracted to the flowers and make an excellent honey from the nectar.

Identification: The entire borage plant is covered with stiff white hairs. The stems are round, branched, hollow, and succulent. The plant grows to about 1 1/2 feet tall. Its deep green leaves are alternate, wrinkled, oval and pointed. Each is about 3 inches long and about 1 1/2 inches across.

The lower leaves have tiny hairs on the upper surface and on the veins on the lower side. Leaf margins are wavy, but entire. The flowers are a vivid blue and star-shaped, with prominent black anthers. The anthers form a cone in the center that is referred to as a beauty spot. The flowers start pink and turn blue, hanging in clusters. The flowers produce four brown-black nutlets.

Edible Use: The leaves, flowers, dried stems, and seeds are all edible and nutritious. You can eat the leaves raw or cooked. I use them in salads or cooked as a pot-herb. The leaves have a salty flavor similar to a cucumber. It is best to use the leaves while young. The more mature raw leaves are very hairy, which some people find unpleasant.

The flowers are nice used raw as a decorative garnish for salads and drinks. They make a refreshing drink when the leaves are brewed as a tea.

Dried stems are often used as a flavoring. The seeds are a healthy source of gamma-linolenic acid (GLA), a beneficial Omega-6 fatty acid, but it is difficult to collect enough for regular use.

Medicinal Use. Regulates Hormones, PMS and Menstrual Issues: Borage treats hormonal imbalances and regulates metabolism. Eating borage with meals regularly helps keep your metabolism running smoothly. Borage reduces symptoms of premenstrual syndrome (PMS), menopause, and regulates the menstrual cycle.

Stress and HPA-Dysfunction ("Adrenal Fatigue"): Borage is a calming herb and is taken to relieve stress. It also helps balance cortisol levels in the body, this aiding the stress response and HPA-Dysfunction (often called Adrenal Fatigue).

Anti-Oxidant Properties: Anti-oxidants in borage helps destroy free radicals in the body, protecting it against aging and cancers caused by free radicals.

Digestive Problems and Irritable Bowel Syndrome: Borage has a soothing effect on the stomach muscles and is a good treatment for irritable bowel syndrome. It reduces inflammation in the intestinal tract and treats gastritis and other digestive problems. It promotes digestion and stabilizes the stomach. Borage also has a mild laxative effect.

Pneumonia: Borage Leaf and Flower Tea or Tincture reduces the symptoms of pneumonia, relieves congestion, and helps the body get rid of excess mucus. However, there are better herbs for these symptoms.

Mouth Ulcers and Sore Throats: Use borage as a mouthwash or gargle to kill bacteria in the mouth and throat. It prevents and treats sore throats and mouth sores.

Urinary Tract and Kidney Infections, Diuretic Properties: Borage acts as a diuretic, removing excess water and toxins from the body. It also works to improve bladder function. Borage flushes the bladder, removing bacteria and relieving bladder infections. Borage also relieves kidney inflammations and restores health of the kidneys. However, I prefer other herbs to treat these, such as Usnea, Oregon Grape and Uva Ursi.

Protects the Brain: The GLA in borage seed oil improves the brains protection against neuro-degeneration. It protects the brain against synaptic failure in Alzheimer's disease and improves resistance to the disease.

Lowers Blood Pressure: Eat borage or drink the juice daily to treat high blood pressure. The GLA content helps to significantly lower blood pressure. Recent studies have confirmed the benefits of Borage for treating hypertension.

Allergies: The anti-oxidants in borage help subdue allergies, reduce inflammation, and suppress the allergic response.

Reduces Fevers: Borage stimulates the sweat glands to produce sweat and cool the body. This property is beneficial for treating fevers in colds, and respiratory illnesses. Arthritis and Gout: Borage is useful for treating inflammation, reducing swelling, and thereby reducing pain. It is effective for reducing inflammation caused by arthritis and gout.

Skin Infections, Wounds, and Rashes: The anti-inflammatory and anti-bacterial properties of borage help keep your skin clear. It is useful in treating wounds and fighting infections or rashes. Use borage tea as a skin wash or use borage as a poultice to treat wounds. A poultice of borage leaves also reduces itching and inflammation from rashes or stings and insect bites. It clears up skin inflammations and the unpleasant symptoms of skin rashes.

Treating Bleeding Gums: Borage fights the infections that cause bleeding gums. Borage helps kill the mouth pathogens and restores health to the gums and mouth.

Macular Degeneration: One cause of macular degeneration is a lack of fatty acids. Borage seeds contain up to 30% GLA, a beneficial fatty acid for treating and preventing macular degeneration.

Improves Milk Production for Nursing Mothers: Borage tea is used to improve milk production in nursing mothers.

Treat Hangovers: Borage Tea made from a combination of dried leaves and flowers is an effective treatment for hangover.

Harvesting: Harvest borage leaves in the late spring and early summer before the plant flowers. Use the leaves fresh or dry them for use throughout the year. Dried leaves lose their medicinal properties over time, so dry a new batch each year. Harvest flowers in the morning in the summer.

Warning: Borage leaves contain a small amount of pyrrolizidine alkaloids and other compounds that are toxic to the liver.

The levels are low and are not a problem for healthy people, but people with liver disease should not use borage in any form. Pregnant women should avoid using borage. In some people, borage causes skin dermatitis. Persons with schizophrenia or epilepsy should avoid using borage.

Bottle Gourd, Lagenaria siceraria

Also known as calabash, white-flowered gourd, and long melon, the bottle gourd is often cultivated for its fruit. When harvested young, the fruit is used as a vegetable. When mature, it is dried, and it can be scraped and used as a bottle, container, or pipe. Bottle gourd is in the cucumber family. It is hard to find in the wild, but easy to cultivate.

Identification: This annual vine grows to be 15 feet (4.5m) long or more. The fruit has a smooth lightgreen skin and white flesh. It grows in a variety of shapes and sizes. It has long densely packed hairs on the stems. These hairs are tipped with glands that produce a sticky sap.

The leaves grow on long stalks and are oval to heart-shaped. Leaves can be unlobed or have 3 to 5 irregular shallow lobes. The flowers are white, growing alone or in pairs. They open at night during the summer and close again in the morning.

Edible Use: Although it is safe to eat in moderate amounts, be aware that young gourds can be bitter. If you think the plant has grown too old or tastes too bitter, throw it away because it might have a buildup of toxins or it may have spoiled. Otherwise, the fruit can be steamed, boiled, fried, used in soups and stir-fries. Young shoots and leaves are cooked as a pot herb.

Medicinal Use: This plant is mainly used for blood sugar control in diabetics, but I know of healers who use it as a heart tonic and as a sedative. It is anti-inflammatory, antioxidant, anti-bacterial, pain relieving, and a tonic for the internal organs.

Diabetes: Bottle gourd helps to lower blood sugar readings in diabetics when taken regularly. Eat a piece of bottle gourd at each meal for blood sugar control. One or two large bites of the gourd are enough to provide the desired benefit.

Headaches: A poultice made by crushing the leaves and applying it to the head over the painful area is useful for relieving the pain of headaches.

Boils, Skin Infections, and Irritations: Bottle gourd has anti-bacterial and anti-inflammatory effects. For these external uses, make poultice from the boiled seeds of the gourd for skin irritations and infections. Cover the poultice with a clean cloth and leave in place as long as possible to reduce swelling and prevent the spread of the infection.

Memory Loss, Depression and Senility: Studies have been done demonstrating bottle gourd for mild depression and memory improvement, including patients with Alzheimer's disease and age-related senility.

Cabbage, Brassica oleracea

The common cabbage is familiar to gardeners across the country, but many don't realize how valuable it is as a medicinal plant. The plant is a biennial or perennial, forming a round head that can reach up to 8 feet (2.4m) when fully mature. Most cabbages are harvested long before they reach such a size. It is in the Brassicaceae (Mustard) Family.

Identification: The leaves are gray with a thick stem. Yellow flowers with four petals appear in the spring. The leaves form a head during the late summer of the first year. Cabbage can also be reddish-purple, green, or white. All varieties have the healthgiving benefits detailed below.

Edible Use: The cabbage is a common vegetable, especially in the winter because it keeps well in the root cellar. It is eaten raw and cooked.

Medicinal Use. Mastitis and Painful Breasts in Nursing Mothers: This is my number one use for cabbage leaves. For painfully engorged breasts and mastitis, use a poultice made from cabbage leaves. Cut out the vein from the cabbage leaf and crush or pound the leaf with a hammer. You'll want your leaf intact but badly bruised to access the healing sulfur compounds and the juice. Apply the bruised leaf to the breast or line the bra cup with the leaf. Repeat as needed until the infection clears.

Treatment for Wounds, Leg Ulcers, Joint Pain, Arthritis, Skin Cancers: Cabbage leaves work well to clean wounds and prevent infection. They are also useful in reducing swelling in painful joints and treating skin tumors. Chop the leaves and crush them to release the health-giving juices and heat them in a very small amount of water. Apply the leaves as a poultice over the affected area. The cabbage detoxifies the skin and underlying tissue, prevents bacterial growth, and reduces inflammation.

Intestinal Problems: Cabbage is useful for treating intestinal problems due to its sulfurous compounds. Fermented cabbage in the form of sauerkraut is even more effective for treating intestinal problems of all kinds.

Diabetes: Sauerkraut juice, mixed with a little lemon juice, helps people control their diabetes and stabilize their blood sugars. The sauerkraut juice stimulates the digestion and pancreas.

Constipation: Cabbage, cabbage juice, and sauerkraut juice all have laxative properties.

Treating Cancer: For treating cancer, especially cancers of the stomach, intestines, pancreas, and prostate, drink cabbage juice or sauerkraut juice twice daily. Finely chopped cabbage should also be eaten as tolerated. Both cabbage juice and sauerkraut juice have many different beneficial compounds that fight cancer and help heal the body.

Recipes: Sauerkraut. Equipment: Large glass jar or crock. I prefer using a fermentation crock, but a glass jar will work, a fermentation weight or a plate that fits in the container, a large bowl or tub for mixing, a plate or tray. Ingredients for 1 gallon (4 liters) of Sauerkraut: 1 large head of cabbage, shredded fine, a few large leaves from the outside of the cabbage, 3 tablespoons pickling salt and 1 tablespoon caraway seeds, optional. Shred the cabbage finely and add 2 TBS of salt. Let the cabbage stand for about 10 minutes to draw out juices. Knead the cabbage for 10 minutes or more to bruise it and release more juices.

Add the remaining salt and the caraway seeds. Pack the cabbage into a large glass jar or crock and add the juices. Cover the top of the shredded cabbage with the whole cabbage leaves. Add a weight to the top of the cabbage to keep it beneath the liquid.

Fermenting crocks use fermenting weights, but a clean plate or another dish can be used. Cover the container with its lid. Place the container in a cool spot on a tray or plate to catch any spills. Leave the cabbage overnight and check it the next day to make sure that all the cabbage is submerged in liquid and skim off any scum that forms.

Continue checking the sauerkraut every other day for 4 weeks. Transfer the sauerkraut to the refrigerator and use within 6 months. Sauerkraut can be canned for longer storage. However, I believe this destroys some of the beneficial enzymes as well as the live culture. I recommande using the sauerkraut with live culture.

Calendula, Calendula officinalis

Calendula or Pot Marigold is a perennial plant in the Aster/Daisy family that is often grown as an annual. It is not originally native to North America but is widely cultivated in flower gardens, self-seeds, and is easy to grow.

Identification: Calendula usually grows 12 to 24 inches (30 cm to 60 cm) tall with branched sprawling or erect stems. The leaves are oblong and lance-like, approximately 2 to 7 inches (5 cm to 18 cm) long, and hairy on both sides. The margins can be smooth, wavy, or even weakly toothed. The flowers are yellow or orange with a 2 to 3-inch (5 cm to 7.5 cm) flower head with two rows of hairy bracts. Flowers appear year-round in warmer climates. Some flowers have multiple rows of ray florets while others have only one. High resin varieties and multirow flowers are said to be better for medicine. The fruit is a small curved achene.

Edible Use: Calendula flowers are edible raw in salads or dried and used as a seasoning. They can be used as a saffron substitute for color but not taste. Tea is made from the petals. The leaves are edible, but are bitter and unpalatable.

Medicinal Use: Calendula can be used as a tea, infused oil, salve, compress, or poultice.

Skin Diseases, Cuts, Rashes, Wounds, Burns, Cold Sores, Herpes, Chicken Pox, and Irritations: Calendula leaves and flowers are soothing to the skin, and I use them to treat all kinds of skin problems like acne, sunburn, and rashes, including diaper rash. The leaves make a healing poultice for minor cuts, scratches, bites, and skin irritations. Place the bruised leaves directly on the skin. The leaves soothe inflamed skin and help it heal. I use the flowers to make a healing salve for skin irritations. The leaves and flowers have anti-bacterial, anti-fungal, anti-microbial, and anti-viral effects as well being an immunostimulant. To treat skin infections, including ringworm, athlete's foot, thrush, diaper rash, and cradle cap, I use Calendula Oil or Salve applied to the affected area several times a day. Note that Calendula is a tonic anti-fungal, weaker than many. I prefer to use a stronger anti-fungal such as black walnut hull powder, Oregano Oil, or Usnea to treat the primary infection and save calendula as a preventative or for chronic situations.

Anti-aging and Collagen Production: Calendula stimulates the immune system, induces collagen production and inhibits collagen degradation. I make an anti-aging blend with Calendula and Cottonwood Buds infused in organic almond oil and use it on my face and neck every day in place of a commercial face cream.

Soothes Muscle Spasms: Calendula relaxes muscles and can prevent spasms. Calendula tea treats abdominal cramping caused by constipation and menstrual cramping.

It is also effective in relieving body aches and pains due to muscle spasms.

Helps Heal Ulcers, Wounds, and Hemorrhoids: Slow healing wounds such as ulcers and hemorrhoids are soothed by the application of calendula as an ointment, gel, or salve. It speeds up healing and wound closure while improving skin firmness and hydration. Calendula increases the blood and oxygen availability in the infected area, which encourages rapid healing. It is antimicrobial and antibacterial.

Stomach and Intestinal Diseases: Calendula works to heal a variety of gastro-intestinal problems including intestinal colitis, GERD, esophageal irritation, peptic ulcers, and inflammatory bowel disease. It soothes the inflammation from infections and irritations while helping heal the underlying problems.

Immune System and Lymphatic System: Calendula stimulates the functioning of the immune system and the lymphatic system, including swollen lymph nodes and tonsillitis, and helps to prevent infections. Additionally, the astringent and antiseptic properties help the body fight off infections and viruses. Calendula also reduces congestion and swelling in the lymph glands.

Menstruation and PMS: Calendula Tea is an effective aid in easing the painful side effects of menstruation. It helps induce the menses, relieves painful cramping, relaxes the muscles, and improves blood flow. Some people claim that it also helps with hot flashes.

Improves Oral Health: Calendula has powerful antibacterial and antimicrobial properties and treats gingivitis, plaque, oral cavities and many other oral health issues.

Inhibits Cancer: Calendula has anti-inflammatory properties which aid the body in fighting cancer, as well as irritations caused by cancer treatments. It activates the lymphatic system against the cancer and helps kill off the cancer cells. It also effectively soothes the skin after radiation treatments.

Liver, Gallbladder, and Whole-Body Detoxification: Calendula helps remove toxins from the body and helps cleanse the liver and gallbladder. The detoxification properties also have a positive effect on the skin and help clear up chronic skin problems such as eczema and acne caused by the body's efforts to rid itself of toxins. For detoxification, try an internal Calendula Extract.

Harvesting: To promote flowering, pick the flowers every two days. Dry them on screens or hang them in a well-ventilated warm area.

Warning: Some people are allergic to calendula. Do not use it if you are allergic to marigold, ragweed, daisies, chrysanthemums, chamomile, echinacea and other plants in the Aster/Daisy family. If you are not sure, start with a small test patch on the skin and increase use gradually if you have no reactions. Do not use calendula internally if you are pregnant or breastfeeding, since safety is unknown. Do not take calendula internally if you are taking prescription medications without the advice of your doctor.

Recipes: Soothing Calendula Salve (Fast Method). Ingredients: half a cup of organic olive oil, 1/3 cup solid organic coconut oil, 3 tablespoons dried calendula flowers, 1 1/2 tablespoons dried chamomile flowers, 1 to 2 ounces (28g to 56g) beeswax. In a double boiler, melt the olive oil and the coconut oil together.

Add the flower petals and allow the mixture to steep for 2 to 3 hours making sure it does not get too hot. Strain out the flower petals. Return the pan to the heat and add the beeswax, stirring. Once the wax melts pour into your containers (adjust amount of beeswax to get the consistency you want). Allow the salve to cool completely before use.

Calendula Extract: Take 1-pint (500ml) loosely packed calendula flowers and 1-pint (500ml) 80 proof vodka or other drinking alcohol of 80 proof or higher. Place the flowers in a pint (500ml) jar with a tight fitting lid.

Fill the jar with alcohol so that the flowers are completely covered. Allow the extract to steep in a cool, dark place for 4 to 6 weeks. Shake daily. Strain out the flowers and store the extract tightly covered in a cool, dark place. Use within 3 years.

California Poppy, Eschscholzia californica

The California poppy has sedative and healing effects but is not psychoactive or narcotic like some poppy species. The California poppy is a species of flowering plant in the Papaveraceae (Poppy) Family, It is native to Western North America. It occurs across a variety of habitats including coastal, foothill, valley, and desert regions, at elevations below 7000 feet (2133m). It is also known as Golden Poppy and Cup of Gold due to its golden color.

Identification: The California poppy is a flowering annual or deep-rooted perennial. It is 1/2 to 2 feet (0.6m) tall, and its foliage is blue-green in color. Its leaves are compound, with three finely divided lobes, and are nearly smooth with no hair. California poppy produces upright flowers on branching stems with four bright orange to yellow petals. The flowers often have distinct, darker orange centers. The seed capsules of California poppy are cylindrically shaped and burst open from the base when ripe. These capsules open explosively to aid in seed dispersal, ejecting the small seeds up to 6 feet (1.83m) from the parent plant. Its tiny round seeds are usually gray to gray-brown in color when mature.

Edible Use: Its leaves are edible if cooked. Caution is advised because other plants in the family are poisonous.

Medicinal Use: The California poppy is a diuretic, relaxes spasms, relieves pain, promotes perspiration, and is sedative. It is non-addictive and can help with opiate withdrawal. It most likely works with GABA receptors. The entire plant is used medicinally, with the root being the most potent part.

Sedative Properties and Antispasmodic: California poppy is a mild sedative that also works well for incontinence, especially for children. It aids in treating sleep deprivation, anxiety, and nervous tension. The sap is somewhat narcotic and works well for alleviating toothaches. Unlike opium poppy, it does not depress the nervous system and it's much milder in action. Take it at bedtime since it induces sleep. It is also an antispasmodic.

Normalizes Psychological Function, PTSD, and Anxiety: California poppy seems to normalize the thinking patterns of people with psychological issues, and is mild enough to use for children. It does not have a narcotic effect, but helps calm the spirit and helps people regain normal function. It works well for anxiety disorders and PTSD.

Suppresses the Milk in Nursing Mothers: When lactation is not desired, apply California Poppy Tea made from the roots as a wash on the breasts to suppress the flow of milk. It helps the milk dry up quickly.

Harvesting: Harvest the entire plant when it is flowering from June to September and dry for use in tinctures and infusions.

Warning: Do not drive or operate heavy machinery, as it is a sedative.

Recipes. California Poppy Infusion: 1 to 2 teaspoons of dried California poppy plant or root, 1 cup boiling water. Make a strong tea by infusing the dried herb in boiling water for 10 minutes and allowing it to cool. Drink one cup of the infusion at night before going to bed. It induces sleepiness.

California Poppy Tincture: 1-pint (500 ml) of 80 proof vodka or other alcohol, or substitute applecider vinegar, dried or fresh California poppy plant. Place the chopped fresh herbs or dried plant into a pint (500ml) jar with a tight-fitting lid, filling the jar 3/4 full. Cover the herbs with alcohol, filling the jar. Store the jar in a cool, dark place such as a cupboard. Shake the jar daily for 4 to 6 weeks. Strain the herbs out of the liquid, cover it tightly and use within seven years.

Carolina Geranium, Geranium carolinianum

Geranium carolinianum, known as Carolina Geranium, Carolina Cranesbill, Crane's Bill Geranium, and Wild Geranium, is native across the US, Canada, and Mexico. This plant is often found in areas with poor soil, clay, and limestone. I often see it near roadsides, abandoned fields, and farmland.

Identification: The Carolina geranium is a winter annual or biennial herb. It is low-growing, usually under 12 inches tall. It has earned the name cranesbill because of the beak-like appearance of the fruit. Its palmate leaves have 5 to 7 toothed lobes, with each lobe divided again.

Leaves are 1 to 2.5 inches (2.5 cm to 6 cm) wide, grayish-green and covered in fine hair. Each leaf usually has five segments, edged with deep teeth. Its pinkishred stems grow erect and are covered in hairs. White, pink, or lavender flowers appear in small clusters on stalks growing off the main stems in April through July. Each flower has five sepals and five notched petals.

One-half inch long fruits, with a longer style, ripen in the fall. Ripe seeds are covered in pits/depressions. The plant has a taproot system that grows close to the surface.

Edible Use: Carolina Geranium is edible raw, cooked, or as a tea. The roots are best boiled for 10 minutes to soften. The cooking water can be used as a tea to relieve stomach upsets. The leaves are astringent and have a strong bitter flavor caused by their high tannin level. Using them young helps relieve some of the bitterness, or change the water out once when you cook them. The tea is often consumed with milk and cinnamon to improve the flavor.

Medicinal Use: The astringent tannic root is the part most often used medicinally, though leaves are also used.

Stops Bleeding, Dries out Tissue: The entire plant is astringent and high in tannins, which causes the contraction of tissues and helps stop bleeding. Use the root or leaves as a poultice on moist wounds and for drying out tissues. As a styptic (to stop bleeding), clean the root or leaves and apply to the wound. Hold the compress tightly for a few minutes until bleeding stops, and then bind the poultice with gauze or a clean cloth. The plant is excellent for use in skin salves to promote skin healing.

Diarrhea and Stomach Upset: Tea made from the root is ideal for treating stomach upsets and diarrhea.

Canker Sores: Wash the canker sore with Carolina Geranium Tea or cover it with a root poultice. The astringent root is drying and reduces canker sores quickly.

Treats Sore Throats: The root is soothing for sore throats. It may have anti-viral properties as well. Hepatitis B: Tinctured Carolina Geranium root has been shown to have the anti-Hepatitis B (HBV) compounds geraniin and hyperin.

Harvesting: Harvest young leaves and use them fresh or dry them for future use. Dig up roots in the late fall when they are plump with stored starch, or if necessary, in the early spring. Clean the roots, slice them thinly and dry for future use or use them fresh.

Recipes: Carolina Geranium Leaf Tea. 2 Tablespoons dried leaves and stems, 2 cups boiling water. Pour the boiling water over the dried leaves and allow the tea to steep, off the heat, for 10 minutes or more. Strain and enjoy.

Carolina Geranium Root Tea: The roots make the most effective medicinal tea. Bring 2 cups of water to a boil and add 2 tablespoons of chopped, dried root. Reduce the heat and simmer the tea for 10 to 15 minutes. Remove from the heat and steep for another 10 minutes. Take up to 3 cups daily.

Carolina Geranium Tincture: Sterilized glass jar with tight fitting lid, ¾ jar cleaned, chopped fresh root or ½ jar dried root, 80 proof vodka or other alcohol to fill jar.

Cheese cloth or fine mesh strainer, glass bowl for straining. Sterilize all jars, utensils, and bowls with boiling water. Pack the jar with herbs: ¾ full for fresh root or ½ full for dried herbs, fill the jar with alcohol, making sure all herbs are covered. Cover tightly with lid.

Store the jar in a cool, dark place. Shake the jar daily for 6-8 weeks. Strain out the root and all sediment. When clean, pour into amber bottles and seal tightly. Label and date the containers Store the bottles in a cool, dark location for up to 10 years.

Chamomile, Matricaria chamomilla

Chamomile is a commonly used useful herb. It is a calming plant, and has sedative properties. It is in Aster/Daisy family.

Identification: Chamomile has daisy-like flowers with a hollow, cone-shaped receptacle. Its yellow cone surrounded by 10 to 20 downward-curving white petals. You can distinguish the plant from similar flowers by the pattern in which the flowers grow, each flower on an independent stem.
The most common way of identifying chamomile is by plucking a small amount of the blossom and crushing it in between your fingers.

Chamomile has a faintly fruity scent. Chamomile grows wild and it is also easy to cultivate in the garden. It thrives in open, sunny locations with well-drained soil. It does not tolerate excessive heat or dry conditions.

Matricaria chamomilla is German chamomile. English chamomile has similar medicinal uses. The two plants can be distinguished by their leaves. German chamomile leaves are very thin and hairy while those of the English Chamomile are larger and thicker. The leaves of the German chamomile are also bipinnate; each blade can be divided again into smaller leaf sections. German chamomile stems are some-what feathery while English Chamomile is hairless. De-pending on the growing conditions chamomile can grow to between 2 feet (0.6m) and 3 feet (0.9m) tall.

Edible Use: I collect both flowers and leaves for medicinal use, but the flowers make the best tea. The flowers have an apple-like flavor, and the leaves have a grassy flavor. You can make a nice liqueur with dried chamomile flowers and vodka.

Medicinal Use: Chamomile is most often taken as a tea but it may also be taken as a tincture or as a dried encapsulated herb.

Digestive Issues: Chamomile relaxes the muscles, including the digestive muscles. This makes it a good treatment for abdominal pain, indigestion, gastritis and bloating. It is also used it for Crohn's disease and irritable bowel syndrome.

Colic: Chamomile is known to be safe for use with babies. Adding a cup of tea to the baby's bath at night soothes colic and helps with sleep.

Muscle Aches: The antispasmodic action of chamomile relieves muscle tension. It soothes aching muscles and body aches.

Insomnia: Chamomile is soothing and sedative. One cup of chamomile tea, taken at bedtime or during the night, helps with sleep. If more help is needed, use a tincture.

Eyewash, Conjunctivitis, and Pinkeye: For eye problems, try an eyewash made by dissolving 5 to 10 drops of Chamomile tincture in some boiled and cooled water or by making a strong chamomile tea. This mixture relieves eyestrain and treats infections. I often pair it with other herbs like Yarrow and Usnea.

Asthma, Bronchitis, Whooping Cough, and Congestion: Use a steam treatment for congestion. Add two teaspoons of chamomile flower petals to a pot of boiling water. Inhale the steam until the phlegm is released. Or add 2 to 3 drops of Chamomile Essential Oil to a vaporizer and use overnight.

Allergies and Eczema: For allergic conditions, including itchy skin and eczema, try Chamomile Essential Oil. The steam distillation process alters the chemical properties of the remedy, giving it antiallergenic properties. Dilute the essential oil in a carrier oil to use directly on the skin or inhale it.

Harvesting: It is best to harvest chamomile during its peak blooming period. I prefer to pick chamomile in the late morning, after the dew has evaporated and before the real heat of the day. Select flowers that are fully open and pinch or clip the flower head off at the top of the stalk. Dry for future use.

Warning: While it is uncommon, some people have an allergic reaction to chamomile. People with allergies to the Asteraceae family, including ragweed and chrysanthemums, should not take chamomile.

Recipes: Chamomile Tea. Ingredients: 1 to 2 teaspoons of dried chamomile flowers or leaves and 1 cup boiling water. Pour 1 cup of boiling water over the chamomile flowers or leaves. Let the herb steep for 5 to 10 minutes. Strain.

Chamomile Liqueur: Ingredients: 1 pint (500 ml) of 80 proof vodka, 1 cup chamomile flowers, 2 tablespoons raw honey or to taste and zest of one lemon. Combine all ingredients in a tightly covered jar and allow the mixture to steep for two to four weeks. Strain.

Chickweed, Stellaria media

Chickweed is an annual plant in the Caryophyllaceae (Pink) Family. This herb is naturalized to many parts of North America. It is sometimes referred to as common chickweed to distinguish it from other plants with the same name. It is also referred to as winterweed, maruns, starweed, and chickenwort among others. It is commonly grown as feed for chickens.

Identification: Common chickweed grows from 2 to 20 inches (5 cm to 50 cm) in height. Its intertwined manner of growing usually covers large areas. Its flowers are white and shaped similarly to a star. The oval leaves have cup-like tips with smooth and slightly feathered edges. Its flowers are small, white, and starshaped. They are produced at the tip of the stem. The sepals are green in color.

Edible Use: The leaves, stem, and flowers are edible raw or cooked.

Medicinal Use. Arthritis: A tea or tincture from this herb is used as a remedy for arthritis. It relieves the inflammation and pain of rheumatoid arthritis. Also try adding a strong tea to a warm bath and soaking to relieve pain, especially on the knees and feet.

Roseola and Other Rashes: Children and adults suffering from roseola are plagued by an itchy rash. Use a poultice of moistened crushed chickweed leaves applied to the rash for relief of pain and itching. Adding a strong tea to the bathwater also helps.

Nerve Pain: Chickweed applied as a poultice or salve helps relieve the pain and tingling caused by surface nerves misfiring.

Constipation and Digestive Problems: Chickweed tea treats constipation. Be careful not to overdo it with the decoction; it has a strong purgative action. Chickweed also has analgesic properties that act on the digestive system to relieve pain, but it does not treat the underlying causes.

Skin Irritations, Dermatitis, Eczema, Hives, Shingles, and Varicose Veins: A salve or poultice made from chickweed works well for skin irritations, especially on itches and rashes. It is also useful for varicose veins, hives, dermatitis, and eczema. You can add the decoction to your bath if the affected area is larger.

Detoxification, Blood Purification, Tetanus, Boils, Herpes, and Venereal Diseases: Chickweed is an excellent detoxification agent and blood purifier. It draws poisons out of the body in cases of blood poisoning, tetanus, or from poisons entering the bloodstream through a wound.

For these purposes make a poultice from equal parts chickweed, ginger root, and raw honey. Blend the mixture to a smooth paste and apply it directly to the wound and the surrounding area.

Cover the poultice and replace it every six hours. Also take chickweed powder or tea to treat the problem from the inside out. This same protocol works for the treatment of boils, herpes sores, and other venereal diseases. Take both internal and external remedies for best results.

Harvesting: Harvest this herb early in the morning or late in the evening. Snip off the upper branches. Use them fresh or dry them for future use.

Warning: Some people are allergic to chickweed. The herb is considered safe, but should not be used by nursing women or pregnant women without the approval from a healthcare professional.

Recipes. Chickweed Decoction: Use fresh chickweed whenever possible to make this herbal decoction. It is an excellent internal cleanser and makes a good wash and external agent. You need 1 cup freshly picked chickweed leaves and 1 pint (500 ml) of water. Bring the water to a boil and add the chickweed leaves. Reduce the heat to low and simmer the leaves for 15 minutes. Cool the decoction and use it internally or externally. The internal dose is 1 to 2 ounces (30 to 60ml).

Chicory, Cichorium intybus

Common chicory is an annual or biannual plant in the Aster/Daisy Family. It originated from Eurasia and is found throughout North America, where it is known as an invasive species in several places. Common chicory is also called blue daisy, blue dandelion, blue sailors, blue weed, coffeeweed, cornflower, succory, wild bachelor's buttons, wild endive, and horseweed.

It is sometimes confused with Curly Endive (Cichorium endivia), a closely related plant often called chicory.

Identification: Chicory is easy to identify by its purple flowers when in bloom. Its stems are rigid with hairy lower stems. Its alternate lobed leaves are coarsely toothed and similar to dandelion leaves in appearance. The lower leaves are covered with hairs and grow up to 8 inches (20 cm) in length. The stems and leaves both exude a milky latex when cut. The plant grows 1 to 3 feet (0.3m to 0.9m) tall and has numerous flower heads, each around 1 to 1 1/2 inches (2.5 cm to 3.75 cm) wide, appearing in clusters of two or three. Light blue-purple (and rarely pink or white) flowers bloom from July thru October. Petals grow in two rows with toothed ends. The blooms are open in the morning but close during the heat of the day. Its root is a thick, fleshy bitter taproot.

Edible Use: The leaves have a bitter taste, which can be reduced by boiling and draining. I prefer young leaves boiled, then sautéed with garlic and butter. The most famous use of chicory is as a coffee additive or substitute. Roast the roots and grind them. Roots may be eaten raw or cooked.

Medicinal Use: Chicory roots and seeds help eliminate intestinal worms and parasites, are antibacterial, antifungal, and hepatoprotective. Roots are being studied for use in cancer. The flowers and leaves are also used medicinally. It is a mild diuretic.

Sedative and Analgesic: The milky juice from the fresh root of chicory is similar to the milky sap of Wild Lettuce (Lactuca spp.), also in this book. They contain lactucin and lactucopicrin, which are sedative and analgesic (pain-killing). They are sesquiterpene lactones, so it is recommended to use the latex as is or, if you want a liquid form, to dry them and then extract the medicine in high proof alcohol or oil versus in water. Pain-relief is similar to ibuprofen.

Antibacterial and Anti-Fungal (Candida): Chicory seed and root extracts are antibacterial and anti-fungal. Seeds work against Staphylococcus, Pseudomonas, E. coli, and Candida. Roots work to kill Staphylococcus, Bacillus, Salmonella, E. coli, and Micrococcus as well as athlete's foot, ringworm, and jock itch. It can be taken internally and externally.

Anti-Parasitic and Malaria: Chicory root alcoholic extractions eliminate intestinal worms and the protozoan responsible for cerebral malaria (Plasmodium falciparum). The roots contain lactucin and lactucopicrin, both anti-malarials.

Liver and Gallbladder Disorders: The leaves, seeds, and roots of chicory are used to treat liver disorders. They are hepatoprotective. They promote the secretion of bile, treat jaundice, and treat enlargement of the spleen. They help fatty liver and to detox the liver.

Diabetes: Chicory leaf tincture, leaf powder, or a whole-plant alcoholic extraction helps regulate insulin levels, stimulate insulin secretion, and lower blood glucose levels.

Digestive Problems and Ulcers: Chicory coffee or tea made from the roots helps treat digestive problems and ulcers.

Skin Eruptions, Swellings, and Inflammations: For external use, wash blemishes with a chicory leaf infusion or apply crushed leaves as a poultice to areas of inflammation. Many people report that chicory infusion used as a wash nourishes the skin and gives it a more radiant and youthful appearance. It can be used as a face and body wash daily.

Harvesting: Only harvest plants that have not been exposed to car fumes and chemical spray along roadsides. Leaves and flowers are easily picked throughout the season. Harvest the roots in the late autumn. Loosen the soil around the base of each plant, grab the plant at the base, and pull up as much of the tap root as possible. Clean and use them fresh or cut and dry them for future use.

Warning: Chicory can cause contact dermatitis in some people. It also causes skin irritations and rashes in some people if taken internally. Avoid chicory during pregnancy; it can stimulate menstruation. Chicory can interfere with beta-blocker drugs for the heart.

Recipes. Chicory Coffee: Clean the roots and chop them into small pieces. Lay them out on a cookie sheet to roast. Roast them in a very slow oven or over a fire. When the roots are completely roasted and dried throughout, grind them into a powder. Store the powder sealed in a cool, dry place. Brew like you would coffee.

Chives, Allium schoenoprasum

Allium schoenoprasum belongs to the Amaryllidaceae (Amaryllis) Family. It is a close relative of garlics, shallots, and leeks. These herbs are often cultivated in home gardens, but also occur wild in many areas. They are widespread across North America, Europe, and Asia. They are mostly used as a culinary herb.

Identification: Chives are bulb-forming plants that grow from 12 to 20 inches (30 cm to 50 cm) tall. Their slender bulbs are about an inch (2.5 cm) long and nearly 1/2 inch (1.25 cm) across. They grow from roots in dense clusters. The stems are tubular and hollow and grow up to 20 inches (50 cm) long and about an inch across. The stems have a softer texture before the emergence of the flower. Chives have grass-like leaves, which are shorter than the stems. The leaves are also tubular or round in cross-section and are hollow, which distinguishes it from garlic chives, Allium tuberosum. Chives usually flower in April to May in southern regions and in June in northern regions. Its flowers are usually pale purple and grow in a dense inflorescence of 10 to 30 flowers that is ½ to 1 inch (1.25 cm to 2.5 cm) wide. Before opening, the inflorescence is typically surrounded by a papery bract. Fruits are small, 3-sectioned capsules. The seeds mature in the summer.

Edible Use: The leaves, roots, and flowers are all edible. Leaves have a mild onion flavor.

Medicinal Use: Chives have similar medical properties to those of garlic but are weaker overall. For this reason, it is used to a limited extent as a medicinal herb. Chives are also a mild stimulant, and have antiseptic and diuretic properties.

Digestion: Chives contain sulfide compounds, antibacterial compounds, and antifungal compounds that are effective in easing digestion and an upset stomach. They also stimulate the appetite.

Lowers Blood Pressure, Cholesterol, and Promotes Heart Health: Like other plants in the onion family, chives contain allicin, which helps reduce the levels of bad cholesterol in the body and improves the circulatory system and heart health. Regular consumption of chives reduces arterial plaques, relaxes the blood vessels, lowers high blood pressure, and decreases the risk of heart attacks and strokes.

Detoxing the Body and Diuretic: The mild diuretic properties of chives help flush toxins from the body and encourage urination.

Anti-inflammatory: Chives have mild anti-inflammatory properties and are a good addition to the diet for people with diseases that involve inflammation, such as arthritis, autoimmune conditions, and inflammatory skin conditions.

Boosts the Immune System: Chives contain a wide range of vitamins and minerals, including vitamin C, which helps boost the immune system and stimulates the production of white blood cells.

Harvesting: Chives can be harvested as soon as they are big enough to clip and use. Snip off the leaves at the base. The plant will continue to grow and can be harvested 3 to 4 times a year when young (the first year) and even monthly as they mature. Store them fresh in the refrigerator or dry them for future use.

Comfrey, Symphytum officinale

Comfrey, is a member of the borage family. The herb is easily grown in your home garden and grows like a weed in many areas. It is also known as knit bone, boneset and slippery root.

Identification: Comfrey is a vigorous perennial herb with long lance-like leaves, each 12 to 18 inches (30 cm to 45 cm) long. The hairy leaves grow from a central crown on the ends of short stems. The plant reaches 2 to 5 feet (0.6m to 1.5m) in height and spreads to over 3 feet (0.9m) in diameter. It can be propagated from cuttings but is not invasive once planted. Comfrey flowers begin as a blue to purple bell, fading to pink as they age. The thick, tuberous roots have a thin black skin.

Edible Use: Comfrey leaves and roots are not edible because they contain small amounts of toxins that should not be consumed. The leaves can be used to make a medicinal tea or gargle.

Medicinal Use: This herb is a valuable remedy that accelerates healing of the skin and wounds. A compress of the roots or leaves can be applied directly to the skin or made into a salve. It inhibits the growth of bacteria, helping to prevent infections, and minimizes scarring. It is mucilaginous and contains the compound allantoin, which boosts cell growth and repair. It also is an excellent anti-inflammatory and relieves pain, inflammation, and swelling in joints and muscles. Comfrey tea is best used to alleviate stomach problems, heavy menstrual bleeding, bloody urine, breathing problems, cancer, and chest pain. Be careful with internal use. It can also be gargled to treat gum disease or sore throat.

Sprains, Bruises and Breaks: Comfrey Salve or comfrey compresses are one of the best remedies for sprains, strains, bruised muscles and joints, and fractured bones. The herb speeds up healing while increasing mobility and relieving the pain and swelling. Apply the salve or a poultice made from crushed comfrey root up to four times a day. Make sure that a broken bone is set before applying comfrey.

Back Pain: Use comfrey root salve to treat back pain. Applied three times a day, it relieves bone and joint pains.

Osteoarthritis: Likewise, external Comfrey Salve is beneficial for knee and joint pain due to osteoarthritis.

Coughs, Congestion, and Asthma: Comfrey Tea treats coughs, congestion, and asthma. The herb reduces the inflammation and soothes the irritation.

Minor Skin Injuries, Burns, Rashes, Eczema, Psoriasis and Wounds: One of the best uses for comfrey is in healing minor injuries to the skin. Rashes, eczema, burns, and skin wounds heal quickly when the herb is used. I prefer to use the root for this purpose, but leaves can also be used. Apply Comfrey Salve three times a day or use bruised leaves or crushed root to make a poultice for the damaged skin. I also use Comfrey Tea or Comfrey Root Decoction as a wash for the area, especially for rashes, acne, eczema, and psoriasis. Do not use for deep wounds or puncture wounds as it heals them too quickly, blocking in infection.

Stomach Upsets, Ulcers of the Stomach and Lungs: Comfrey is used to treat internal ulcers and the bleeding they cause. The comfrey stops the bleeding and helps the wounded tissue heal. You can drink the tea or use the decoction.

Harvesting: Comfrey leaves are best harvested in the spring or early summer, before the plant blooms. They can be harvested in several cuttings and dried for later use. The roots can be dug at any time as needed. Leave behind part of the roots to encourage continued growth and an additional crop the next year.

Warning: Harmful toxins in comfrey are believed to cause liver damage, lung damage, or cancer when used in highly concentrated doses. For this reason, many healers do not recommend internal use of comfrey. However, small doses have been used safely in herbal medicines for hundreds of years with no reported ill effects. Use internally with caution or under care.

Comfrey should not be used by pregnant or breastfeeding women.

Both oral use and skin application could be hazardous and could cause birth defects. Do not use comfrey if you have liver disease or any liver problems. Comfrey heals wounds very quickly. As such, it is recommended that bone fractures and bone breaks are properly set before using it. This also applies for puncture wounds, as its rapid healing can seal in the bacterial infection.

Recipes. Comfrey Salve: You'll need: Comfrey root and/or leaves to fill a pint (500ml) jar, 1 cup Organic Olive Oil and 1/4 cup of beeswax, or more. Allow the comfrey leaves and root to dry, removing excess moisture. This can be done in a low oven, dehydrator, or by leaving them out in a warm place for a few days. Turn the oven on to its lowest setting.

Place the dried leaves and chopped root pieces into a pint (500ml) jar. Add 1 cup of olive oil and place the open jar in the oven. Allow the oil to warm and infuse for 90 minutes. Remove the jar from the oven and cover with a cloth to cool. When cool, place the lid on the jar and allow it to steep for 2 to 3 weeks in a cool, dark place. Strain the oil, removing the leaves and roots.

Combine the oil and the beeswax in a pot and warm gently until the beeswax is melted (4:1 ratio of oil to beeswax). Test the consistency of the oil by dipping a small amount onto waxed paper or aluminum foil and place in the freezer for five minutes. If the oil is thick enough, pour the mixture into a jar or wide mouth container. If not add a little more beeswax and test again.

Continue until desired consistency is reached. If the mixture is too thick you can warm it again and stir in a little more oil. Note: use an old non-aluminum pot to heat the oil and wax. It is difficult to clean. I have a small pot that I use only for this purpose.

Common Flax, Linum usitatissimum

Also known as Linseed, this is a useful plant for making medicine, oil, and fabric. Many people take it as a nutritional supplement. It is in the Linaceae (Flax) Family.

Identification: Common Flax is an annual. While rarely found growing wild, it is usually easy to find a cultivated crop or to grow yourself. The mature plant is 3 to 4 feet (0.9m to 1.2m) tall. A loose cluster of bluepurple stalked flowers grows at the tips of the branching stems. Each ¾ to 1 inch (2 cm to 2.5 cm) wide flower has 5 ovate petals surrounded by 5 erect, bluetipped stamens with a green ovary. The 5 sepals have a lance-shape. Flax has simple, alternate, erect green leaves that are 1/2 to 1 1/2 inches (1.25 cm to 3.75 cm) long and very narrow. They are stalkless and have smooth margins. Its stems are mostly unbranched and erect, and has multiple round, smooth stems growing from its base. Flax fruit is a round, dry, 5-lobed capsule that is 1/4 -1/2 (0.75 cm to 1.25 cm) inch in diameter.

Edible Use: The sprouts and seeds can be eaten raw or cooked. Careful eating the sprouts raw as they can stop up the bowel. Chew seeds well to access their nutrition, as they don't digest well whole.

Medicinal Use. As a Nutritional Supplement: Flax seed is rich in dietary fiber, protein, omega-3 fatty acids, and other nutrients. I grind flax and chia seeds fresh and eat them daily for health. I find that the fresh seeds are better as oil goes rancid quite quickly.

Cholesterol Control: Ingesting crushed flaxseeds on a daily basis is a good way to lower your cholesterol and LDL.

Autoimmune Issues: Flax seeds are high in omega 3 fatty acids, alpha-linolenic acid (ALA), and lignans. These compounds help regulate immune response, suppress inflammation, have neuroprotective effects, act as antioxidants, and modulate hormonal influences in autoimmune conditions.

Respiratory Problems: Flax seed oil helps with respiratory problems, including ARDS (acute respiratory distress syndrome). Its anti-inflammatory effects help coughs, sore throat, and congestion.

Constipation: For constipation, try two teaspoons of ground flax seed every morning, taken with a full glass of water.

Skin, Boils, Abscesses, Herpes, Acne, Burns: A warm poultice of flax seed oil on a cotton ball or applied directly helps heal these common skin problems. Flax is an excellent anti-inflammatory both internally and externally. For boils, add Lobelia inflata root to flax seed oil and apply it directly to the boil or use as a poultice.

Balancing Hormones: Flax seed contains lignans, a type of phytoestrogen. This helps balance female hormones, especially in post-menopausal women, and helps with symptoms of menopause.

Cancer: Flax seed and flax seed oil work as a complementary treatment as well as for the prevention of breast cancer and prostate cancer, where they seem to reduce PSA (prostate specific antigen) levels. Flax seeds help decrease breast cancer risk, lower the risk of metastasizing, and help to kill cancer cells in postmenopausal women. Consult with your oncologist.

Harvesting: Flax seed is harvested in the same manner as wheat. Harvest when the plant and fruits are dry and the seedpods begin to split. Shake over a sheet and sift. You may have to crush the seedpods to access the seeds.

Warning and Recommendations: Ground and powdered flax seed go rancid very quickly. I keep my flax seed whole until I need them, then grind or crush only the needed amount. Drink plenty of water with flax seeds.

Couch Grass, Agropyron (Elymus) repens

Couch Grass is often considered a simple weed and a nuisance; however, it has a list of medicinal properties that can't be ignored. It is also called dog grass, witchgrass, quack grass, and twitch grass. It can grow up to 3 feet (0.9m) tall and is part of the Poaceae (Grass) Family.

Identification: The crawling tubular root is elongated while the leaves are slender. Each short stem produces five to seven leaves and possibly a flower spike at the terminal. Each flower spike is composed of oval-shaped spikelets less than an inch (2.5 cm) long. The flowers appear in late June through August. The seed heads look like a stalk of grain. The roots are elongated, thin, tubular and whitish in color with yellow ends. Couch grass grows aggressively and is capable of crowding out agricultural crops and is often found on cultivated land. It likes loose and sandy soils and will die out as the soil becomes compacted.

Edible Use: The grain has food value as fodder for animals, and I am told that the root is sometimes eaten when food is scarce. I've never tried it. The roots can also be ground and roasted to make a coffee substitute.

Medicinal Use: Use the rhizomes of this plant to make a tincture, infusion, or decoction.

Urinary Tract Problems, Kidney Stones, Cystitis and Gallbladder Diseases: Couch grass is effective at treating urinary tract problems including inflammations, infections, and slow and painful urination caused by muscle spasms of the bladder and urethra. It soothes the mucous membranes and relieves the pain. It is a diuretic that increases the production of urine. It also works to dissolve kidney stones and gravel and treat cystitis and diseases of the gallbladder. Try using couch grass in combination with Usnea and bearberry to treat urinary tract infections.

Swollen Prostate: The herb is effective for treatment of swollen prostate glands, especially from gonorrhea. It is often combined with saw palmetto for this use.

Gout: Try couch grass decoction for treating gout.

Rheumatoid Arthritis: The diuretic properties, anti-inflammatory properties, and analgesic properties of couch grass make it effective in treating rheumatoid arthritis.

Jaundice: The anti-inflammatory properties and diuretic properties, combined with the benefits to the urinary tract and gallbladder, make couch grass a good choice for treating jaundice. It helps the body eliminate toxins and allows it to heal.

Recipes. Couch Grass Decoction: Ingredients: 4 ounces (113g) couch grass roots, chopped and 1-quart (1 Liter) water. Bring the water and the roots to a boil and reduce the heat to a simmer. Simmer the roots, uncovered, until the liquid is reduced by half, leaving approximately 2 cups of liquid. Store in the refrigerator for 3 days or freeze for longer periods.

Dandelion, Taraxacum officinale

Most children relish the opportunity to blow a puff of dandelion seeds into the wind. This wonderful plant is commonly regarded as a weed and can be found growing in sidewalk cracks and across untended roadsides and lawns. There are some look-alike flowers, so be sure of your identification before harvesting the plant. It is in the Aster/Daisy Family.

Identification: Dandelion is a perennial herbaceous plant native to North America. It grows from a tap-root that reaches deep into the soil. The plant grows up to a foot in height and flowers from April to June. It produces a yellow flower head consisting of florets. Leaves grow from the base of the plant in an elongated shape with highly jagged edges. The edges are said to resemble a lion's tooth, giving the plant its name.

Edible Use: The entire plant is edible and nutritious. The young leaves are best for greens, since the leaves grow more bitter with age. Young leaves can be cooked or eaten raw. Dandelion root is sometimes dried and roasted for use as a coffee substitute. The roots can also be cooked and eaten. They are bitter, with a taste similar to a turnip. Dandelion flowers make a nice salad garnish or can be battered and fried. Unopened flower buds are prepared into pickles similar to capers. Flowers can also be boiled and served with butter. Dandelion leaves and roots make a pleas-ant, but bitter tea. Flowers are fermented to make dandelion wine. Leaves and roots are used to flavor herbal beers and soft drinks.

Medicinal Use: The entire dandelion plant is used medicinally. The bitter roots are good for gastrointestinal and liver problems, while the leaves have a powerful diuretic effect. The plant makes a great general tonic and benefits the entire body. It is high in vitamins, minerals, and antioxidants. I use dandelion tea and tincture for internal use.

Digestion Problems, Liver and Gallbladder Function: Dandelion root is used to aid digestion and benefits the kidneys, gallbladder, and liver. It stimulates bile production, helping with the digestion of fats and toxin removal. Use it to treat jaundice and raise energy levels after infections. It removes toxins from the body and restores the electrolyte balance, which improves liver health and function.

I do a 2-week liver cleanse with my homemade Liver Tonic – a Dandelion Root and Milk Thistle seed tincture blend – every 6 months for general health. It also helps prevent gallstones. Dandelion contains inulin, a carbohydrate that helps maintain healthy gut flora and helps to regulate blood sugar levels. The plant is rich in fiber, which adds bulk to the stool, reducing the chances of constipation, diarrhea, and digestive issues.

Liver Protection and Healing: Vitamins and antioxidants in dandelion protect the liver and keep it healthy. It helps protect the liver from toxins and treats liver hemorrhages. Dandelion tea is used to treat non-alcoholic fatty liver disease. My Liver Tonic Blend (Dandelion Root and Milk Thistle Seed extract) reversed a patient's liver disease to the point that she no longer needs a liver transplant. This blend is also good for cirrhosis and hepatitis.

Diuretic and Detoxifying the Body: Dandelion leaves are a powerful diuretic and blood purifier. They stimulate the liver and gallbladder while eliminating toxins through the production and excretion of urine. They also help flush the kidneys. Even though dandelion is a diuretic it helps replace lost potassium and other minerals that are lost when water and salts are expelled.

Skin Wounds, Corns, and Warts: Fresh dandelion juice applied to the skin helps wounds heal and fights the bacteria and fungi that would otherwise cause infections. Dandelion sap, sometimes called dandelion milk, is useful to treat itches, ringworm, eczema, warts, and corns. Apply dandelion sap directly to the affected skin. Dandelion tea can be used as a wash on the skin to help healing. Dandelion sap is also useful in treating acne. It inhibits the formation of acne blemishes and reduces scarring. Some people are allergic to dandelion sap, so watch for signs of dermatitis on first use.

Osteoporosis and Bone Health: The calcium and vitamin K found in dandelion can protect bones from osteoporosis and arthritis. It helps stabilize bone density and strengthen the bone.

Controls Blood Sugar: Dandelion has several effects that are beneficial to diabetics. Dandelion juice stimulates the production of insulin in the pancreas, which helps regulate blood sugar levels and prevent dangers blood sugar swings. The plant is a natural diuretic which helps remove excess sugars from the body. It also helps control lipid levels.

Urinary Tract Disorders: The diuretic nature of dandelion helps eliminate toxins from the kidneys and urinary tract. The herb also acts as a disinfectant, inhibiting bacterial growth in the urinary system.

Prevents and Treats Cancer: Dandelion extracts are high in antioxidants, which reduce free radicals in the body and the risk of cancer. Its role in removing toxins from the body is also helpful. Researchers have shown that Dandelion Root coupled with Burdock Root have potential in treating cancer.

Prevents Iron Deficiency Anemia: Dandelions have high levels of iron, vitamins, and other minerals. Iron is an important part of the hemoglobin in blood and essential for healthy red blood cell formation. Using dandelion and eating the greens helps keep iron levels high.

Treating Hypertension: As a diuretic, dandelion juice helps eliminate excess sodium from the body and bring down blood pressure. It also helps reduce cholesterol ratios and raises the "good" HDL levels.

Boosts the Immune System: Dandelion boosts the immune system and helps fight off microbial and fungal agents.

Mastitis and Lactation: Dandelion has tradition-ally been used to enhance milk production and for treatment of mastitis. Check in with your doctor for this use.

Fights Inflammation and Arthritis: Dandelion contains antioxidants, phytonutrients and essential fatty acids that reduce inflammation in the body. This relieves swelling and related pain in the body. Inflammation is the root cause of many diseases, such as arthritis. Taraxasterol, found in dandelion roots, has shown great promise for Osteoarthritis.

Harvesting: I prefer to gather dandelion leaves in the spring when they are young and less bitter. I dry them for later medicinal use. Often, they grow in lawns or parks that have been sprayed so be careful where you harvest them.

For roots, I prefer the roots of plants that are 2-years old or older. The roots are larger and more medicinally potent. Grab the plant at the base and pull the entire plant up. The root is a deep taproot and will require some force.

You can also dig around the plant at a modest distance to help remove the entire root. As many gardeners know, leaving just a bit of the root will allow the plant to regrow.

So, if you want more dandelions simply leave part of the root intact. Plants dug in the autumn have more medicinal properties and higher levels of inulin.

Warning: Dandelion is generally considered safe, although some people may be allergic to it. Do not take dandelion if you are allergic to plants from the same family, or similar plants such as ragweed, chrysanthemum, marigold, yarrow, or daisy. Do not take dandelion if you are pregnant and consult your doctor if nursing.

Consult your doctor before taking if you are taking prescription medicines. Some people have reported dermatitis as a result of touching the plant or using the sap. Do not use dandelion if you are allergic.

Recipes: Dandelion Tea. Ingredients: 1/2 to 2 teaspoons of roasted dandelion root, in small pieces and 1 cup of boiling water. Pour boiling water over roasted or dried dandelion root and allow it to steep for 20 minutes. Strain the tea and drink.

Do not add sweeteners, as they reduce the herb's effectiveness. Milk may be used to taste, if desired.

Drink 3 cups per day for general medicinal use.

Dill, Anethum graveolens

Dill is a familiar aromatic herb cultivated in herb gar-dens across the country. It is in the Apiaceae /Umbelliferae (Celery/Carrot) Family.

Identification: Dill grows to 30 inches (75 cm) tall with a slender, hollow, and erect stem and feathery leaves. Leaves are finely divided and delicate in appearance, and are 4 to 8 inches (10 cm to 20 cm) long. They are similar to fennel in appearance.

Numerous tiny yellow or white flowers appear on umbrellas that are 3/4 to 3 1/2 inches (1.875 cm to 8.75 cm) in diameter as soon as the weather turns hot.

The seeds are small, up to 1/5 of an inch (0.625 cm) long with a ridged surface.

Edible Use: Dill is widely enjoyed as an herb, especially with fish and in pickles. The leaves, seeds, and stems are edible.

Medicinal Use. Colic: Colicky babies respond well to a dill infusion. The dill soothes the stomach and calms the baby. This is a popular colic remedy because it is easily attained, effective, and known to be safe for children.

Digestive Issues, Irritable Bowel Syndrome, Menstrual Cramps, and Muscle Spasms: Dill Leaf Infusion relieves cramping and muscle spasms including those in the digestive tract. It relieves the symptoms of painful spasms without treating the underlying cause. Use it to give immediate relief while looking for the cause of the problem. A Dill Seed Infusion or Dill Tincture may also be used.

Stimulates Milk Flow: Dill Infusion helps nursing mothers increase their milk flow. It has a beneficial calming effect on both mother and child.

Halitosis: Temporary bad breath is easily solved by chewing on dill leaves or seeds, but the problem can be completely alleviated by chewing the seeds daily. Over the long term the seeds attack the causes of the problem causing a permanent solution.

Flatulence: For abdominal flatulence, take Dill Seed Infusion before each meal.

Harvesting: Harvest leaves throughout the summer until the flowers appear in late summer. Gather leaves in the late morning after the dew has dried and use them fresh, freeze them, or dry them for later use. I collect the seed heads once the flowers are fully open, if needed, or I allow them to completely ripen for seed collection. The brown seeds are collected and dried for storage.

Warning: Consumption of dill can cause sensitivity to the sun in some people. People sometimes have a rash appear after exposure to sunlight.

Recipes. Dill Leaf Infusion: Ingredients: 1 Tablespoon chopped dill leaves and 1 cup boiling water. Pour the boiling water over the dill leaves and cover the cup. Let it steep until cool enough to drink, then strain out the leaves.

Dill Seed Infusion: You need 1 to 2 tablespoons dill seeds and 1 cup water. Bring the seeds and water to a boil, turn off the heat and cover the pot. Allow the infusion to steep for 15 minutes. Cool and strain out the seeds. Take one cup before each meal for digestive issues.

Dock (Curly/Yellow), Rumex crispus

Docks and Sorrels, genus Rumex, is a group of over 200 different varieties in the Polygonaceae (Buckwheat) Family. Here I am referring specifically to Rumex crispus and its medicinal use, but broad-leaved dock, Rumex obstusifolius, is used in a similar manner. Curly Dock is a biennial herb that grows across the globe. The plant is also called yellow dock, sour dock, narrowleaved dock, and curled dock.

Identification: Flower stalks grow from the base (similar to a rosette) with smooth, leathery, fleshy leaves growing in a large cluster at the apex. Leaves are wavy or curly on the edges and have a coarse texture. These leaves can grow up to 2 feet (0.6m) long and are only 3 inches (7.5 cm) wide, making them long, narrow and wavy. Small veins curve out toward the edge of the leaf and then turn back towards the central vein. Leaves farther up the plant may vary in size and appearance. On older leaves the central vein is sometimes tinged with red.

The flower stalk is approximately 3 feet (0.9m) in height with clustered flowers and seeds. Tiny green flowers grow in dense heads on the flower stalk during the second year.

The 3-sided seeds are brown, shiny, and covered by a papery sheath that looks like heart-shaped wings. The root is a long yellow, forking taproot that regenerates the plant each year.

Edible Use: Curly dock has a lemony flavor and its leaves are used as a cooked vegetable. Young leaves can be eaten raw (old ones can too but they don't taste as good). Leaves contain varying amounts of oxalic acid and tannin. The seeds can be pounded into a flour. The root is generally not eaten but it is used for medicine.

Medicinal Use: Curly dock is a purifying and cleansing herb. All parts of the plant can be used, but the roots have the strongest healing properties.

I often crush dock leaves to put on stinging nettle stings. My grandmother showed me this trick when I was a child visiting her in England and I've been using it ever since. They tend to grow near each other, which is very useful.

Constipation and Diarrhea: Curly dock is a gentle and safe laxative for the treatment of mild constipation. It can also cause or relieve diarrhea, depending on the dosage and other factors such as harvest time and soil conditions.

Skin Problems: Curly dock weed is useful externally to treat a wide variety of skin problems due to its cleansing properties.

Taken internally, it is a tonic. It's dried or pounded root can be used as a poultice, salve, or powder applied to sores, wounds, or other skin problems.

Liver, Gall Bladder and Detox: Curly dock root is a bitter tonic for the gall bladder and liver. It in-creases bile production, which helps the body with detoxification. It is helpful for any condition that can benefit from purifying and cleansing the body from toxins. It is often combined with Greater Burdock to create a stronger detoxifying effect.

Harvesting: Harvest the root early in autumn and dry it for later use. Dig up the entire plant and root if possible and wash the root lightly. Cut before drying. Harvest leaves from spring through summer as needed. Look for leaves that are fresh and curled. Avoid leaves that are brown or full of bug holes. Also avoid areas that are near highways or that have been sprayed with pesticides.

Recipes. Curly Dock Tincture: You need fresh curly dock root, grated, 80-proof vodka or other drinking alcohol and a glass jar with tight-fitting lid. Place the grated root in a clean glass jar. Fill the jar, covering the root completely, with 80-proof alcohol.

Allow the tincture to steep for 6 to 8 weeks, shaking gently every day. Strain out the root pieces and place the tincture in a clean glass jar. Store in a cool, dark place for up to 7 years.

Echinacea angustifolia and E. purpurea, Purple Coneflower

Echinacea is commonly called Purple Coneflower. It is a pretty, purple sunflower-like flowering plant that has strong medicine. It is native to North America and be-longs to the Asteraceae (Daisy) Family. It is widespread and easy to cultivate in the garden. Echinacea grows wild in open rocky prairies and plains.

Identification: Purple coneflower is a perennial herb that is 6 to 24 inches (15 cm to 60 cm) tall with a woody, often branching taproot. This plant has one to several rough-hairy stems that are mostly unbranched. The leaves are alternate, simple, and narrowly lance-shaped.

The stem leaves are widely spaced and attached alternately to the lower half of the stem. Edges of leaves are toothless and have three distinct veins along its length. Stem and leaves are rough and hairy to touch. Its stems may be purple or green tinged. Echinacea Flowers look like lavender sunflowers. Its flowerheads are 1 ½ to 3 inches (3.75 cm to 7.5 cm) wide and are at the ends of long stalks. They bloom in summer. The disk flowers are 5-lobed, brownishpur-le in color, and are situated among stiff bracts with yellow pollen. Its fruits are small, dark, 4- angled achenes.

Medicinal Use: This herb has a modulating effect on the body's natural immune system, encouraging it to operate more efficiently. It raises the body's resistance to bacterial and viral infections by stimulating the immune system. It also has anti-inflammatory and pain-relieving functions.

Do not use internally if you have an autoimmune condition. Most people seem aware that Echinacea is an herb for preventing and healing colds and the flu, but these plants can do a lot more. The root and leaves are used medicinally.

Urinary Tract Infections: The anti-microbial and anti-inflammatory effects of Echinacea make it an ideal choice for the treatment of urinary tract infections. It is a standard UTI treatment and is often combined with goldenseal root. Do not take either of these herbs if you have an autoimmune condition.

Colds and the Flu: Echinacea is known to reduce the impact of the common cold and the flu. People who begin taking Echinacea extract or tea immediately upon feeling sick heal much more quickly than those who do not.

In general, people who take Echinacea get well up to 4 days faster than those who don't (note that the same holds true for blue elderberry). For best results, they should begin taking Echinacea as soon as they notice symptoms, taking a double dose three times on the first day and then take three regular doses each day during the illness.

Allergies and Respiratory Diseases: Echinacea helps to relieve allergies by stimulating and balancing the immune system. It is especially helpful in relieving asthma attacks. While it doesn't cure asthma, it reduces the severity of the attack and helps the patient get over attacks. It is also useful for treating bronchitis.

For Infections, Burns, Wounds and as an Anti-Fungal: Echinacea is an antibiotic, antifungal antiviral, and it stimulates the immune system. It is helpful to relieve infections of all kinds. It is used both externally and internally.

Snakebite, Insect and Spider Bites, and Stings: Echinacea is used to treat spider bites and in-sect stings. It does a good job of neutralizing the poison and reducing the pain. It is said to be useful for snake-bites, as it is a strong anti-inflammatory.

Harvesting: Harvest the roots in autumn when the plant has died back. Dig up the entire plant, watching for branched roots. Scrub the dirt from the root and dry it for later use.

Warning: Do not use internally long-tem as it may cause digestive upset. People with autoimmune conditions should not use Echinacea internally as it is an immune-system booster and may lead to a flare-up.

Recipes. Echinacea Tincture: 1-pint (500ml) of vodka or rum, at least 80 proof, 1 cup of loosely packed Echinacea leaf and root, chopped fine, 1-pint(500ml) glass jar with a tight-fitting lid.

Put the loosely packed Echinacea leaf and finely chopped root into the jar. Fill with 80 proof vodka or rum and tightly fasten the lid. Keep the herb covered and shake the jar daily for 2 months. Add more alcohol when needed to keep the jar full. Strain the herbs. Keep the extract covered in a cool, dark place.

Elecampane, Inula helenium

Elecampane, a member of the sunflower family Asteraceae, is also commonly known as horse-heal, horse-elder, wild sunflower, starwort and elfdock. According to legend, the plant sprung up where the tears fell from Helen of Troy. The plant was considered sacred to the Celts and was thought to be associated with the fairy folk.

Elecampane is found in moist soil and shady places. It is cultivated in North America and is naturalized in the eastern United States growing in pastures, along road-sides, and at the base of eastern and southern facing slopes.

Identification: Elecampane is an upright herb that grows up to 6 feet (2m) in height. The large rough leaves are toothed and can be egg-shaped, elliptical, or lance-shaped. Lower leaves have a stalk, while the up-per ones grow directly on the stem. Each leaf is up to 12 to 20 inches long (15cm-30cm) and 5 inches (12cm) wide. The upper side of the leaf is hairy and green, while the underside is whitish and velvety.

Flower heads are up to 3 inches (7 cm) in diameter and contain 50 to 100 yellow ray flowers and 100 to 250 yellow disc flowers. Elecampane blooms from June to August. The flowers are large, bright yellow, and resemble a double sunflower. The brown aromatic root branches below ground. It is large, thick, mucilaginous, and bitter with a camphoraceous odor and a floral background scent.

Edible Use: The root has been used in the making of absinthe and as a condiment. It stimulates pungent and bitter tastes, but it also has a sweet flavor due to its high polysaccharide content (inulin). Inulin, not to be confused with insulin, is a prebiotic that is used to feed and support healthy gut bacteria.

Medicinal Use: The elecampane root is the part most often used medicinally. Asian traditions also use the flowers, but I have had best results with the roots.

Elecampane root is useful fresh and dried. It can be in-fused into honey, extracted in alcohol, made into cough syrup, or made into a tea.

In most cases, it is best to start with a small dose and slowly increase it until the best results are obtained without nausea or overly drying effects.

Elecampane contains alantolactone and isoalantolactone, which is antibacterial, antifungal, and acts as a vermifuge (against parasites). These compounds also demonstrate anticancer activity, helping with apoptosis (programmed cell death).

Asthma, Bronchitis, Mucus, Whooping Cough, Influenza, and Tuberculosis: Elecampane root is useful as an expectorant and cough preventative in asthma, bronchitis, whooping cough, and tuberculosis. It lessens the need to cough by loosening phlegm and making the cough productive. It is beneficial for any respiratory illness with excess mucus discharge. Not recommended for dry coughs. It soothes bronchial tube linings, reduces swelling and irritation of the respiratory tract, cleanses the lungs, and fights harmful organisms in the respiratory tract. For acute coughs, use small, frequent doses. It is also useful to support lung health in asthma patients (as is mullein).

Stimulates Digestion and Appetite: While elecampane is mostly valued for its effects on the respiratory system, it is also valuable for treating digestive system problems. It is warming, draining, and bitter.

Use elecampane for poor digestion, poor absorption, poor appetite, mucus in the digestive system, excess gas, and lethargy or sluggishness of the digestive sys-tem.

Elecampane strengthens digestion and improves ab-sorption which is beneficial in malnourished or under-nourished patients. It also treats nausea and diarrhea.

Type 2 Diabetes: The high inulin content in elecampane is helpful for patients with high blood sugar and for type 2 diabetes patients. Inulin slows down sugar metabolism, reduces blood glucose spikes and decreases insulin resistance. It may also reduce inflammation associated with diabetes.

Intestinal Parasites: Elecampane is a vermifuge that eliminates intestinal parasites from the body, including hookworm, roundworm, threadworm, and whipworm.

Cancer: Elecampane contains alantolactone and isoalantolactone, which have been shown to help with programmed cell death (apoptosis) for certain cancers.

Harvesting: Harvest fresh elecampane root in the fall after the plant has produced seed, or in the early spring before leaves appear. I prefer roots that are two to three years old. Older roots are too woody, and younger roots lack their full medicinal potential. It is best to dig up some of the larger horizontal roots and leave the remaining roots so the plant can continue growing.

Warning: Large doses of elecampane can cause nausea, vomiting, and diarrhea.

Avoid use of elecampane during pregnancy since it can cause contractions and is a uterine stimulant.

Skin rashes have been reported in sensitive people. Persons with known allergies to plants in the Aster family should avoid using elecampane.

Elecampane can lower blood sugar and could interfere with blood sugar control in diabetics.

There are indications that elecampane may interfere with blood pressure control in some patients. Monitor blood pressure carefully while using elecampane. Do not use elecampane within 2 weeks before or after a scheduled surgery. It may cause drowsiness – no not use with sedatives.

Evening Primrose, *Oenothera biennis*

Evening primrose is also known as evening star and sun drop. Evening primrose gets its name because its flowers usually open at dusk, after the sun is no longer on them. It grows in eastern and central North America and has naturalized to Europe. It is in the Ona-graceae (Evening Primrose) Family.

Identification: *Oenothera biennis* is a biennial plant. In its first year, the leaves can grow up to 10 inches (25 cm) long. Leaves are lance-shaped, toothed, and form a rosette. In its second year, the flower stem has alternate, spirally-arranged leaves on a hairy, rough flower stem that is often tinged with purple.

The leaves are reminiscent of willow leaves. This erect flower stem sometimes branches near the top of the plant and grows from 3 to 6 feet (0.9m to 1.8m) tall. It flowers from June to October.

The bright yellow flowers are partially to fully closed during the heat of the day. Flowers have four petals and are 1 to 2 inches (2.5 cm to 5 cm) across. They grow in a many-flowered terminal panicle. The fragrant flowers last only 1 to 2 days. Seedpods are long and narrow.

Edible Use: All parts of evening primrose are edible, including the flowers, leaves, stalks, oil, root, and seedpods. Roots can be eaten either cooked or boiled. Its flowers and flower buds are good raw in salads. Young seedpods can be cooked or steamed. Second year stems can be peeled and eaten fresh. Its seeds are edible and oily. Leaves aren't usually eaten due to their texture but they can be if boiled a few times.

Medicinal Use: Evening primrose oil comes from the seeds of the evening primrose, which contain gamma linolenic acid (GLA) - an omega 6 fatty acid also found in borage. Flowers, roots, bark, and leaves are also used medicinally.

Balancing Women's Hormones, PCOS, PMS, and Menopause: Evening primrose oil helps balance hormones in women. It naturally treats symptoms of PMS, including breast tenderness, water retention and bloating, acne, irritability, depression, moodiness, and headaches.

It is also useful in the treatment of polycystic ovarian syndrome (PCOS), helping with fertility and in normalizing the menstrual cycle. It helps ease the symptoms of menopause as well, like hot flashes, moodiness, and sleep disturbance.

Hair Loss in Men and Women: Evening prim-rose attacks the hormonal causes of male pattern bald-ness and androgenetic alopecia in women. By balancing the hormones, it prevents further hair loss and, in some people, helps hair grow back. It is best used both internally and externally (rub on the scalp daily along with diluted rosemary essential oil).

Skin Diseases, Eczema, Psoriasis, Acne: Evening primrose oil works well for people with skin problems such as acne, eczema, dermatitis, and psoriasis. It balances the hormonal causes of these diseases, reduces inflammation, and promotes healing while reducing symptoms such as itching, redness, and swelling.

Arthritis and Osteoporosis: Evening primrose oil is a good supplement for people with rheumatoid arthritis and osteoporosis. It is anti-inflammatory and reduces pain and stiffness. It also balances the hormones that cause bone loss in osteoporosis. It also seems to help with calcium absorption and is best combined with fish oil.

Gastro-Intestinal Disorders: The bark and leaves are astringent and healing. They are effective in treating gastro-intestinal disorders caused by muscle spasms of the stomach or intestines. They calm the spasms and allow better digestion.

Whooping Cough: Evening primrose is an expectorant. A syrup made from the flowers helps treat whooping cough symptoms and is easier than a tincture or tea to get young children to swallow. Boil the flowers in a small amount of water, strain, and sweeten with raw honey.

Asthma and Allergies: Use leaf and bark tea to treat asthma. The tea relieves bronchial spasms and opens the airways. It does not cure the asthma, only treats the symptoms. It seems to work best for asthma with allergic causes.

Blood Pressure and Cholesterol: Regular consumption of evening primrose oil helps reduce blood cholesterol levels and lowers blood pressure.

Best results are achieved by long-term use; it is not in-tended for acute situations.

Diabetic Neuropathy: Evening primrose oil helps treat nerve pain specifically due to diabetes.

Harvesting, Preparation, and Storage: The seeds of evening primrose ripen from August to October. Collect them when ripe and press for oil before they dry out. Flowers must be picked in full bloom.
Gather the leaves and stem "bark" when the flowering stems have grown up. Strip the "bark" of evening prim-rose and dry for later use; the leaves are also harvested and dried at that time. Dig the roots in the second year when they are larger and more potent.

Recipes. How to Make Cold-Pressed Evening Primrose Seed Oil: Grind fresh seeds. You can use a flourmill, sausage grinder, auger type juicer, coffee grinder, or blender to grind the seeds into a paste. It may take several passes through the grinder to get a fine grind. Add a tiny amount of water only if necessary, to facilitate grinding. Roll the ground seeds into a ball and knead them by hand to release the oil, catching it in a small bowl. Knead and squeeze the seeds until the oil is released, this may take some time. Place the seed paste into a seed bag or use a coffee filter and tighten it to release even more oil into the bowl. When you have gathered as much oil as possible, filter it through a fresh filter to remove any remaining seed remnants. The standard dosage for internal use is 1 gram of oil daily, broken into 2 to 3 doses.

Strong Evening Primrose Tea. (1-ounce bark and leaves, crushed or chopped into small pieces, 1-pint (500 ml) of water). Bring the water and herbs to a boil and reduce the heat to a low simmer. Simmer the herbs for 10 minutes. Allow the tea to cool and strain out the herbs. Keep the tea refrigerated until needed and use within three days.

Fennel, Foeniculum vulgare

Fennel is a commonly used vegetable in the Apiaceae /Umbelliferae (Celery/Carrot/Parsley) Family. It has a licorice flavor and is very fragrant. It is found across the United States and Canada. I grow it in my garden, but am also able to find it along roadsides, riverbanks, and pasture lands.

Identification: Fennel is a flowering perennial herb with yellow flowers. It looks a lot like dill, except for the bulb. The leaves are feathery, and finer than dill leaves. The stems are erect, smooth and green and grow to a height of eight feet (2.4m).
The leaves are finely dissected with threadlike segments. Most, but not all varieties form a stem-bulb that sits on the ground or is lifted by a segment of stem. Leaf branches fan out from the stem, forming the bulb. Flowers appear on umbels, 2 to 6 inches (5 cm to 15 cm) in diameter. The umbels are terminal and com-pound, with each section containing 20 to 50 tiny yellow flowers. The fruit is a small seed, approximately 1/5 to 1/3 inch-long (0.6 cm to 0.9 cm) with grooves along its length.

Edible Use: The stems, leaves, and seeds are edible. I prefer to roast the bulbs and use the seeds for seasoning.

Medicinal Use: The seeds and root are used to pre-pare remedies, but eating the plant is also healthy.

Digestive Problems: An infusion made from the seeds is effective in the treatment of digestive problems. Take it after meals for the treatment of indigestion, heartburn, and flatulence.

It is also effective for constipation and stomach pains. In addition to using the infusion, if you have digestive problems add fennel seeds to your cooking.

Nursing Mothers and Colic: For the treatment of colic, have the mother drink Fennel Infusion. It not only relieves the baby's colic, but it also increases the milk flow. Non-nursing babies can take a spoonful of the infusion to relieve the symptoms.

Sore Throats, Laryngitis, Gum Problems: I also use Fennel Infusion as a treatment for sore throats. Gargle with the infusion to treat the infection and pain. This treatment is also effective for sore gums.

Urinary Tract Problems, Kidney Stones:
For urinary tract infections, kidney stones, and other urinary tract problems, use a decoction of the fennel root.

Menstrual Problems and Premenstrual Tension: Fennel has the ability to regulate the menstrual cycle and the hormones affecting it. I prescribe Fennel Seed Tea for a variety of menstrual problems including cramping, PMS, pain fluid retention and other menstrual symptoms. Fennel contains estrogen-like chemicals that work to restore the hormonal balance

Detoxifying, Diuretic: Fennel is a strong diuretic and detoxifier. It cleans toxins from the body and flushes them out through the urinary tract. Drink Fennel Seed Tea up to three times daily to detoxify the body and remove excess fluids.

Eyesight, Eyewash, Conjunctivitis, Eye Inflammations: To strengthen eyesight, eat fennel with your meals.

For inflammations and eye infections, use Fennel Seed Tea as an eyewash. It treats conjunctivitis, infections and reduces inflammations of the eye.

Harvesting: Harvest fennel seeds in autumn when they are fully mature. Dry them and store in an air-tight container in a cool, dark place.

Warning: Rarely people have had problems with photo-dermatitis while taking fennel seed. Fennel has hormonal effects and should not be consumed by pregnant women.

Recipes. Fennel Infusion: You need 1 teaspoon crushed fennel seeds and 1 cup boiling water. Pour the boiling water over the fennel seeds and allow the infusion to steep, covered, for 10 to 15 minutes. Drink 3 cups daily. Take after meals for digestive issues.

Fennel Root Decoction: To make the decoction get 2 ounces (56g) chopped fennel root, fresh and 1-quart (1 Liter) water. Bring the fennel root and water to a boil and turn the heat down to a simmer. Simmer the decoction for 1 hour. Turn off the heat and strain out the root. Store the decoction in the refrigerator for up to 1 week.

Feverfew, Tanacetum parthenium

Feverfew is an herb that is widely used for migraines. It grows along roadsides, in rocky and disturbed soil, and is cultivated in some home herb and ornamental gardens. Also known as Chrysanthemum parthenium, wild chamomile, and bachelor's buttons. It is a member of the Aster/Daisy Family.

Identification: Feverfew grows into a bushy shape approximately 1 to 3 feet (0.3m to 0.9m) tall. It has round, leafy stems that grow from a taproot. The leaves are yellow-green and pinnately divided into slightly rounded divisions.

The upper leaves are more lobed and toothed than lower leaves. Leaves have a distinctive bitter aroma and taste. Flowers bloom in summer.

The flowers look like small daisies with a large yellow disk and short white rays. The center disk is flat, unlike chamomiles, which have conical central disks.

Edible Use: Feverfew leaves are edible but are very bitter.

Medicinal Use: The leaves and flowers are used medicinally. Typical doses are 2 to 3 leaves per day, with a proportionally reduced dose for children over the age of three.

Migraines and Tension Headaches: Taking feverfew regularly works well as a preventative for migraine headaches, as does butterbur. It must be taken regularly to work.

Feverfew may work in a few ways: as an anti-inflammatory, by inhibiting smooth muscle contraction, as an analgesic, and by inhibiting blood platelet aggregation. It may also help via other mechanisms still being studied.

Use the flowers and leaves fresh or dried. To prevent migraines, chew 1 to 4 leaves per day, or drink 1 cup of Feverfew Leaf Tea daily, or use a daily tincture.

For people with migraines simply keep dried leaves or a feverfew tincture on hand with you.

If mouth sores develop from chewing leaves regularly, switch to a powdered or tinctured form. The tea, leaf or tincture may also be used as a treatment for tension headaches.

Fevers, Cold and Flu Pain (and Colic): Fever-few gets its name from its traditional use treating fevers. Hot Feverfew Tea helps break a fever and treats the aches and pains associated with cold and flu. It is anti-inflammatory and analgesic. For colic in babies and young children, try just a few drops of a cold infusion.

Menstrual Cramps and to Regulate the Menses: Feverfew is both a uterine stimulant and a pain reliever and is particularly good at relieving painful menstrual cramping and in bringing on menses.

Feverfew shouldn't be used if you are pregnant, as it can stimulate uterine contraction and directly affect the baby.

Harvesting: Harvest feverfew leaves and flowers shortly after the flowers appear in early summer. Dry a supply for future use. You can also powder the dried leaves and encapsulate them.

Warning: Some people have an allergic reaction to feverfew and dermatitis can also occur with skin con-tact. Chewing the leaves can cause mouth sores in some people. If you are allergic to ragweed, marigold, or chrysanthemum, you may also react to feverfew.

Do not use during pregnancy as it causes contractions. Do not use on people who have blood coagulation problems.

Recipes. Feverfew Tea: Steep 1 heaping teaspoon of feverfew leaves and flowerheads in 1 cup of hot water. Allow the infusion to cool to lukewarm, then drink it or apply as directed.

Garlic, Allium sativum

Garlic has strong medicinal value, and it tastes great. Most people would benefit greatly by eating more garlic, no matter how good or bad their health. I use garlic for nearly everything.

Most of the garlic that I use now is cultivated. It is found in nearly every herb garden and kitchen garden across the country and is easily found at supermarkets. Don't fall for prepared garlic, however. Chop it fresh and make your own garlic products for maximum health.

Identification: The garlic plant grows to about 2 feet (0.6 meters) tall. It is a bulbous herb with four to twelve long, flat, sword-shaped leaves growing from an underground stem. The bulbs are rounded and contain approximately 15 smaller cloves. Each clove and the bulb is covered by a thin white or pinkish papery coat. Flowers appear in a cluster at the top of a 10-inch (25 cm) flower stalk. Flower stalks grow from a common point on each plant. The flowers are green-white or pinkish with six sepals and petals. Propagation is primarily by bulbs. Seeds are rarely produced.

Edible Use: The bulbs are the only part of the garlic eaten and are usually used for seasoning or as a condiment.

Medicinal Use: For internal use, I usually recommend that people simply eat more garlic in their foods. For best results, garlic should be chopped fine and al-lowed to rest for 10 minutes or so before cooking. Eating it raw is even better.

Chopping, and allowing time for the sulfurous com-pounds to develop in the garlic, will make it more potent. Some people complain of a strong garlic smell in the sweat when consuming garlic. This is a natural response and indicates that the body is using the beneficial components. To alleviate this complaint, eat fresh parsley with the garlic.

Taking Garlic as Medicine: In general, use garlic in any way that best suits you. People who don't like the strong flavor can put it into capsules, but I like using it fresh and chopped fine or crushed to release the beneficial sulfurous compounds.

You can also take it as a tincture. For people who like garlic, try chewing one whole raw clove at each meal or drinking garlic juice daily.

Treating Viral, Bacterial, and Parasitic Infections: Garlic is a potent antibiotic, antifungal, and anti-parasitic plant. Use garlic to treat infections of all kinds, including colds, flu, sore throats, bronchitis, stomach flu, and intestinal worms.

Thrush, Yeast, and Fungal Infections: Use garlic preparations topically to treat thrush infections and other types of yeast or fungal infections. Spread a paste of garlic on the affected area several times a day and eat garlic regularly to clear the infection internally.

Digestive Problems: Garlic improves digestion and is useful to relieve excessive gas, bloating, and other digestive upsets.

Lowers Blood Sugars in Diabetics: Garlic helps lower blood sugar in diabetics by improving the function of the pancreas and increasing the secretion of insulin.

This helps the body regulate blood sugar levels and alleviates the problems associated with high blood sugar. To be effective, garlic needs to be eaten at every meal in significant quantities. Adding a couple of cloves of pickled garlic to the meal is usually enough to get the full benefits.

Bronchitis, Whooping Cough, Congestion of All Causes: Garlic has a strong decongestant effect and expectorant action. It is useful for maladies where phlegm or mucous is a problem. Garlic also

Taking Garlic as Medicine: In general, use garlic in any way that best suits you. People who don't like the strong flavor can put it into capsules, but I like using it fresh and chopped fine or crushed to release the beneficial sulfurous compounds.

You can also take it as a tincture. For people who like garlic, try chewing one whole raw clove at each meal or drinking garlic juice daily.

Treating Viral, Bacterial, and Parasitic Infections: Garlic is a potent antibiotic, antifungal, and anti-parasitic plant. Use garlic to treat infections of all kinds, including colds, flu, sore throats, bronchitis, stomach flu, and intestinal worms.

Thrush, Yeast, and Fungal Infections: Use garlic preparations topically to treat thrush infections and other types of yeast or fungal infections. Spread a paste of garlic on the affected area several times a day and eat garlic regularly to clear the infection internally.

Digestive Problems: Garlic improves digestion and is useful to relieve excessive gas, bloating, and other digestive upsets.

Lowers Blood Sugars in Diabetics: Garlic helps lower blood sugar in diabetics by improving the function of the pancreas and increasing the secretion of insulin.

This helps the body regulate blood sugar levels and alleviates the problems associated with high blood sugar. To be effective, garlic needs to be eaten at every meal in significant quantities. Adding a couple of cloves of pickled garlic to the meal is usually enough to get the full benefits.

Bronchitis, Whooping Cough, Congestion of All Causes: Garlic has a strong decongestant effect and expectorant action. It is useful for maladies where phlegm or mucous is a problem. Garlic also reduces fevers and kills off the underlying infection. It is also useful for bronchial asthma where the breathing passages have swollen making breathing difficult.

Elevated Blood Cholesterol Levels and Blood Pressure: Garlic effectively lowers blood cholesterol levels and blood pressure when consumed regularly.

Corns, Warts, and Acne: For corns, warts, and acne, rub a paste made from fresh mashed garlic on the affected spot. Garlic actually softens and soothes the skin and kills the viral or bacterial infection causing the problem.

Recipes: Garlic Infusion. Chop or grind garlic cloves and allow them to rest for 10 to 15 minutes before continuing. Place the garlic into a pot and cover with water. Heat the water gently to a simmer, then turn off the heat. Allow the garlic and water to steep overnight. Use 2 to 4 ml of this infusion, 3 times a day with meals. Keep the Infusion in the refrigerator for up to three days or in the freezer for up to a month.

Garlic Tincture: Chop 1 cup of garlic cloves fine and allow to rest for 10 to 15 minutes. Place the garlic cloves in a pint (500ml) jar with a tight-fitting lid. Cover the chopped garlic with apple cider vinegar, preferably with the mother (live vinegar). Allow the jar to steep for 4 to 5 weeks, shaking it several times a week. Take 1 tablespoon of garlic tincture with each meal.

Goldenrod, *Solidago* spp.

Goldenrods comprise about 100 species or more that grow throughout North America in open areas like meadows, prairies, and savannas. I primarily use *Soli-dago canadensis*, which is the most common golden-rod in North America. It is in the Aster/Daisy Family and is also known as goldruthe, woundwort, and soli-dago. Goldenrods take the blame for a lot of allergies, but most of it is undeserved. There are people allergic to goldenrod and they should not use the plant. How-ever, most of the allergies are caused by ragweed and other similar flowering plants. Goldenrod are pollinated by bees and do not release pollen into the air like the ragweeds. Furthermore, Goldenrod can be used against allergies caused by ragweed.

Identification: I often find goldenrod in open areas and along trailsides. I identify it by its unique aroma, taste, and its visual properties – like its height and its large sprays of yellow flower clusters. Crushing a goldenrod leaf releases a salty, balsam-like fragrance. Any goldenrod species can be used medicinally; however, it is necessary to differentiate the plant from similar toxic plants, including ragwort and groundsel. If you are unsure of your identification, use a local field guide. Goldenrod plants have alternate, simple leaves that are usually toothed. They can also be smooth or hairy.

The leaves at the base of the plant are longer, shortening as they climb the plant, with no leaf stem and 3 distinct parallel veins. The shape can vary from species to species. The stems are unbranched, until the plant flowers. Flower heads are composed of yellow ray florets arranged around disc florets. Each flower head may contain a few florets per head or up to 30, depending on the species.

The flower head is usually 1/2 inch (1.25 cm) or less in diameter, although some varieties are larger. The inflorescence is usually a raceme or a panicle. Plant size varies by species, usually growing 2 to 5 feet (0.6 meters to 1.5meters) tall. Some varieties spread aggressively by runners, while others grow in clumps that expand outward each year.

Toxic Look-Alikes: Goldenrod has many look-alikes and some of them are deadly. Groundsel, life root, staggerweed, and ragwort are regional names for deadly look-alike plants in the Senecio genus. Ragwort and groundsels usually have fewer and smaller flower heads and bloom earlier in the season. These are not hard rules, however, so it can be difficult to identify the plants and distinguish them from other local varieties. You should be very sure of your plant identification before harvesting.

Edible Use: Goldenrod flowers are edible and can be eaten lightly fried or in a salad. It is also used as a flavoring for alcoholic beverages such as cordials and mead, and in fermented homemade soda. Leaves can be cooked and eaten like spinach.

Medicinal Use: I use the leaves and flowers in my medicinal preparations; however, the roots are also used. I use goldenrod to made medicinal tea and tinctures. For children, it can be infused into raw honey or made into a syrup.

Urinary Tract and Kidneys: Goldenrod has astringent and antiseptic properties, that are useful in treating urinary tract infections and bladder infections. It is also effective in restoring balance to the kidneys and in prevention of kidney stones. It is a good choice for chronic conditions and long-term use, though care should be taken as it is a diuretic. Other treatments might be more useful for acute UTI and kidney infections.

Skin, Wounds, and Stopping Bleeding: Goldenrod is an herb of choice to treat and help heal skin wounds, burns, open sores, cuts, boils and other skin irritations. The herb acts as an anti-inflammatory, antibacterial, and antifungal. It helps wounds heal quickly and soothes the irritation. I use goldenrod decoction as a wash, make a poultice, or sometimes use the powdered dried leaves directly on skin wounds. Its common name of "woundwort" came from its ability to stop bleeding when applied to a wound (its dried, powdered form works best as a styptic). You can also use goldenrod to make an ointment or salve. Roots were traditionally used for burns.

Colds, Allergies, and Bronchial Congestion: Goldenrod Tincture is a good choice for treating the symptoms of seasonal allergies and colds. It calms runny eyes and noses, and the sneezes that are triggered by summer and fall allergies.

It is an antiseptic and an expectorant and contains quercetin and rutin, which are natural antihistamines. It also treats sore throats. Goldenrod can also be taken as a tea when needed. For treating a sore throat, try combining it with sage.

Once cooled a bit, the tea can be used as a gargle for laryngitis and pharyngitis (sore throats). Goldenrod helps the body get rid of respiratory congestion caused by allergies, sinus infections, colds and the flu. It works much like Yerba Santa to dry bronchial and respiratory secretions and to expel existing mucous.

Diarrhea: Goldenrod stimulates the digestive systems while calming internal inflammation and irritation that causes diarrhea. It is anti-inflammatory and anti-microbial, so it attacks the symptoms and causes.

Boosts the Cardiovascular System: Golden-rod is a good source of rutin, a powerful antioxidant that improves the cardiovascular and cerebrovascular system. It supports circulation and increases capillary strength. Peoples with this need drink Goldenrod Tea daily, as long as they do not have problems with blood pressure.

Yeast Infections and Anti-Fungal: Golden-rod's antifungal properties make it effective against yeast infections such as *Candida*. Drink the tea or take the decoction daily and use powdered goldenrod, as needed, for external infections. A gargle can be used for oral thrush (Usnea also works well for thrush).

Joint Pain: This herb is anti-inflammatory, and works well to reduce pain and swelling, especially in the joints. It is useful to treat gout, arthritis, and other joint pains. Take internally and topically apply a poultice or wash directly to the affected joints.

Harvesting: Harvest healthy leaves and flowers that are free of powdery mildew or other diseases. Pick the leaves throughout the spring and summer and harvest flowers in the late summer or early autumn, just as the flowers open. Leave some flowers on the plant to pro-duce seeds and guarantee a crop the next year. Roots are harvested in early spring or autumn. Hang the plants to dry or use a dehydrator on the lowest setting to dry them for long-term storage.

Warning: Goldenrod is a diuretic and can be overly drying when used long-term as a daily beverage or tea. Do not use goldenrod during pregnancy or when nursing. Consult your doctor if you have a chronic kidney disorder. Do not use goldenrod if you are allergic to any members of the Asteraceae family.
Be sure of your plant identification. There are poisonous look-alikes. Goldenrod can increase blood pressure in some people.

Recipes. Goldenrod Tea: You will need 2 cups of boiling water and 1 Tablespoon of fresh goldenrod or 2 teaspoons of dried goldenrod. Bring the water to a boil and pour over the goldenrod. Allow the herbs to infuse for 15 minutes. Strain and serve. Use up to three times a day. This tea is slightly bitter. Adding an equal amount of mint to the herbs improves the flavor.

Goldenrod Decoction: Ingredients: 1-ounce goldenrod herb (leaves or flowers), 1-pint (500ml) of water. Place the herbs in a non-reactive pot with the water over medium heat. Bring the mixture to a boil. Turn the temperature down to a low simmer for 20 minutes. Cool the decoction and strain out the herbs. Store in the refrigerator for up to 3 days. Use 1 to 2 tea-spoons per dose, 3 times a day.

Greater Burdock, *Arctium lappa*

Arctium lappa belongs to Asteraceae (Daisy) Family. It is commonly known as greater burdock, edible bur-dock, lappa, beggar's buttons, thorny burr, or happy major. It is a Eurasian species and is cultivated in gar-dens for its root, which is used as a vegetable. This plant has become an invasive weed in many places in North America. It is a giant weed with much medicinal potential.

Identification: Greater burdock is a biennial plant. It is tall, and can reach 10 feet (3meters). Its stems are branched, rough and usually sparsely hairy. It flowers from July to September. The fleshy tap-root of this plant can grow up to 3 feet (0.9 meters) deep. Greater Burdock forms a 1.5-inch-wide (3.75 cm) single flower-like flat cluster of small purple flowers surrounded by a rosette of bracts. Leaves of greater burdock are alternate and stalked. They are triangular–broadly oval, usually cordate, and have undulating margins. They have a white-grey-cottony underside and first year growth is in rosettes.

The fruit is flattish, gently curved and is grey-brown in color. It has dark-spotted achene with short yellow hooked hairs on tip. Greater burdock is found almost everywhere, especially in areas soils that are usually rich in nitrogen. Its preferred habitat is in disturbed areas.

Edible Use: The leaves, stems, seeds, and roots are all edible. Young first-year roots and leaves are good raw in salads, but they become too fibrous as they mature and need to be cooked before eating.

The leaves and stalks are also good either raw or cooked. I prefer to remove the outer rind before cooking or eating. The sprouted seeds are also eaten.

Medicinal Use: Greater Burdock is antibacterial and antifungal, helps with digestion and gas, is a diuretic, and regulates blood sugar. It is a powerful detoxifier. The dried root is most often used for medicine, but the leaves and fruit can also be used.

Detoxing and Liver Cleanser: Its root is particularly good at helping to eliminate heavy metals and other resilient toxins from the body.

It helps with conditions caused by an overload of toxins, such as sore throat and other infections, boils, rashes, and other skin problems.

Cancer Treatment: Greater burdock is known to kill cancer cells. It flushes away toxins from the body, increases blood circulation to normal cells, protects the organs, and improves the health of the whole body. It is used to treat breast cancers, colon cancer, and even the deadly pancreatic cancer with good results.

I feel confident that it would be effective against other cancers as well. In treating cancer, the greatest success seems to come when herbs are used in combination to kill the cancer cells and support the body. Try using greater burdock in combination with sheep sorrel and slippery elm to kill the cancer and detox the body during treatment. Remember to also eat a highly nutritious diet with a high concentration of vegetables and fruits and limited meats and fats.

Turkey Tail and Reishi Mushrooms are other cancer gotos for me. Dosage: Mix 1/4 cup of Anti-Cancer Decoction with 1/4 cup of distilled water. Drink 3 times a day: 2 hours before breakfast, 2 hours after lunch and before bedtime on an empty stomach. Wait at least 2 hours after taking the decoction before eating again.

Anemia: Greater burdock has a high concentration of bioavailable iron. People with iron deficiency anemia are able to increase their iron levels rapidly by taking daily supplements of greater burdock powder or eating greater burdock as a vegetable.

Skin Diseases: Greater burdock is a very soothing herb for the skin. It has mucilaginous properties that enhance its ability to cure skin diseases such as herpes, eczema, psoriasis, acne, impetigo, ringworm, boils, insect bites, burns, and bruises. Use greater burdock tea as a wash and take it internally to clear the body of the toxins that are causing the skin problems. For bruises, burns, and sores, crush the seeds and use as a poultice on the affected skin.

Diabetes: Greater burdock root helps improve digestion and lower blood sugar in diabetics. For this use the fresh root is best, but 1 to 2 grams of dried powdered root can also be taken 3 times daily.

Strengthens the Immune System and Protects the Organs: This herb strengthens the immune system and the lymphatic system, which helps rid the body of toxins and ward off diseases. It also cleans the blood. It cleand and protects the spleen and helps it remove dangerous pathogens from the body. It improves blood quality, liver health, blood circulation, and fights inflammation.

Stimulates the Kidneys, Relieves Fluid Retention: Greater burdock stimulates the kidneys, helping get rid of excess fluids in the body. This reduces swellings, increases urine output, and flushes waste and toxins from the body. Greater Burdock Tea is a natural diuretic.

Osteoarthritis and Degenerative Joint Disease: The anti-inflammatory properties of greater burdock are powerful enough to reduce the inflammation of osteoarthritis. Patients show remarkable improvement when they consume three cups of Greater Burdock Root Tea daily.

Improvement is slow and steady, taking about two months to achieve maximum benefits.

Sore Throats and Tonsillitis: For acute tonsillitis and other sore throats, try Greater Burdock Tea. It relieves pain, inflammation, coughing, and speeds healing. The greater burdock also acts as an antibacterial to kill the harmful bacteria and cure the infection.

Harvesting: The root must be harvested before it withers at the end of the first year. The best time is after it seeds until late autumn when the roots become very fibrous. Immature flower stalks are harvested in late spring before the flowers appear. Care must be taken when harvesting the seeds. They have tiny, hooked hairs that can latch onto the mucus mem-branes if inhaled.

Recipes. Anti-Cancer Decoction: To make 1-gallon (4 liters) you need 1-ounce greater burdock root, powdered, 3/4 ounces (21g) sheep sorrel, powdered, 1/4 ounces (7g) slippery elm bark, powdered and 1-gal-lon (4 liters) distilled water. Equipment: 8-pint (4 Liters) canning jars and lids, sterile, large pot, capable of holding 1 gallon (4 liters) or more, with a tight-fitting lid and boiling water canner.

Bring the greater burdock, sheep sorrel, and slippery elm bark to a boil in 1 gallon (4 liters) of distilled water, tightly covered. Boil the herbs, tightly covered, for 10 minutes, then turn off the heat and stir the mixture.

Cover tightly and let the decoction steep for 12 hours, stirring again after 6 hours. After 12 hours, bring it back to a boil and pour it through a fine mesh strainer or a coffee filter. Pour the decoction into pint (500ml) jars while still hot, leaving ½ inch (1.25 cm) headroom. Cap the jars. Process the jars in a boiling water bath for 10 minutes.

The decoction will keep for 1 year in sealed jars. Store in the refrigerator after opening. Dosage: Mix 1/4 cup of the decoction with 1/4 cup of distilled water. Drink 3 times a day: 2 hours before breakfast, 2 hours after lunch and before bedtime on an empty stomach. Wait at least 2 hours after taking the decoction before eating again.

Henbane, Hyoscyamus niger

Henbane is poisonous, so it is advised that you use it with caution. Although native to Europe, it has been cultivated in North America for many years. It's a beautiful plant with a foul smell, and a member of the Solanaceae (Nightshade) family.

Identification: *Hyoscyamus niger* grows from 1 to 3 feet (0.9 meters) tall. A mature henbane plant has leafy, thick, hairy, widely-branched, erect stems. It is an annual and biannual and the biannual growth is used for medicine. Its foul-smelling lobed alternate leaves are grayish-green or yellowish-green in color and have white veins. They spread out like a rosette and are coarsely toothed, large, and wide, growing up to 6 inches (15 cm) wide and 8 inches (20 cm) long. The 5-petaled flowers are a funnel shape and are brownish-yellow in color with dark purple veins. Flowers have a long-spiked inflorescence arrangement in upper leaves with young flowers at the pointed end. Flowers are up to 2 inches (5 cm) across. It flowers from June thru September. The 5-lobed, urn-shaped fruit is 1 inch (2.5 cm). Each fruit is packed with hundreds of tiny black seeds. The roots of henbane are whitish in color. The main taproot is stout and branched. Henbane does not tolerate waterlogged soils. It likes pastures along fencerows and roadsides.

Medicinal Use: Because the plant is poisonous, it is important that all medicines be made precisely and the strength carefully regulated. I prefer to use this plant externally, where there is no danger.

The plant has strong pain-relieving qualities, and is used externally for muscle pains caused by strain or sprain. It has some good applications internally, but I do not recommend using it internally without the close supervision of a medical professional. The above ground parts are used for medicine.

Internal Use: The plant is used to relieve irritable bladders and the pain of cystitis. It is a mild diuretic, hypnotic, and anti-spasmodic. The hypnotic action is the same as belladonna, but with milder effects. Use with great care or find an alternative! Use can be fatal.

Gout, Neuralgia, and Arthritis Pains: External pain from gout, neuralgia, and arthritis are effectively treated with a poultice made from fresh henbane leaves. Crush the leaves and place them directly over the painful area.

Hemorrhoids: Try a poultice of crushed henbane leaves to reduce the swelling and pain of external hemorrhoids.

Harvesting: Collect the leaves, stems and flowers from the biennial plants when in full flower at the start of summer.

Warning: Henbane is poisonous. Use with great care and do not use internally.

Woods, Shrublands, and Groves

Amaranthus caudatus

Amaranthus caudatus is a brilliantly beautiful plant. Its tails of bright red flowers make it easy to locate, even at a distance. It is also called loves-lies-bleeding, tassel flower, velvet flower, foxtail amaranth, pendant amaranth, and quilete. It is in the Amaranthaceae (Amaranth) Family. Amaranthus caudatus is widespread throughout North America. It often grows in disturbed ground.

Identification: Amaranthus caudatus is an annual flowering plant. It grows from 3 to 8 feet (0.9m to 2.4m) tall in full sun with a spread of 1 to 3 feet (0.3m to 0.9m). It blooms from July until the first frost. The red flowers are very small and have no petals. They bloom in drooping terminal tassel-like panicles that are 1 to 2 feet (0.3m to 0.6m) long. The seeds ripen in September.

Edible Use: The leaves and seeds of Amaranthus caudatus are edible. Amaranth leaves can be eaten raw or cooked. The seeds are used as a grain. They do not need to be cooked, but are good toasted in a little oil. The seeds are also good when sprouted.

Medicinal Use: The plant is astringent, anti-parasitic, and diuretic.

Diabetes: People with diabetes can substitute Amaranthus for rice and also eat the seeds and leaves as often as possible. It has anti-diabetic properties that help regulate blood sugar and brings it down significantly.

Lowers Cholesterol: Amaranthus seeds and oil are a healthy choice for those with hypertension, cardiovascular disease, and high cholesterol.

Sore Throats, Mouth Sores, and Canker Sores: A gargle made from dried and powdered Amaranthus leaves is an effective treatment for sore throats and canker sores. To make a gargle, boil 2 tablespoons of powdered amaranth leaves in 1 cup of water for 10 minutes. Let it cool and gargle and swish with it three or more times a day.

Heavy Menstrual Bleeding and Stopping Bleeding: Amaranthus caudatus is a powerful blood clotting agent and works to stop excess menstrual bleeding. Boil 1 tablespoon of root powder in 1 cup of water. Let it cool, then consume. For external bleeding, dust the affected area with the root powder. It quickly stops nosebleeds and bleeding from other small wounds.

Vaginal Infections: Use an Amaranthus leaf and root powder decoction internally, and use externally as a douche to treat vaginal discharge.

Warning: Amaranthus caudatus should not be used by people who have gout, rheumatoid arthritis, or kidney disorders. It should not be given to pregnant women, nursing mothers, or babies.

American Ginseng, Panax quinquefolius

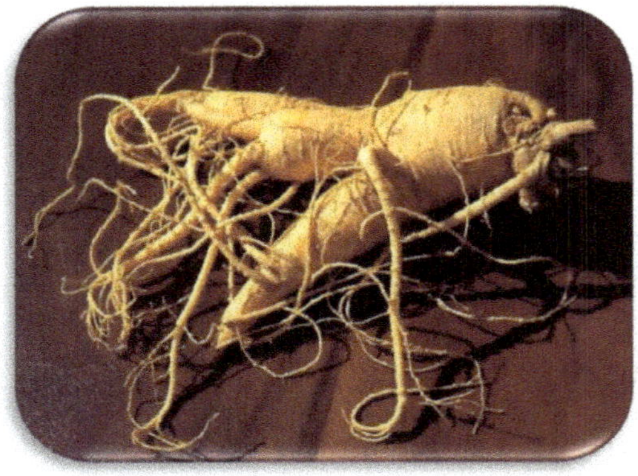

American ginseng, also known as Panax ginseng, is in the Araliaceae (Ginseng/Ivy) Family. It is native to eastern North America and cultivated widely elsewhere. Its aromatic root forks as it matures.

Identification: Plants grow 6 to 18 inches (15 cm to 45 cm) tall. Its leaves are palmate and divided into 3 to 7 (usually 4 or 5) lance-shaped, sharp-toothed leaflets. The flowers are whitish greenish, and fruits are pea-sized red berries with two seeds each. The neck of the rhizome shows scars left by each year's growth. Counting the leaf scars ages the root. Its medicinal compounds, called ginsenosides, increase in concentration as the root ages. In general, harvest roots 4 years or older.

Medicinal Use: Panax species have a well-deserved reputation as powerful adaptogens. They help the body recover from the effects of stress and adrenal fatigue, much like Reishi or Ashwagandha. It is also used as an aphrodisiac and for erectile dysfunction. American ginseng is a relaxant, while the Asian version, P. ginseng, is said to be more stimulating. The mature root and leaves can be chewed, powdered and put into capsules, extracted in alcohol as a tincture, or made into a tea.

Diabetes: Ginseng has many benefits for diabetics. American ginseng helps regulate blood sugar. Taking take 2 to 5 drops of American Ginseng tincture before each meal helps prevent post-meal spikes in blood sugar levels. It is recommended starting with 2 drops and monitoring blood sugar levels. Increase the dosage one drop at a time, as needed, up to 5 drops per meal, depending on the potency of your tincture. American ginseng contains a class of compounds called ginsenosides, which possess antioxidant and anti-inflammatory properties, two important factors in the progression of diabetes. American ginseng also promotes the secretion of insulin, necessary for regulation of blood sugar levels. Ginseng helps lower high blood pressure in diabetics. Regular use gives some protection to the heart and retina from diabetes-induced damage.

Cold and Flu: American Ginseng helps fight the common cold and flu when taken regularly. People who take ginseng daily report fewer colds and less severe cold and flu symptoms.

Tonic for Fatigue, Stress, Memory, and Concentration: American ginseng has properties that boost energy and stamina and reduces fatigue caused by failing health and everyday stresses. It also betters cognitive performance, and enhances memory.

Erectile Dysfunction: American ginseng is an effective treatment for erectile dysfunction when taken on a regular basis. Favorable results are only seen when the herb is taken daily over the long term. It seems to work by opening up necessary blood vessels for improved blood flow.

Other Uses for American Ginseng: Since Panax is a tonic and reduces the stress on the body, it is effective for use in many different diseases and conditions. It is said to raise the spirits and to improve sleep, mood, and general outlook on life. It is also an antispasmodic.

Harvesting: Like all plants, the ginseng root needs to be treated with great respect. Do not harvest the roots before the berries ripen and the seeds set, in late summer or early autumn. When uncovering the neck of the root, look for four or more leaf scars, one scar for each year of age. Roots less than four years old do not contain enough beneficial properties to be effective. Note the location of younger roots and leave them in the ground or dig them up for relocation. The root branches underground, so dig carefully, and excavate a large area. Use the root fresh and dry some for future use.

Warning: Avoid American Ginseng if taking warfarin or other blood thinning therapies. Not recommended for pregnant or breastfeeding women. Ginseng should not be taken if someone has a hormonerelated condition such as endometriosis, fibroids, or cancers of the breast, ovaries, uterus, or prostate. Do not use ginseng for people with heart disease except under the close supervision of a healthcare professional. Ginseng may decrease the rate and force of heartbeats. Occasional side effects include headaches, anxiety, upset stomach, and sometimes trouble sleeping.

Recipes. American Ginseng Tea: Here is a simple ginseng tea with cooling properties. It keeps the body balanced and improves mental alertness. Avoid taking ginseng tea close to bedtime. You'll need 1/2 ounce of American Ginseng root fibers, 3 cups of water, a few grains of salt (optional). Bring the water to a boil. Add ginseng and simmer for 5 to 10 minutes. Season with salt, if desired. Strain the tea and allow it to cool. Serve at room temperature or cold.

American Ginseng Extract: Use 8 ounces (230g) of American ginseng root, pounded into fibers or ground, with 1- quart (1 Liter) of 80 proof or better alcohol and infuse it for 6 to 8 weeks.

Angelica, Angelica archangelica

According to legend, an angel revealed in a dream how to use angelica to cure the plague. It was reverently called "The Root of the Holy Ghost" and was believed to ward off witchcraft and evil spirits. It is also called Wild Celery.

Angelica is a useful medicinal plant, but care must be taken to identify the plant correctly before using it. It is similar in appearance to other poisonous plants like water hemlock and giant hogweed. Please note the distinguishing features listed below and be sure you have the correct plant before harvesting.

The plant is found in the North Eastern parts of North America and in Northern Europe and grows in moist, cool woodlands, along stream banks, and in shady places. It is widely cultivated as an ornamental and medicinal plant. There are many varieties, but it is the Angelica archangelica that is used medicinally. It is in the Apiaceae/Umbelliferae (Carrot/Celery) Family.

Identification: Angelica is a biennial plant that dies after it sets its seed in its second year. During the first year, the plant puts out leaves, but most of its growth and its flowering stage occurs in the second year. It grows from 4 to 6 feet (1.2m – 1.8m) tall and occasionally up to 10 feet tall (3m), with large dark green bipinnate leaves. Each leaf contains many leaflets, divided into three main groups.

Each subdivision is further divided into three groups. The leaves are finely serrated. The lower leaves are the largest, up to 2 feet wide (0.6m). The leaf stalks are flattened and fluted. Stems are curved inward with sheathing that forms an elongated bowl that holds water. Stems are dark purple, round, smooth and hollow and are 1 to 2 inches (2.5cm-5cm) across.

The small, plentiful white, yellowish, or greenish-white flowers grow in large, compound umbels, up to 6 inches wide (15cm). The star-shaped flowers appear in July after the second year.

The fruit are small, oblong and pale yellow. Each is 1/6 to 1/4 inch (0.4cm – 0.6cm) in length when ripe and they reside in round heads that are up to 8 to 10 inches (20cm – 25cm) in diameter. The root is branched, thick, and fleshy with small rootlets. The root is 3 to 6 inches (7.5cm – 15 cm) long.

Edible Use: The fresh root is rumored to be poisonous, but cooked and crystalized pieces of root and stem are used as decorative pieces for cakes and are used for flavoring in alcoholic beverages. Young shoots and leaves are edible raw or cooked. The flavor is sweet and similar to celery with a slight licorice taste. Use the shoots in salads or boil them like a pot herb. Use angelica stems when young and tender. Preserve them in sugar or candy them for use as a decoration on sweet treats. Angelica root must be dried and preserved for later use. Do not use it fresh.

Medicinal Use: The entire plant is used medicinally. Leaves, stems, and flowers are crushed and used in a bath or as a poultice. The medicine from the roots is best extracted using alcoholic tinctures. Roots can be dried and powdered for medicinal use.

Respiratory Issues: The herb is well known as an expectorant and is used to treat bronchitis, asthma, colic, coughs, and the common cold. The root is best used for respiratory ailments, but stems and seeds are also usable when necessary. A tincture or a tea will work as an expectorant.

Digestive Aid, Stimulates Appetite, and Intestinal Infections: Angelica stimulates the appetite, improves digestion, soothes colic, and reduces the production of intestinal gas. It also increases the production of stomach acid. It has been used as a cure for the plague, dysentery, cholera and intestinal infections. The herb is anti-bacterial and kills the bacteria that cause many gastric illnesses, like E. coli.

Nerve Pain: Rub angelica directly on the skin to treat neuralgia or nerve pain. It acts as an anesthetic.

Joint Pain: The anti-inflammatory properties of Angelica are useful for treating arthritis, gout, swelling, and for broken bones. For joint pain, a poultice made from crushed leaves is effective.

Anti-Seizure Effects: Recent studies show that Angelica archangelica protects the body against chemically induced seizures. Angelica essential oil exhibits anti-seizure effects, probably due to the presence of terpenes in the oil.

Sore Throats and Mouth Sores: The antibacterial and anti-inflammatory properties of the root is useful in treating sore throats and mouth sores. Use an Angelica Infusion as a gargle or wash several times a day.

Menstrual Problems: Angelica regulates female hormones, regulates the menstrual cycle, and controls menstrual discharge.

Acne: Anti-bacterial and anti-inflammatory compounds in angelica help prevent and control acne. Use an angelica decoction or angelica tea as a face wash.

Anxiety: Recent studies showed that angelica has an antidepressant and anti-anxiety effect. It reduces stress and improves relaxation.

Cancer: Angelica archangelica has been shown to be effective against breast cancer cells. It reduces proliferation of the cancer cells and reduces tumor growth. Research is ongoing into its anti-tumor properties.

Anti-Fungal: Powdered angelica root is used to treat athlete's foot and other fungal infections.

Improves Circulation: Angelica strengthens the heart and improves blood circulation throughout the body.

Harvesting: While all the parts of the herb are useable for culinary and medicinal purposes, they are useable only during certain parts of the year. The roots are best harvested in the fall or winter of the first year. The stem and leaves are best in the spring or early summer of the second year, before the flowers appear. Dry the roots at or below 95 F and store in an airtight container.

Warning: Some people are allergic to Angelica. Avoid using angelica with anti-coagulant drugs. Do not use during pregnancy or breastfeeding. People with Diabetes should not use Angelica

Recipes. Angelica Tea or Decoction: Add 1/2 teaspoon of powdered angelica root to one cup of boiling water. Simmer for 10 to 15 minutes. Turn off the heat and let the tea steep for another 8 to 10 minutes. Strain out the root and store the decoction in a glass jar for later use. Use as a wash for skin problems or drink a cup after meals.

Candied Angelica: Trim angelica shoots and cut into strips. Blanch the strips in boiling water, then cook them in sugar syrup, gradually increasing the amount of sugar. Dry them and store in a sealed container. Keep the syrup for other uses.

Arnica cordifolia, Heartleaf Arnica and A. montana

Heartleaf arnica, also known as mountain tobacco, is one of the many Arnica species used for medicine. It is a member of the Daisy/Aster Family. It grows in high meadows, coniferous forests, and the western mountains at elevations from 3500 to 10,000 feet. It is native to western North American from Alaska to California and New Mexico, and east to Michigan. It is relatively easy to cultivate in the garden.

Identification: Arnica is a rhizomatous perennial growing from one or more erect stems. It grows between 12 and 20 inches (30 cm to 50 cm) tall. The stems are hairy with two to four pairs of heartshaped to arrowhead-shaped leaves. Cordate leaves are often produced on separate short shoots, are coarsely toothed and wither when the plant flowers. The leaves on the upper part of the plant are hairy, like the stalk. Lower leaves have rounded tips. The flowers are small and yellow, forming 1 to 5 daisy-like flowering heads per plant, and each flower head has a golden yellow disc with 10 to 15 yellow rays. The rays are pointed and about 1 inch (2.5 cm) long. The entire flower head is about 2 1/2 inches (3.7 cm) in diameter. The seeds form in a small, hairy achene, about 1/2-inch (1.25 cm)-long. Flowers appear from May to August.

Medicinal Use: Use the flowers externally to reduce inflammation, reduce bruising, and for pain. It is antimicrobial and antiseptic. It can be used in small doses internally with great care.

How to Use Arnica on Skin: I often use Arnica externally on the skin as a salve or oil to promote healing in sprains, muscle pulls, contusions, and bruises. Use a diluted oil or salve on areas that need tissue stimulation and healing. Arnica treats common skin problems like infections, itching, and eczema.

Arthritis: Arnica is excellent at relieving arthritis pain, especially in cold weather. It warms the area and stimulates blood flow, and is anti-inflammatory. Rub arnica salve into the painful joint, or apply it as a poultice of bruised leaves or flowers.

Frostbite and Chilblains: Because it is warming and stimulates blood flow to an area, Arnica is used for the treatment of frostbite and chilblains. Use a poultice of leaves or flowers, or a salve or oil made with Arnica.

Bruises, Black Eyes, Muscle Aches, Inflammation, Sprains, Phlebitis, Carpal Tunnel, and Swelling: Arnica applied topically is useful in the treatment of a wide variety of external conditions. It reduces inflammation, warms the skin and muscle, relieves pain, and promotes healing. It is excellent for any strains, sprains, swellings, carpal tunnel, muscle soreness, and to reduce bruising.

Sore Throat and Toothache: For a sore throat or a toothache, try chewing the root. If the mouth is too sore for chewing, mash it and apply it to the swollen area. Gargling Arnica Tea is also effective for some people.

Other Uses of Arnica: Some people use Arnica to make homemade cigarettes, known as mountain tobacco.

Harvesting: When harvesting from the wild, pick flowers sparingly, never harvest rhizomes or roots; this destroys the plant. The plant will grow back as long as the rhizome survives in place. I prefer the flowers for medicinal use but leaves and stems also contain beneficial properties. Pick flowers in the early afternoon, after the morning dew has evaporated.

Warning: Arnica can be highly toxic if taken internally. I do not recommend internal use, except homeopathically. Avoid using undiluted Arnica preparations topically on open wounds, as it can cause inflammation and irritation. Dilute the oil and extracts with a carrier solution or oil if using on broken skin.

Arrowleaf Balsamroot, Balsamorhiza sagittata

Arrowleaf balsamroot, also known locally as the Oregon Sunflower, is a tough plant. It grows in grasslands, steppe, and scrubland areas, often on hillsides, in the western part of North America. It is in the Aster/Sunflower/Daisy Family.

Identification: Arrowleaf Balsamroot grows 1 to 2 feet (0.3 to 0.6 meters) tall. Its basal silver-green leaves grow up to 2 feet (0.6 meters) long and are arrow-shaped. Larger leaves are at the base of the plant and the leaves get smaller toward the top of the stem. Leaves are "wooly" and covered in fine white hairs. Flower stems grow from the root crown to 6 to 30 inches (15 cm to 75 cm) tall. Each flower stem has one flower head that resembles a sunflower with 8 to 25 yellow rays surrounding a disc. This plant grows from a deep taproot reaching 8 feet (2.4 meters) into the ground. It also has deep lateral roots that extend up to 3 feet (0.9 meters) around the plant.

Edible Use: This plant is an excellent food source. Its leaves can be eaten raw or cooked. Peel the stems before eating to get rid of the tough exterior. The seeds are nutritious and can be roasted like sunflower seeds. The root is eaten steamed or can be dried and pounded into a flour. The root can also be used as a coffee substitute.

Medicinal Use: The leaves, stems and roots contain medicinally active compounds. It acts internally as a disinfectant and expectorant.

Stimulates the Immune System: Taken internally, arrowleaf balsamroot roots enhance the action of the immune system, works as an antimicrobial, and stimulates the activity of white blood cells.

Toothaches, Sore Mouths, and Body Aches: Traditionally used to treat toothache pain and sore mouths by chewing on the root. Inhaling root smoke is said to treat body aches.

Sore Throat, Bronchial Congestion, Coughs, and TB: Balsamroot Tincture made from the dried or fresh root treats sore throats and loosens phlegm. Try putting your tincture into warm water and drink as a tea. You can also make cough syrup by simmering the root in raw honey (recipe below). Chew on the root to ease sore throat pain. Root infusions are used traditionally to treat tuberculosis and whooping cough.

Soothes Skin Burns, Wounds, Eczema, and Bruises: Use the balsamroot leaves as a compress on the skin to relieve pain and help heal burns, wounds, bruises, and rashes. Dry and powder the leaves or bruise and mash fresh leaves and place them on the skin or infuse them in oil for a salve.

Fungal Infections, Ringworm, Jock Itch, and Athlete's Foot: Use the dried and powdered root as an antifungal to heal common fungal infections. Apply the powder and leave in place to heal ringworm, jock itch, and athlete's foot.

Stomach Problems: The root, leaves, and stems are soothing for the digestive tract. Try a tea made from the entire plant.

Harvesting: Leaves and stems are easily harvested by cutting the stem and leaf from the plant. The root is more difficult because there is a very deep taproot as well as lateral roots and it often grows in rocky soil. Harvest the root in mid-spring to mid-August. You'll probably need to dig out a large area to get most of the root. Bring good tools and only take what you need from this slow-growing plant.

Recipes. Balsamroot and Raw Honey Cough Syrup: You'll need 3 to 4 Tablespoons of fresh Arrowleaf Balsamroot root, chopped into small pieces, and 1 cup raw honey. Bring the honey to a simmer and add the chopped balsamroot. Keep the heat at a low simmer for 2 to 3 hours. Strain the warm honey to remove the root pieces. Place in a clean jar and label and date. Use 1 to 2 teaspoons every 2 to 4 hours or as needed.

Bearberry, Arctostaphylos uva ursi, or Arbutus uva ursi

Also called kinnikinnik, uva ursi, hog cranberry, mountain cranberry, upland cranberry, bear's grape, and red bearberry, this herb is a small evergreen shrub that grows in northern North America and in higher elevations throughout the Appalachian Mountains. It likes acidic dry soils, especially sandy and gravel rich soils. It is in the Ericaceae (Heath) Family. It is commonly used in smoking mixtures.

Identification: The alternate paddle-shaped leaves are small and shiny with a thick, stiff feel. The underside is lighter in color than the green topside. Leaves are up to an inch (2.5 cm) long and have rounded tips. The leaves are evergreen, changing from dark green to a reddish-green and then to purple in autumn. The small dark brown buds have three scales.

Bearberry has small white or pink, urn-shaped flowers that appear in terminal clusters from May to June. They mature into pink to bright red fleshy drupes. The fruit is 1/4 to 1/2 inch (0.75 cm to 1.25 cm) in diameter and can remain on the plant until winter. Each mealy fruit contains up to five tiny hard seeds.

The root system has a fibrous main root with buried stems that give rise to the stems of the herb. These trailing stems form layered mats with small roots and have stems growing up 6 inches (15 cm) tall when mature, with a reddish- brown bark. Younger branches are white to pale green.

Edible Use: Bearberry fruits are edible, but they are not tasty, so they are rarely eaten or used in cooking. They are sometimes used in pemmican.

Medicinal Use: The leaves and berries are used for medicine. I usually use it in tincture form for internal use.

Urinary Tract Infections, Nephritis, Kidney Stones, Cystitis, and Gout: Bearberry leaves treat kidney (nephritis), bladder (cystitis), and urinary tract infections extremely well. It is a diuretic, increasing the urine volume, and it has antiseptic properties that reduce bacteria populations in the kidneys, bladder, and urinary tract. It relieves bladder inflammation and helps relieves the pain of stones. It also reduces uric acid in the body, and thus is useful in treating gout.

Bearberry leaves work best for urinary tract problems when the urine is less acidic or even slightly alkaline. Use at the first sign of infection. I often use it for UTIs as a blended tincture with Usnea, Goldenrod, and Oregon Grape Root, and also drink unsweetened cranberry juice or take a concentrated cranberry supplement. To decrease acidity, follow a vegetable-based diet, eliminating meat and milk products from the diet until the problem is eliminated.

Painful Sex in Women and the Urinogenital System: Bearberry tea or tincture treats long-term inflammation of the urethra in women. The tannins in the berries and leaves have a strong astringent action and reduce inflammation in the urogenital system.

Vaginal Infections: Bearberry is an effective internal treatment against vaginal infections, including yeast infections. It has astringent and anti-inflammatory effects that help soothe the vaginal region. You can also use the leaf and berry tea as a douche or sitz bath twice a day.

Post-Partum Use and Uterine Hemorrhage: Drinking Bearberry Tea soon after giving birth helps increase uterine contractions and prevents hemorrhages. It helps prevent post-partum infections and helps incisions heal. It can also be used as a douche or sitz bath due to its astringent and tightening effects. Not for longer-term internal use if the mother is breast-feeding.

Prevents Scurvy: Bearberry berries and leaves are rich in vitamin C, which is necessary to prevent Scurvy. In winter months it can be difficult to find adequate sources of vitamin C. Drinking bearberry tea or eating its berries adds vitamin C to the diet.

Stomach and Intestinal Cramping: Bearberry has muscle relaxant properties that soothe stomach and intestinal cramping. It also has antiseptic properties that are effective against the most common causes of diarrhea and stomach upsets.

Harvesting: Bearberry leaves can be picked from mid-spring to mid-autumn. Pick the mature berries before the first frost.

Warning: Bearberry should not be used by people with high blood pressure, by pregnant women, or women who are nursing. Bearberry can induce nausea in some people and can cause stomach irritation. Soaking the bearberry leaves overnight before use may help. Not for continued long term use. Best used for acute treatment.

Recipes. Bearberry Leaf and Berry Tea: *Soaking the leaves and berries before brewing the tea removes some of the tannins and helps reduce digestive discomfort if using internally. You can also use the leaf only. 3 Tablespoons of dried leaves and berries, chopped, 1- quart (1 Liter) water. Soak the dried leaves and berries in cold water overnight or for up to one day. Drain. Bring a quart (liter) of water to a boil. Add dried leaves and berries. Reduce the heat to a simmer and cover tightly. Simmer the tea for about five minutes. Turn off the heat. Allow the tea to steep, tightly covered for 30 minutes. Strain. Drink one cup, two to three times daily, lukewarm on an empty stomach.

Bee Balm, Oswego Tea, Monarda didyma

Bee Balm is also known as Oswego Tea, horse mint, Indian nettle, Red Bergamot and Scarlet Bergamot. It gets the name Oswego tea because of its use by the Oswego Tribe. It is in the Lamiaceae (Mint) Family and is easily cultivated in the garden. This is a great herb to plant to attract hummingbirds, bees, and butterflies. It is a perennial and grows naturally in much of North America, Europe, and Asia.

Identification: Bee balm has straight, ridged, square stems and grows to 3 feet (0.9 meters) tall. Its course opposite leaves can be smooth or have a thin coating of fine hairs. The leaves have a strong fragrance and are 3 to 6 inches (7.5 cm to 15 cm) long. Their showy flowers range in color from deep pink to bright red to purple. They are approximately 1 ½ inches (3.75 cm) long and are grouped in dense heads of many flowers. They bloom in mid to late summer. The plant spreads on underground shoots, increasing the size of the plant every autumn. The plant in the center will begin to die back after three to four years.

Edible Use: Oswego tea is made from dried leaves of the bee balm plant. The leaves and flowers are edible. Bee balm flowers are lovely as a garnish in salads, and dried leaves can be used like sage to flavor meats.

Medicinal Use: Leaves and flowers are used medicinally.

Menstrual Problems: Bee balm is an anti-spasmodic, and large doses of bee balm tea cause the uterus to contract, bringing on the menstrual period. However, it can also cause miscarriage and thus should be avoided during pregnancy

Colds, Sore Throats, and Congestion: Bee balm leaves are useful for treating colds, sore throats, and nasal and chest congestion in the form of a tea or in a steam vaporizer. Breathe in the vapors to open sinuses and clear congestion from the lungs.

Fevers: Oswego/Bee Balm tea is a mild diuretic, expelling water from the body through both sweat and urination. Sweating helps cool the body and reduce fevers.

Nausea, Vomiting, Flatulence, and Stomach Problems: Like most mints, bee balm has a soothing effect on the stomach and can calm flatulence, nausea, and vomiting. However, it is not appropriate for use with nausea caused by pregnancy. Large doses can cause miscarriage.

Nervine for Calm: Bee balm works similarly to Lemon Balm as a nervine, though it is less powerful than Lemon Balm for this use.

Stings, Scrapes, and Rashes: Bee balm is wonderful in a healing salve and helps soothe bites, stings, and rashes.

Harvesting: Pick the leaves in the mid to late morning after the morning dew has dried. Pick your yearly supply during the summer and dry them for future use. Collect the flowers when they are beginning to fully open. Dry them and store them in a sealed jar in a dark place.

Recipes. Oswego Tea: You'll need 1 teaspoon Oswego Tea/Bee Balm Leaves and 1 cup boiling water. Pour the boiling water over the tea leaves and allow the tea to steep for 5 to 10 minutes. Strain out the leaves and drink.

Black Cohosh, Actaea racemosa

I find black cohosh to be a very valuable herb for menopause, and I rarely use it for other uses, except as a supplementary herb. It balances hormones, which helps many conditions without curing them. Black cohosh is in the Ranunculaceae (Buttercup) Family. Black cohosh is native to eastern North America. It is found as far south as Georgia and west to Missouri/Arkansas and the Great Lakes region. It grows wild in small woodland openings.

Identification: Black cohosh is a perennial with large compound leaves that grow from its rhizome. It grows up to 2 feet (0.6m) in height with distinctive serrated basal leaves that can be 3 feet (0.9m) long, growing in sets of 3 leaflets. Flowers bloom from June to September on an 8-foot tall stem, with racemes (flower clusters) up to 20 inches (50 cm) long. These white flowers occur in tight clusters with a white stigma surrounded by long stamens.

The flowers have no petals or sepals. A distinguishing feature is the sweet, putrid smell of the flowers that attracts flies, gnats, and beetles. The fruit is a 1/4-inch to 1/2-inch (0.74 cm to 1.25 cm) long dry follicle containing several seeds.

Medicinal Use: I mainly use black cohosh root for menstrual problems and menopause, although it is also useful for digestive problems and as a sedative. The best benefits are achieved when black cohosh is taken regularly long-term. Often it takes a month or more before benefits are noticed. The root is used medicinally. Menopause,

Menstrual Problems, Improved Ovulation, and PCOS: Black Cohosh works to balance hormones in women, helping to relieve menopausal symptoms such as hot flashes, moodiness, night sweats, headaches, heart palpitations, vaginal dryness, and mental fog. It is also used for menstrual problems, painful intercourse, decreased sex drive, and Polycystic Ovary Syndrome (PCOS) and has been shown to improve ovulation in women.

Osteoporosis: By balancing hormones, black cohosh reduces bone loss caused by osteoporosis in women.

Reducing Anxiety and Aiding Sleep: Black cohosh has a sedative effect that calms the nervous system and reduces anxiety. It promotes restful sleep.

Digestive Problems: For digestive problems, crush a small piece of black cohosh root and boil it in a small amount of water. Drink the water to relieve stomach pain and intestinal problems. It helps improve digestion and elimination and prevents gastric ulcers. Black cohosh is only moderately effective for other digestive problems. There are better remedies out there.

Warning: People who are allergic to aspirin, have liver problems, have issues with seizures, or have a high risk of blood clots or stroke should not use black cohosh. Pregnant and breastfeeding women, women with endometriosis, uterine cancer, or breast cancer should not take black cohosh.

Bleeding Heart, Dicentra formosa

Bleeding heart is a calming herb and is useful for the nervous system after a shock or an accident. It is also known as Pacific Bleeding Heart and Western Bleeding Heart. It is in the Papaveraceae (Poppy) Family and grows in moist areas of coniferous forests in the Pacific Northwest.

Identification: Bleeding heart is a perennial with fern-like, lacy, divided leaves. It grows from a rhizome and reaches 18 to 24 inches (45 cm to 60 cm) tall when mature. Heart-shaped dangling pink flowers bloom in clusters from mid-spring through autumn. Flower stems reach above the leaves, each with 5 to 15 blooms. Seeds form in pointed, pea-like pods. Depending on the weather, the plant may go dormant during the hot summer months. They have shallow rhizomes that are easy to harvest but are also sensitive to foot traffic.

Medicinal Use: Use bleeding-heart with great care and in small doses as it is a very potent narcotic and is toxic in higher doses. The root is mostly used, though the flowers and leaves also have medicinal properties.

Toothache: The root is good for relieving toothache pain. Chew the root and place it on the painful tooth.

Bruises, Sprains, Joint Pain, Nerve Pain: A compress made with Bleeding Heart Decoction or by heating root pieces in water and applying them as a poultice is effective in relieving nerve and muscle pain and helping bruises and sprains to heal.

Shocks to the Nervous System, Anxiety, and Nervous Disorders: Bleeding heart root decoction and tincture are both effective in relieving anxiety and nerves. It is effective in calming people after a shock, loss, or trauma. The plant has sedative and narcotic properties.

Muscle Tremors: Compounds in bleeding heart are calming and relaxing for the nervous system. They relax the muscles and suppress muscle tremors exhibited in some nervous system disorders.

Diuretic: This diuretic herb helps flush toxins and other poisons from the blood, liver, and kidneys. However, there are safer herbs for this use.

Increases Metabolism and Stimulates Appetite: Bleeding heart calms the nervous system while increasing the metabolic process, often giving you more energy and an increased appetite.

Cancer and Swollen Lymph Nodes: Bleeding heart tincture has been used traditionally for the treatment of cancer, swollen lymph nodes, and enlarged glands.

Harvesting: Bleeding heart is a rare plant and is becoming endangered in some areas. Check the status in your area before collecting and do not overharvest. Use it sparingly because it is rare in the wild, or, even better, grow your own supply so that you do not disturb the plants growing in the wild. Gather the roots of bleeding heart in the summer, if the plant goes dormant, or in the autumn when the leaves begin to change and after the seed pods have matured.

Warning: Avoid using bleeding heart during pregnancy or breast-feeding. Use bleeding heart sparingly, a little goes a long way. Do not use if you have liver disease. Do not use in combinations with other sedative and note that it can cause a false positive for opiate use on a drug test. Consult a medical professional before use.

Recipes. Bleeding Heart Tincture: Finely chopped fresh or dried bleeding-heart rhizome to fill ½ a jar, 80 proof or better alcohol such as vodka or brandy. Place the rhizome pieces into a clean jar with a tightfitting lid. Cover the herb completely, filling the jar with alcohol. Cap and label and place it in a cool, dark cupboard. Shake the jar daily for 6 to 8 weeks while the tincture steeps. Strain, label, and store. Usual dosage is 10 to 20 drops of fresh tincture, and 15 to 30 drops if using dried roots. Use with care.

Bloodroot, Sanguinaria canadensis

Bloodroot is mainly for the treatment of skin cancers, ulcers, and wounds that won't heal. I have always known the herb as bloodroot, but it is also called redroot and red puccoon. The juice is red and quickly dyes the skin and has been used by the Algonquin Tribe to paint the skin for ritual. It is in the Papaveraceae (Poppy) Family. Use with great caution! This herb grows in eastern North America in moist thickets and dry woods and on floodplains and near streams.

Identification: Bloodroot is a stemless, rhizomatous wildflower that blooms in early spring. The herb grows from 6 to 10 inches (15 cm to 25 cm) tall. The leaves go dormant in mid to late summer. When the bloodroot flower is sprouting, it's usually wrapped by one deeply-scalloped, grayish-green, palmate basal leaf. Bloodroot has a hermaphroditic flower that has 8 to 12 fragile white petals, yellow stamens, and two sepals positioned below the leaves, which fall off after the flowers open. The root is a blood-red rhizome that will branch out and grow new rhizomes.

Medicinal Use: Caution is advised. Bloodroot is a toxic plant, and serious problems can arise. Use small doses only as advised by a medical professional or find an alternative plant. The root is used medicinally.

Skin Cancers, Ulcers, Moles, Skin Tags, Warts, Eczema and Other Skin Conditions: Treating skin problems is what bloodroot does best. However, use with great caution and in moderate amounts as it will also kill healthy cells and can cause permanent scarring and sloughing of the skin. Traditionally, people made and applied a salve from bloodroot to the affected area.

They covered it with a bandage and left it in place for a week or so. Usually, only one application is required, but extensive areas, deep lesions, or other tough cases may require repeated application.

The bloodroot kills the cancerous or damaged cells and covers the area with a scab. Leave it alone to heal, and check the area to be sure that all of the cancer is removed so that it doesn't return. The bloodroot also has anti-inflammatory, anti-bacterial, anti-fungal, and anesthetic properties that help the skin to heal while relieving pain. The salve can be used to remove skin tags, warts, moles and other unwanted skin lesions. Apply the salve directly to the lesion, keeping it well away from the healthy skin. If you decide to use this plant do so with great caution and in small doses. I use a facial mask once a month with a very small amount of bloodroot in it (along with other ingredients). This is a good example of my utilizing it in small and infrequent doses. Treating

Respiratory Problems: Bloodroot is a bronchial muscle relaxant used to treat asthma, whooping cough, influenza, and as a treatment for croup.

Gastrointestinal Problems: Bloodroot powder treats gastrointestinal bleeding, abdominal cramps, nausea, and vomiting. In large doses, it acts as an emetic, causing the very problems it treats. Use with great care or find an alternative herb. Diphtheria,

Tuberculosis, and Respiratory Illnesses: Small doses of bloodroot decoction are an antibacterial agent useful for the treatment of bacterial diseases such as diphtheria, tuberculosis, asthma, bronchitis, and pneumonia. For respiratory illnesses, it has the added benefit of cleaning out the mucus and congestion and suppressing coughs. However, I prefer other, safer remedies. For sore throats, you can dilute the decoction in a glass of water and use it as a gargle.

Menstrual Problems: Small doses of Bloodroot Decoction are beneficial for treating menstrual problems including excessive bleeding and cramping. Again, I prefer other plants for this purpose.

Dental Care: Extracts from bloodroot help fight infections like gingivitis and prevent the formation cavities, tartar, and plaque. Add a drop of bloodroot decoction to your toothpaste for this purpose or use a diluted tea as a rinse.

Harvesting: Wear protective gloves to protect your hands from staining red and to avoid the medicine being absorbed through your skin. Best harvested in autumn when the strength of the plant is returning to the root and the tops are dying back. Dig up the root and the surrounding area, removing the rhizomes. Leave a few behind for next year's plants. Dry for future use.

Warning: Great caution is advised. Bloodroot is a toxic plant that can cause tunnel vision, nausea, and death. Do not use bloodroot if you may be pregnant or if you are nursing. It may also cause permanent scarring or disfiguration when used topically.

Blue Cohosh, Caulophyllum thalictroides

Blue cohosh is also known as squaw root or papoose root for its use to induce labor. It is a perennial member of the Berberidaceae (Barberry) Family. Do not confuse it with Black Cohosh. They are very different. It is found on the floor of hardwood forests in eastern North America. It prefers moist soil, hillsides, and shady locations with rich soil.

Identification: A single smooth stalk, 1 to 3 feet (0.3m to 0.9m) tall, grows from the rhizome, and contains a single three-lobed leaf and a fruiting stalk. Its leaflets are serrated at the tip and the leaves turn a bluish-green hue when mature. It has deep blue fruits.

Medicinal Use. Childbirth: The root has oxytocic properties that promote childbirth. Do not take during pregnancy until 1 to 2 weeks before the due date and only under a doctor's care. It causes powerful uterine contractions that are regular and productive, encouraging a quick and easy birth. It also has a calming effect, helping the mother relax between contractions and reducing pain.

Menstrual Problems: Blue cohosh root is used for menstrual problems, including delayed menstruation, cramping, and profuse hemorrhage.

Harvesting: Harvest blue cohosh root in late autumn, when it stores its strength. You can also harvest the rhizomes in the spring, just as the new growth begins, if needed. Dry and store the roots for future use.

Warning: Do not use during pregnancy. Do not use for estrogen-sensitive diseases such as endometriosis, fibroids, and certain cancers. Blue cohosh can elevate blood pressure so careful using for heart patients and people with high blood pressure. Excessive dosage can cause nausea, vomiting, and a lack of muscle coordination.

Butterbur, Arctic Sweet Coltsfoot, Petasites frigidus

Butterbur, or Sweet Coltsfoot, is a plant that grows in moist areas throughout the Northern Hemisphere. The name butterbur reportedly came about because the leaves were used to wrap butter for keeping. It is also called bog rhubarb. It is in the Aster/Daisy Family. Note that Arrowleaf coltsfoot (P. frigidus var. sagittatus) has the same medicinal properties as butterbur; it has arrow-shaped leaves. Butterbur or Sweet Coltsfoot is not the same plant as Tussilago farfara, known commonly as coltsfoot and also in this book, though they are closely related.

Identification: Butterbur or sweet coltsfoot flowers appear in February and March, before the larger basal leaves that arrive in late spring. The flowers have a sweet scent, and are often the first flowers seen in the New Year in the cold wetlands in the North. A cluster of white to purple-pink flower heads appears on the tip of a fleshy stalk, which is covered with sheathed leaves. The flowers give way to silver-white seed heads and its large basal, rhubarb-like leaves arise near the flowering stalk directly from an underground rhizome. The basal leaves are palmately divided and their underside is "wooly" with white hairs.

Edible Use: The flowers, flower stalks, and leaf stalks are edible in limited amounts when cooked. The ash (after burning the aerial part) is a good salt substitute.

Medicinal Use: The roots, mature leaves, and stems are all used medicinally. It is antispasmodic, anti-inflammatory, a vasodilator, and mucilaginous. I use it as a tea or a tincture. Only collect mature leaves, as young leaves contain small amounts of pyrrolizidine alkaloids, which are hepatotoxic.

Allergies: Butterbur leaf is very effective for allergies, including hay fever, reducing histamine and leukotriene release. It has been shown to be as effective as many prescription allergy medications without causing drowsiness.

Bronchial Spasms, Chronic Coughs, and Spasmodic Airways and Asthma: Butterbur leaf is useful against asthma and restricted bronchial passages. It reduces the sensitivity and the frequency of attacks. As an antispasmodic, it reduces spasms of the bronchial tract while also relieving inflammation, and is excellent for any chronic cough like those caused by emphysema or bronchitis.

Migraine Headaches: The herb relaxes vasoconstriction and relieves inflammation that can trigger migraine headaches. Like feverfew, it is best taken daily as a preventative rather than as a rescue treatment, though it works as a cure as well. I often pair it with Feverfew in tincture form. Taken daily, butterbur leaf reduces the incidents of migraines.

Inflammation and Muscle Sprains: The plant is a strong anti-inflammatory and antispasmodic. Externally a root poultice can be used to treat inflammation and pain due to a muscle sprain or strain.

Harvesting: Harvest roots in spring. Harvest the leaves and stems throughout the summer once they are fully grown. Young leaves contain small amounts of pyrrolizidine alkaloids, which are hepatotoxic.

Warning: Avoid using butterbur if you have liver problems. Do not use if you are pregnant or breastfeeding, or for children under age 7. Adverse reactions can include GI symptoms, nausea, flatulence, and gassy stomach. Allergies are possible.

California Buckwheat, Eriogonum fasciculatum

California Buckwheat is in the Polygonaceae (Buckwheat) Family. It is a wild buckwheat species and is commonly known as eastern Mojave buckwheat. This shrub is a native to the Southwestern United States and Northwestern Mexico. It grows on dry slopes, canyons, and washes in scrubland and coastal areas.

Identification: Eriogonum fasciculatum is varied in appearance. Sometimes it is a compact bramble and sometimes it is a spreading bush approaching 6 feet (1.8m) in height and 10 feet (3.0m) wide. It has numerous flexible slim branches. Its leaves and are 1 1/2 to 2 inches (3.75 cm to 5 cm) long and less than 1/2 inch (1.25 cm) wide. Leaves grow in a whorled cluster at nodes along the branches. They are wooly and leathery on the undersides and roll under along the edges. Its flowers are dense clusters that are 1 to 6 inches wide (2.5 cm to 15 cm). Each distinct flower is white and pink and only a few millimeters across. It blooms from May to October. It has light brown small seeds.

Edible Use: The seeds are eaten raw or dried for later use. Seeds can be ground into a powder and used as a flour. Young sprouts can also be consumed, and the seeds can be sprouted to eat.

Medicinal Use: The seeds, leaves, flowers, and roots are all used for medicine. Older, mature plants are more potent. The roots are dried and ground for medicine and a strong, thick tea is made from the leaves or the roots.

Wound Care: The leaves, flowers, and roots are used for skin wounds. Fresh leaves or flowers can be applied as a poultice. Ground leaves and ground roots are mixed with water or oil and applied as a poultice. California Buckwheat Tea can be used as a wash.

Colds, Coughs, and Sore Throats: A mild leaf tea works for colds, coughs, and sore throats. The hot root tea can also be used for colds and laryngitis.

Diarrhea and Stomach Illnesses: For diarrhea and other stomach troubles, use a strong decoction made from the roots of California Buckwheat. It cleans out the system and gets rid of irritants.

Oral Care: For sore gums or for use as a mouthwash, use a weak leaf tea. It is a mild pain reliever and calms inflammation. Swish a mouthful of tea around for a few minutes, then spit it out.

Headaches: For headaches and other aches and pains, use a strong tea made from the leaves. It relieves the immediate pain and flushes toxins from the system.

Heart Health: A tea made from dried flowers or dried roots helps prevent heart problems.

Harvesting: The seeds mature in early autumn and dry right on the plant. Wait until the seed pods have dried and turned to a rusty brown before harvesting. Once dried, they can easily be hand-stripped from the plants into open tubs or bags. Harvest older roots as they contain more medicine.

Recipes. Strong California Buckwheat Root Tea: 1 tablespoon California buckwheat shredded root, 1 pint (500 ml) of water. Mix the root into the water and bring to a boil. Reduce the heat to a simmer. Cover and simmer the tea for 15 minutes.* Strain and serve warm or cold. *For a weaker tea, reduce the brewing time to 5 minutes

California Buckwheat Leaf Tea. 1 teaspoon California buckwheat leaves, dried or 1 tablespoon fresh, 1 cup boiling water. Pour the boiling water over the leaves and steep for 5 to 10 minutes. Strain.

Cardinal Flower, Lobelia cardinalis

Cardinal flower is a beautiful showy plant with brilliant red flowers. This plant is hard to miss. It is in the Campanulaceae (Bellflower) Family. It grows in wet soil, swamps, stream banks, and along rivers.

Identification: The flowers are a cardinal red color and are 2-lipped with five deep lobes. They grow on an erect raceme approximately 2 to 3 feet (0.6m to 0.9m) tall and flower during the summer and autumn. The toothed lanceolate to oval leaves grow 8 inches (20 cm) long and 2 inches (5 cm) wide.

Medicinal Use: Traditional uses for cardinal flower are below. It isn't used as often as it used to be in herbal medicine but is still an important plant to know. All parts are used medicinally.

Bronchitis: Cardinal flower is used as an expectorant for bronchitis.

Epilepsy, Diphtheria, Tonsillitis: The anti-inflammatory and narcotic properties of the roots help it treat convulsive and inflammatory diseases such as these. It relaxes spasms and allows the body to heal.

Eye Diseases: A weak tea made from 1 teaspoon of root or leaves per cup of boiling water is useful as an eye wash.

Sprains, Bruises, and Skin Irritations: As an external application for relieving pain and encouraging healing in sprains, strains, bruises, and other surface irritations, try Cardinal Flower tea or a Lobelia Seed Vinegar Preparation. It relaxes the muscles and speeds healing though I do prefer other plants for this use.

Warning: Some other plants in the Lobelia genus are toxic, so it is wise to be careful in the use of cardinal flower since it could potentially be toxic in larger doses. Symptoms of toxicity would include nausea, vomiting, diarrhea, excessive saliva, weakness, dilation of pupils, convulsions or coma.

Lobelia Vinegar Preparation: Use the fast method only in emergencies. A slower maceration is best. Ingredients: 4 ounces (113g) powdered Lobelia seed and 1-quart (1 Liter) of vinegar. Macerate the vinegar and seed powder for seven days, shaking daily. Filter mixture through a coffee filter to remove the seed powder. Store in a cool, dry place. Fast Method: Place the vinegar and seed powder in the top of a double boiler and cover. Bring water to a simmer in the lower pot. Warm the vinegar mixture this way for 1 hour. Cool and strain.

Cat's Claw, Uncaria tomentosa

Cat's Claw, or uña de gato, grows in Central and South America, where it grows profusely in the rainforest. The root and vine bark are imported here for medicinal use. It is a useful plant and I try to keep a supply on hand. It is in the Rubiaceae (Bedstraw/Madder) Family.

Identification: Cat's claw, Uncaria tomentosa, is a tropical woody vine whose hooked claw-shaped thorns give it its name. The vine grows to a length of up to 100 feet (30meters), climbing anything in its path.

The bright green elongated leaves grow in opposing pairs. They have a smooth edge that may be rounded or come to a point. The flowers are yellow, trumpet shaped, and have five petals. The barbs are hookshaped and curled like a cat's claw.

Medicinal Use: The inner bark of the vine or root is used. It is taken as a powder, in capsules, as a tea, or as a double-extracted tincture.

Cancer Treatment and Prevention: Cat's claw prevents and helps treat cancer. It contains anti-inflammatory, anti-oxidant, and anti-tumor properties that prevent cancer cells from developing in the body. It helps the immune system fight existing cancerous cells by enhancing white blood cell function. People in chemotherapy report that it helps relieve pain and other symptoms related to chemotherapy drugs.

Irritable Bowel Syndrome, Crohn's Disease, Colitis, Ulcers, and Other Gastrointestinal Issues: Cat's Claw helps support the digestive system, relieving inflammation in the stomach and intestines. It has anti-bacterial, anti-fungal, and antiviral properties that help rid the body of the underlying causes. It fights diseases of the intestines, stomach, and liver while restoring the body's natural flora and healing the digestive system.

Anti-Inflammatory and Autoimmune Conditions: Inflammation is a cause of many body diseases, including autoimmune diseases, arthritis, and heart disease. Reducing swelling in joints, wounds, and bodily organs helps the body heal faster and reduces pain. They are still researching its use in certain autoimmune diseases, and some recommend not taking it if you have an autoimmune issue due to the way it boosts the immune system.

Osteoarthritis and Rheumatoid Arthritis: The anti-inflammatory effects of this herb are very beneficial for osteoarthritis and rheumatoid arthritis. It calms the inflammation, reduces swelling, and relieves the associated pain.

Powerful Anti-Viral: Cat's claw is useful in treating viral diseases due to its quinovic acid glycosides. It is used to treat herpes, Epstein-Barr, hepatitis B and C, HPV, HIV, Dengue Fever, and other viral diseases. I would try it against any of the tropical viral diseases, given the need.

Helps the Body Heal, Chronic Fatigue Syndrome: Its anti-inflammatory and anti-bacterial properties help the body from getting an infection and calm the body's response to the damage, helping it heal. It also helps people with Chronic Fatigue Syndrome.

Lowers Blood Pressure: Cat's claw increases circulation throughout the body and helps lower blood pressure for people with hypertension.

Supports the Immune System and Help for Mold Exposure: Cat's claw contains isopteropodin, which helps increase the body's white blood cell count, eliminates free radicals from the body, and helps fight infection. Its anti-inflammatory and antioxidant properties also help with mycotoxin exposure.

Regulates Female Hormones and the Menstrual Cycle: Cat's Claw helps regulate the female hormones that keep the menstrual cycle regular and helps to alleviate bloating, cramping, and mood changes that are associated with it. If you are pregnant or trying to conceive avoid this plant. It can cause miscarriages and may prevent conception.

Detoxification: Cat's claw is beneficial in detoxifying the whole body and cleansing the blood and lymph. It is excellent at removing toxins, drugs, heavy metals, and other foreign substances from the body. It also boosts the effectiveness of the kidneys, spleen, pancreas, and digestive system due to its cleansing effects.

Warning: Do not take cat's claw if you are pregnant, nursing, or trying to get pregnant. Do not take if you have an autoimmune disorder. It may cause a flare-up. Consult your health professional if you are taking blood thinners or any other prescription drugs as it interacts with some of them. Side effects can include nausea, diarrhea, and dizziness.

Cleavers/Bedstraw, Galium aparine

Cleavers, also called Bedstraw, catchweed, sticky weed, and goosegrass, is an annual plant that grows in damp, rich soils along riverbanks and fence lines in eastern and western North America and is found worldwide. It is in the Rubiaceae (Bedstraw) Family. You often find the plant and its seeds stuck to your clothing like Velcro after walking through it.

Identification: A climbing hairy, almost sticky, stem grows from a thin taproot to a height of 2 to 6 feet (0.6m to 1.8m). The plant has coarse leaves with a variable shape. The leaves grow in whorls around the stem, and the stem, leaves, and fruit are usually covered with small, spiny hairs. Its leaves may be oblong to lance-like or even linear. Cleavers flowers are small and white or greenish-white in color and flower from early summer until autumn. The flowers have a sweet smell.

Edible Use: Cleavers are edible. I prefer them cooked as their hairs and hooks get stuck in my throat when I eat them raw. Their seeds can be roasted as a coffee substitute. They are a good green to juice and drink.

Medicinal Use: Cleavers are astringent, anti-inflammatory, diuretic, detoxifying, febrifuge and promote sweating. It is effective both internally and externally. I use the leaves for medicine and infuse them cold into oil, water, or a tincture. Do not boil.

Rejuvenate the Skin, Slow the Signs of Aging: Cleaver tea is said to have a toning effect to tighten skin and smooth out wrinkles when applied externally.

Detoxify the Body, Drain the Lymphatic System, and Swollen Glands: Cleavers are a diuretic. They work well to remove toxins from the body and to clean the lymphatic system.

Skin Disorders, Acne, Psoriasis, Eczema, Abscesses, and Boils: Cleavers works internally and externally to improve the condition of the skin, detoxify the blood and lymph, and reduce inflammation associated with these conditions. They are also antibacterial, which helps treat the underlying infections. Use both internally and externally for these conditions.

Kidney Stones, Bladder and Urinary Tract Infections: Cleavers are very effective at treating bladder infections, urinary tract infections, and kidney stones. It dissolves stones, clears obstructions, and flushes them out of the body. The antibacterial action is effective at curing the underlying infections.

Cancr: Research has been done that supports the use of cleavers to treat tumors, especially those of the breast, skin, head, neck, bladder, cervix, prostate, and lymphatic system.

Chickenpox, Measles, and Fevers: To treat chickenpox and the measles, try cleavers internally to treat the disease and externally on the skin to relieve the itching and general discomfort from the rash. Cleavers also helps bring down the accompanying fever.

Stop Bleeding, Burns, and Sunburns: Freshly picked cleavers leaves are excellent for stopping bleeding in wounds, cuts, or other surface bleeding. Apply the leaves directly to the wound. It also reduces inflammation and speeds healing. The leaves can be made into a poultice for larger wounds.

Tonsillitis, Sore Throat, Glandular Fever, and Prostate Problems: Cleaver juice works well for glandular problems like tonsillitis, glandular fever, and for prostate problems and prostate cancers. When fresh juice is not available an infusion can be used, although it is not usually as effective as the juice for these issues.

Harvesting: Harvest cleavers in spring to mid-summer and use fresh or dry for later use.

Recipes. Cleaver Juice. Fresh cleavers leaves and water. Wash the fresh leaves thoroughly and place them in a blender with a small amount of water. Use only as much water as needed to blend. Blend the leaves into a pulp and strain out the juice with a fine sieve. I recommend making a large batch of juice and freezing the extra. Most people drink 2 cups daily to treat cancers and tumors.

Club Moss, Lycopodium clavatum

Club moss is a vascular spore-bearing plant and propogates via spores. It is in the Club Moss Family, Lycopodiaceae, and is not a true moss but is more closely related to ferns and horsetail. Club Moss is found worldwide and is also called staghorn, ground pine, and running pine,

Identification: The yellow-green leaves are scalelike and short and taper to a fine feathery point. The 3 to 4-foot-long, ground-hugging stem of this plant is highly branched with small, spirally arranged scaly leaves. The stem runs along the ground producing roots at frequent intervals. It resembles the seedling of coniferous trees, though there is no relationship between them. Its spores grow on two or sometimes three yellow-green barrel-shaped cones that are on small, 6- inch (15 cm) stalks.

Medicinal Use: Mostly the spores are used in medicine, but sometimes an extract of the entire plant is used.

Respiratory Problems: Club moss spore decoctions are used to treat ailments like chronic lung, bronchial disorders, and other respiratory issues.

Congestion, Colds, and Flu: Club moss spores act to dry out mucous membranes and relieve congestion. Try a 1/4 teaspoon of the spores mixed into a glass of water three times a day until the congestion clears.

Urinary Tract Disorders: Club moss is a diuretic, increasing the amount of urine expelled and flushing toxins from the body. To treat urinary tract problems, use a decoction of the whole plant. Common usage is 1 to 2 tablespoons of the decoction 3 to 4 times a day.

Skin Conditions: Club moss spores treat many different skin conditions, including allergic reactions, sunburns, psoriasis, eczema, fungal infections, chickenpox, contact dermatitis, hives, and insect bites and stings. Make a salve with the spores of club moss. The spores can also be applied lightly as a powder and rubbed into wounds, folds of skin, or anywhere that you prefer not to use oil. The powder absorbs moisture and helps heal wounds.

Rheumatoid Arthritis: A decoction of the entire plant is said to help rheumatoid arthritis symptoms.

Flatulence: Both constipation and flatulence can be treated with spores from club moss. As little as 1/4 teaspoon mixed with water eases symptoms and resolves the problem.

Kidney Diseases: Club Moss Decoction made from the whole plant is used to treat kidney disease and related disorders. It works to eliminate kidney stones and cleanse the system.

Wound Treatment: Open wounds and sores that refuse to heal are well served by the application of club moss spores. Apply the spores as a powder and rub it into the affected area.

Harvesting: Harvesting of club moss should be done when the spore heads are dry, mature, and ripened, though the spores can also be harvested while still green. For a ripe plant just cut off the plant and spread them on a sheet to dry until the cones open. Shake them and collect the spore powder. To collect the spore heads from green cones, cut off the cones and break them open. Place the cones in a paper bag and place them in a cool, dry place to open. When the cones open, shake out the spores and remove the remaining plant material.

Warning: Club moss contains small amounts of alkaloids, which are a toxic substance and can cause paralysis to the motor nerves if consumed in large amounts.

Recipes. Club Moss Decoction: 1 ounce of ground or finely chopped club moss plant, 2 cups of water. Bring the water to a boil and add the club moss plant. Turn the heat down to a slow simmer and simmer the decoction for 15 minutes. Allow the decoction to cool and strain out the herb. Keep the decoction in the refrigerator and use within 3 days. Use a maximum of one cup daily, split into 4 or more doses.

Club Moss Salve. 5 ounces (150ml) of organic olive oil or other carrier oil, 1 ounce (28g) of shaved beeswax, 1 tablespoon of club moss spore powder. Heat the olive oil gently over very low heat in a double boiler. Add the club moss spore powder. Keep the oil on very low heat for 20 to 30 minutes while the spores release their medicine into the oil. Add the shaved beeswax and stir until the salve is thoroughly mixed. Do not strain out the spores. Pour the salve into a sanitized jar and cover it tightly. Keep the salve refrigerated if in a very hot climate. Apply 2 to 3 times daily, as needed.

Coltsfoot, Tussilago farfara

Coltsfoot is in the Aster/Daisy Family, and is closely related to Butterbur. It is native to Eurasia but has naturalized in the US and Canada. It is also known as coughwort, podbel, and son-before-the-father.

Identification: Coltsfoot is a rather unusual perennial. The flowers look like dandelion, but they appear early, in April, and die before the leaves appear. It grows between 4 and 6 inches (10 cm to 15 cm) tall and is usually found in open areas with disturbed soil. The top of the leaf is smooth, while the underside is covered with white downy hairs. Leaves at the top of the plant are green, while those closer to the ground are white or grayish in color. These basal leaves are 2 to 10 inches (5 cm to 25 cm) long and serrated on the edges. The single bright yellow flowers are a little over a half inch (1.25 cm) across and look like dandelion. Its small white root spreads underground.

Edible Use: Coltsfoot flowers and leaves are edible. They are good in salads (in small amounts only). Young leaves are also used in soups or stews. To use the leaves as a vegetable, wash them after boiling to get rid of the bitterness. Dried or fresh leaves and flowers can be used to make an aromatic tea.

Medicinal Use: Both the leaves and flowers have medicinal value, although the flowers have the highest concentrations of medicinal compounds. People rarely use the roots, but they have medicinal properties as well. This plant has anti-inflammatory and anti-tussive properties, due to it containing mucilage and tannins.

Asthma, Whooping Cough, Laryngitis, Coughs, Emphysema, and Bronchial Congestion: The botanical name Tussilago means 'cough dispeller,' and it does the job well. Use it to relieve congestion and expel mucous. It is especially useful for chronic coughs like emphysema and whooping cough. Coltsfoot Decoction, taken throughout the day, is used as a remedy for chronic coughs of all causes.

Eczema, Sores, and Skin Inflammations: The flowers, prepared as a poultice, are helpful applied directly onto skin inflammations, sores, and eczema.

Warning: Coltsfoot leaves contain small amounts of toxic compounds, which are destroyed by cooking. Eat raw leaves sparingly and boil, drain, and rinse leaves when using as a vegetable.

Recipes. Coltsfoot Decoction. 1-ounce coltsfoot leaves, 1-quart (1 Liter) water, raw honey, as desired. Combine the coltsfoot leaves and water over mediumhigh heat and bring to a boil. Reduce the heat and boil the decoction until the water is reduced by half. Cool and strain the decoction to remove the leaves. Sweeten the decoction with raw honey as desired. It can be bitter, depending on the age of the leaves. Drink 1/4 cup at a time, throughout the day or as needed to provide relief.

False Hellebore, Indian Poke, Veratrum viride

There are several plants that go by the name of False Hellebore or Indian Poke. This is Veratrum viride, not Phytolacca acinosa or other pokeweeds. It is in the Lily Family. It is found in pastures, meadows, open woods, damp soils, and swamps. It grows throughout most of eastern and western North America (not mid).

Identification: False Hellebore is an erect perennial herb that grows 2 to 7 feet (0.6m to 2.1meters) tall. The leaves are broad on the lower part and spirally arranged on the stout stem. Leaves are 4 to 14 inches (10 cm to 35 cm) long and 2 to 8 inches (5 cm to 20 cm) wide. The leaf blade of this plant is widest near the middle and tapering at both ends (ovate). The leaves are feathery on the underside. The flowers are arranged on a large branched inflorescence approximately 1 to 2 1/2 feet (0.7m) long. The flowers are ¼ to ½ inch (0.75 cm to 1.25 cm) long with six green to yellow-green tepals.

The ovary is positioned above the sepal attachment and produces flat, winged seeds. The fruit splits along two or more seams when dry to release seeds. The fruit grows up to 1 1/4 inches (3.2 cm) long.

Medicinal Use. Treating High Blood Pressure and Rapid Heartbeat: False Hellebore Root contains chelidonic acid and other alkaloids. Some of the alkaloids expand peripheral blood vessels and lower blood pressure by slowing the heartbeat. Several pharmaceutical drugs for high blood pressure and rapid heartbeat have been developed from False Hellebore compounds. This herb is highly effective, so only very small doses should be used since an overdose is potentially deadly. I prefer other home methods than this plant for lowering blood pressure and heart rate, as the strength can vary from plant to plant and in how it is made. If you choose to use False Hellebore for this purpose, start with very small doses of the decoction and have very close medical supervision.

Reducing Fevers in Acute Diseases: In acute disease situations such as peritonitis and acute pneumonia, a decoction of False Hellebore acts as a febrifuge (brings down the fever). However, do not forget the other effects of the decoction and use it sparingly under complete medical supervision. I much prefer Yarrow to bring down a fever.

Body Pain, Arthritis, and Muscle Pains: A decoction of the leaves or roots, diluted with water, works as a wash to reduce or relieve shoulder pains, intense arthritis pain, severe aches of the muscles and body parts, pains at the rear portion of the neck and fast electric shock in all parts of the body. Alternately, use a salve made from False Hellebore as a rub to relieve pain.

Other Uses: The roots of False Hellebore are slightly soapy and can be used to do laundry. Grate the root and add it to water.

Harvesting: Wear gloves when harvesting. Pick individual leaves and leave the plant intact. Dry the leaves for storage. Harvest rhizomes only from mature plants. Collect the roots in autumn and dry them for future use.

Warning: Take precaution and use only small doses, if you use it internally at all. False Hellebore is considered to be very toxic. Veratrum viride contains numerous toxins that may cause vomiting and nausea. If the poison is not evacuated, vertigo and cold sweats start, respiration slows, blood pressure and cardiac rhythm falls, and the heart fails eventually leading to death.

Recipes. Indian Poke Leaf Decoction: 1 ounce chopped Indian poke Leaves, 1 pint (500 ml) of water. Cover the chopped leaves with water and bring to a boil. Turn off the heat and allow the leaves to steep for 10 to 15 minutes. Strain out the leaves and store the decoction in the refrigerator for up to 3 days or freeze.

False Solomon's Seal, Maianthemum racemosum (Smilacina racemosa)

False Solomon's Seal, also called Solomon's plume and feathery false lily of the valley, is a flowering plant that grows across continental North America. It is a useful plant, but often gets overlooked in favor of more versatile plants. I recommend you get familiar with this plant since it grows almost everywhere. It has been moved from the Lily Family to the Asparagus Family.

Note that this is a different plant than true Solomon's Seal. You can easily tell them apart when flowering as False Solomon's Seal has terminal feathery flower clusters with red berries while Solomon's Seal carries their bell-shaped flowers and dark blue berries on the underside of their stem. It likes moist forests.

Identification: False Solomon's seal grows up to 3 feet (0.9m) tall from underground rhizomes, producing single unbranched arching stems with large leaves that are up to 6 inches (15 cm) long and half as wide. They have smooth margins and parallel veins. The stem is green, softly hairy and, when in flower, ends in a cluster of feathery white flowers. Each flower has 6 tepals, 6 stamens, a pistil, and short style. Their small star-shaped flowers appear in mid-spring. The flowers produce round, green fruits that turn red or red and purple-striped when mature. Each berry has a few seeds.

Edible Use: The fruit are eaten raw or cooked. They have a bitter-sweet flavor and are a good source of vitamin C. Eat in small quantities only, larger amounts have a laxative effect. Young shoots are eaten raw or cooked as a green vegetable. The roots are eaten cooked. Soak the root first in water, change the water and cook. Eat like potatoes.

Medical Use: False Solomon's seal root is used medicinally for a variety of problems. The roots and leaves of False Solomon's seal are used to make tincture, salve, tea, or capsules. It is a lubricating plant and the rhizomes contain saponins.

Sore Throats and Oral Irritations: A strong root tea is valuable for sore throats and other mouth irritations. Try the root tea double in strength and use it to gargle several times a day until all irritation is gone.

Coughs: Make an infusion of leaves as a cough remedy. Sweeten with raw honey for extra soothing power.

Congestion: For bronchial congestion, try breathing in the steam while making a root decoction. Then use the decoction internally to treat symptoms.

Regulating the Menstrual Cycle and Hormonal Swings: False Solomon's Seal Root Tea or Root Tincture is used to regulate the menstrual cycle, to relieve symptoms of menstrual disorders, and help with swings in hormone levels.

Stomach Complaints: An infusion of the root is used to relieve stomach pain and soothe the digestive system.

Stop Bleeding and Treat Wounds: Use a poultice from the crushed leaves or root and apply it to wounds, scrapes, rashes, cuts, burns, and insect bites. Its anti-inflammatory nature reduces the irritation in the area and soothes the skin. Dried powdered root stops bleeding in skin wounds. You can also use the tea as an external wash.

Arthritis: To relieve arthritic pain and to reduce swelling in the joints, mix the dried powdered root with water to make a thick paste. Rub the paste on the affected joint. It acts as an analgesic and anti-inflammatory to help heal the joint. Taking an internal decoction of False Solomon's Seal leaves also soothes arthritic joints.

Harvesting: Harvest leaves, stems and berries by plucking them from the plant whenever they are available. Use only healthy leaves. Dig the rhizomes in autumn and slice them before drying for future us

Wild Comfrey, Hound's Tongue, Cynoglossum virginianum

Wild Comfrey is also known as blue houndstongue, as its leaves are said to look like a dog's tongue. It is native to eastern North America and much of Europe. It primarily grows in deciduous forests and open upland areas.

Note that this is not the same plant as Comfrey (Knitbone), Symphytum officinale, which is also in this book, though they are both in the Borage Family.

Identification: Wild comfrey grows on an erect simple stem with fine hairs on both the leaves and stem. The alternate leaves are simple, 4 to 8 inches (10 cm to 20 cm long and 1 to 3 inches (2.5 cm to 7.5 cm) wide with smooth edges.

The leaves are larger and stalked at the lower end of the stem and grow in a rosette. As you move up the stem the leaves are smaller, clasp the stem, and are unstalked. It is biennial. The blue-purple to white flowers appear in late spring/early summer. Each flower has five deep lobes connected to an ovary, which is connected to the style. Flowers are approximately 1/3 inch (0.8 cm) across and have ragged edges. Fruits are produced in mid-late summer. There are one to four prickly nutlets per flower, each having one seed that is covered with bristles that cling to clothing. The plant grows from a taproot.

Medicinal Use: While both the root and the leaves can be used medicinally, the root is more powerful and best used fresh. Note that this is a different plant than the medicinal comfrey, also in this book. I do not use this particular wild comfrey species as reports of medicinal uses are not backed up by as much research. I do use comfrey, Symphytum officinale, quite often.

Itchy Skin: Wild Comfrey Root Decoction is said to treat itchy skin.

Burns, Bruises, and Contusions: Wild comfrey leaves have been used as a poultice for burns, and bruises. Again, I prefer Symphytum officinale and don't use Wild Comfrey.

Warning: Avoid large doses and long-term use, which can result in liver problems.

Arbors and Bushes

American Basswood or American Linden, Tilia americana

Tilia americana belongs to the Malvaceae (Mallow/ Hibiscus) Family. It is most commonly known as American Basswood, American Linden, and American Lime Tree. The common name of this plant is from "bastwood," referring to use of the inner bark, the "bast," for weaving rope and baskets. The tree is a native to eastern and mid North America.

Identification: American Basswood is a large deciduous tree that reaches a height of 60 to 100 feet (18m to 30m). It has a trunk diameter of 3 to 6 feet (0.9m to 1.8m) at maturity. It has gray furrowed bark with flat ridges.

Leaves of American Basswood are deciduous, alternate, and unevenly heart-shaped. Leaves are 4 to 6 inches (10 cm) long, about 3 inches (7.5 cm) wide, thick and slightly leathery, with sharply serrated margins. They are usually smooth and hairless on both sides but occasionally have soft downy hairs on the lower surface. Yellowishwhite fragrant flowers grow in drooping clusters of 5 to 20 and are about ½ inch (1.25 cm) wide. It flowers May thru June for about 2 weeks. Fruits are small dry round nutlets that ripen in autumn, with each fruit bearing one seed.

Edible Use: Edible parts of this plant include its flowers, leaves, seeds, bark, and sap. Leaves and flowers can be eaten raw or cooked. The leaf buds are especially delicious. The inner cambium (bark) can be eaten raw or ground into a flour. The tree can be tapped like a maple but it takes a lot more sap to make a syrup. The flowers make a nice tea.

Medicinal Use: Skin Treatments Burns. A poultice or tea made from the inner bark of American basswood works well for burns, sunburns, boils, and other skin irritations. It softens skin and relieves inflammation, infection, and itching.

Sedative, Anticonvulsant, and Nerve Pain: American Basswood is a sedative, an antispasmodic, and an analgesic. It helps with nerve pain, anxiety, insomnia, and seizures. A tincture made from the leaves and flowers effectively treats seizures and other problems related to the nervous system.

Hypertension, High Cholesterol, and Heart Tonic: An American Basswood flower and leaf tincture helps lower high blood pressure. Its calming effects extend to the cardiovascular system as they relax the blood vessels. It also helps lower blood cholesterol levels and helps regulate irregular heartbeats.

Coughs and Throat Irritation: The flowers and leaves are used to treat coughs, laryngitis, and throat irritations, though Tilia cordata, the European littleleaf linden, is the tree most often used for this.

Conjunctivitis, Eye Infections, and Eyewash: Try an infusion made from fresh American basswood leaves to clear up eye infections and conjunctivitis. A recipe for American Basswood Infusion Eyewash is below.

Dysentery, Heartburn, Stomach Complaints, and Diuretic: American Basswood Tincture is good for stomach ailments, heartburn, and dysentery. For stomach issues, use a tincture of flowers and leaves. The inner bark infusion has diuretic properties and promotes urination. Recipes.

American Basswood Infusion Eyewash: 1 teaspoon American basswood leaves, crushed but not ground and 1 cup distilled water. Bring the water and fresh leaves to a full boil, then reduce the heat and simmer for 10 minutes. Strain the infusion to remove all of the plant material. Allow the mixture to cool completely before using. Use fresh.

Ash, Fraxinus americana or Fraxinus excelsior

The ash tree, also known as the American Ash (F. americana), Common Ash, Weeping Ash, White Ash, and European Ash (F. excelsior), is a tall, fast-growing tree that can reach up to 100 feet (30m) in height. The tree grows tall and thin when young, and it spreads and becomes more rounded as it ages. It is in the Oleaceae (Olive) Family.

Identification: In the early spring, before the leaves have fully formed, the branches display clusters of flowers, with male and female flowers on separate plants. It has large 8 to 12 inch (20 cm to 30 cm) dark green opposite pinnately compound leaves that each have 5 to 11 oval-shaped leaflets. The leaflets are 2 to 5 inches (5 cm to 12.5 cm) long, stalked, and shiny green on top and pale green below. Margins may be slightly toothed. The fruit is a tan winged achene, called a samara, one to two inches (5 cm) long. Each fruit contains a single seed.

Medicinal Use: Leaves, seeds, inner bark, and sap are used for medicine.

Childbirth, PCOS, Uterine Fibroids: Ash Leaf Extract is used as a tonic after childbirth. It is used homeopathically for PCOS and uterine fibroids.

Fevers, Stomach Cramps, Laxative: Ash tree inner bark has tonic and astringent properties. It can be taken as a tea to treat fevers and stomach cramps. Ash Leaf Tea is a diuretic and useful for flushing excess water and toxins from the body. The inner bark is a laxative.

Harvesting: Gather the leaves during the summer when the leaves are fully open, but before they begin to change color. Gather the bark in the spring.

Warning: Ash can cause vomiting when taken internally. Use caution. Ash is very potent and should not be combined with other medicines without the advice of a doctor or qualified health professional. Do not give ash to pregnant women, nursing mothers, or young children. Do not use ash for people with kidney or liver problems.

Ash Tree Bark Tonic: 1 teaspoon dried inner bark of the ash tree, 1 cup boiling water. Add the inner bark to the boiling water and turn off the heat. Allow the tonic to brew for 15 minutes. Strain out the bark.

Balsam Fir, Abies balsamea

The balsam fir is popular as a Christmas tree. It is also known as the Canada balsam, fir pine, silver fir, or silver pine. It is easily recognized by its cone-shape, short needle-like leaves, and its fir fragrance. It is in the Pinaceae.

Identification: Most balsam firs grow 45 to 65 feet (13.7m to 19.8m) tall when mature. The Christmas trees sold for indoor use are only a few years old and still immature. The tree grows in the classic Christmas tree shape, although trees grown for sale are shaped. In nature, the tree forms a narrow crown that is more rounded than the single point that most commercial trees have.

Leaves are short dark green, flat needles, each approximately an inch (2.5 cm) long and silver-blue on the underside. The bark is smooth and grey with resinfilled blisters that form a rough, scaly appearance on older trees. Seed cones are about 1 1/2 inch- to 3 inches-long (3.75 cm to 7.5 cm) and dark purple, turning brown and opening to release the seeds when mature. The seeds are winged and release in September.

Medicinal Use: The leaves and twigs can be used to make medicinal teas, tinctures, and extracts, and the pitch is used as it is or to make a medicinal tea. It has antibiotic, analgesic, and anti-cancer properties. The distilled essential oil and extracted oil are also valuable medicines. The distilled essential oil is strongest, but extracted oil can be used if distillation equipment is not available.

Healing and Infections: Cuts, Sores, Wounds, and Abrasions. Balsam fir pitch or resin is easy to use as is as on cuts, sores, and wounds of all kinds. Cover the affected area with the pitch. It forms a protective cover, helps prevent and heal infection, and helps wounds heal quickly. It has antiseptic and healing properties. For large cuts, use the stickiness to "glue" the edges of the wound together to help it heal once it is clean. Infused oil can also be applied for infection.

Chapped Lips and Cold Sores: In winter, smear a little balsam fir pitch on your lips to prevent chapping. If your lips are chapped, or if you have a cold sore, the pitch helps the area to heal quickly.

Bronchitis, Coughs, and Sore Throats: For bronchial and chest congestion, coughs, tuberculosis, and sore throats, use either Balsam Fir Tincture or Balsam Fir Pitch Tea. If using tea, sip as needed to calm sore throat pain, coughs, and bronchial spasms. Another treatment for bronchial congestion is to add balsam needles to water and use it in a sweat bath or sauna. The essential oils in the needles will sweeten the air and loosen phlegm from the lungs, easing breathing.

Gonorrhea: Balsam Fir Pitch Tea is useful for curing the sexually transmitted disease Gonorrhea. Anti-Cancer Agent: Balsam fir essential oil has many anti-cancer and anti-tumor properties. The oil stops the growth of cancer cells, prevents cancer from spreading, and kills existing tumor cells. The oil also has anti-inflammatory properties, which calm the inflammation in the nearby skin. Common dosage is to take one to two drops of distilled balsam fir essential oil in a tablespoon of organic olive oil or add one to two drops to a cup of balsam fir tea. Take two to three times daily. Start with one drop, then increase it to two when you are sure you are not allergic. Balsam fir essential oil can be used along with conventional cancer treatments.

Painful Muscles and Body Aches: Balsam fir essential oil is an excellent pain killer for muscle and body aches. Put a small amount of the diluted essential oil (always dilute essential oils in a carrier oil) onto the achy area and massage it into the skin.

Harvesting. To Harvest Balsam Fir Pitch: The pitch is found in blisters on the tree bark. Simply open the blisters with a knife, cutting gently into the blister. If the blister is forcefully popped, the pitch can spray out. The pitch is clear, runny, and sticky. In cold weather, it is thick and almost gel-like in texture. I collect the pitch into a small glass jar with a tight lid.

To Harvest Balsam Fir Leaves: The young leaves and shoots are best for making teas and tinctures. It is best to harvest leaves and young shoots in the spring. Use them fresh to make tinctures and dry some leaves for use throughout the year.

Recipes. Balsam Fir Pitch Tea: Dissolve a small amount of balsam fir pitch, approximately 1/8 to 1/4 teaspoon, into a cup of warm water or an herbal tea. Drink pitch tea as needed to calm throat pain and bronchial spasms.

Extracted Balsam Fir Oil (Cold or Warm Extraction). Cold Extraction: Balsam fir leaves, twigs, and/or bark, dried, organic olive oil, or another suitable carrier oil. Fill a glass jar 2/3rds full of dried balsam fir needles and small pieces of twig or bark. Cover the fir needles and twigs with organic olive oil, filling the jar to within ½ inch (1.25 cm) of the top. Stir the oil and herbs to make sure no air pockets remain. Place the jar in a sunny window for 6 to 8 weeks. Strain the oil through a fine sieve to remove the leaves, twigs, and bark. Store in a cool, dark place, and use the oil within one year.

Warm Extraction: Place the herbs and oil in the top of a double boiler. Fill the bottom of the double boiler with water and heat to a low simmer. Heat the oil and herbs slowly for 2 hours, checking frequently Simmer. Do not boil. Strain the oil through a fine sieve or cheesecloth. Discard the herbs. Store in a cool, dark place, and use the oil within one year.

Balsam Poplar, Populus balsamifera

Balsam poplar is a member of the Salicaceae (Willow) Family. It is also commonly known as bamtree or eastern balsam poplar. It has similar uses as Cottonwood Trees (also in this book). It is most commonly found in Northern North America. It likes moist sites along rivers and in floodplains.

Identification: If you live in an area where balsam grows, you probably already know this tree. Populus balsamifera is a deciduous tree growing up to 100 feet (30m) tall. It has brown bark on the branches in the first year that turns grey as it ages. This fast-growing tree can grow several feet in height each year. The simple, toothed, alternate leaves are narrow to broadly oval-shaped and pointed. They are 3 to 5 inches long and 1.5 to 3 inches (4.5 cm to 7.5 cm) wide.

Their bases taper in a heart shape and are usually rounded at the base. The underside is whitish or pale green and the tops are a shiny green. Its flowers are borne in catkins. The male catkins are 1 to 2 inches (2.5 cm to 5 cm) long. The female catkins are nearly 3 inches (7.5 cm) long. Their blooms form in mid-spring. Their fruits are eggshaped capsules with two to three carpels each. They are usually hairy.

Edible Use: You can dry the inner bark of balsam poplar and grind it into a flour to use as a thickener or add it to flour for making bread. Catkins can be eaten raw or cooked.

Medicinal Use: The inner bark, leaf buds, and resin are most often used.

Coughs, Colds, Bronchitis, and Respiratory Diseases: The inner bark and buds of balsam poplar have proven to be a highly effective treatment for respiratory illness. The anti-inflammatory effects soothe swollen airways, while the herb expels mucus and relieves pain and fever. It also has anti-microbial effects that combat the causes of the disease. When treating severe congestion, try a steam treatment. Put poplar balsam buds into boiling water and breathe in the cooled steam. This releases the phlegm and gives quick relief. Arthritis: Balsam poplar reduces the pain and inflammation of arthritic joints. For joint pain, try drinking inner bark tea daily and using the buds as an external infused oil or salve.

Skin Conditions: For skin diseases, inflamed skin, cuts, wounds, burns, bruises, acne, rashes, and other related skin conditions, balsam poplar is a good herbal treatment. The resin from the buds soothes and moisturizes irritated skin and burns, and the tea makes a good wash for general skin irritations. It relieves pain and itching while calming the inflammation. The resin can be used fresh or extracted with alcohol.

Harvesting and Warning: See Cottonwood

Bayberry and Wax Myrtle, Myrica carolinensis and M. cerifera

Southern Bayberry/Wax Myrtle fruit is a favorite among the local bird populations. It grows in wet bogs, marshes, and thickets near sandy coasts They also grow along the banks of the great lakes. The wax is used for candle-making and provides the "bayberry scent". It is in the Myricaceae (Wax Myrtle) Family.

Identification: The plant is an evergreen shrub, sometimes deciduous, growing 6 to 12 feet (1.8m to 3.65m) tall. It has long elongated leathery dark green leaves with jagged edges, hanging from thin, small trunks. The shrubs produce either all male or all female flowers. Male flowers have 3 to 5 stamens, while female flowers produce globular fruit that is coated with wax. Flowers appear in the spring to early summer, and fruit follows in the late summer and fall. Another bayberry, Myrica pensylvanica, grows further north, but the range overlaps. You can easily tell the shrubs apart by examining the leaves. The Myrica pensylvanica leaves are greener and lack hairs on the fruit wall and papillae. They are also rounder at the tips, while the Southern Bayberry come to a point. Myrica pensylvanica does not have all of the healing properties of Myrica carolinensis. Below Bayberry and Wax Myrtle are used interchangeably and taxinomically they are often lumped together under M. *cerifera*.

Edible Use: The berries can be eaten raw or cooked and the leaves can be used for flavoring like bay leaves.

Medicinal Use. Bayberry root bark, leaves, and berries are used.

Diarrhea, Colitis and Digestive Issues: Try bayberry root mixed in a glass or water for bowel and digestive issues. It is effective in the treatment of diarrhea and colitis. When bayberry root is not available, you may use the leaves.

Dysentery and Ulcers: A concentrated extract made from the bayberry fruit is used.

Common Cold and Sore Throats: Powdered bayberry root in a glass of cold water makes a soothing gargle for sore throats and colds. Cold bayberry leaf tea can also be used. The root bark is an astringent that brings blood to the area to speed healing.

Reduce Fevers: Those same qualities that bring blood to the surface and speed healing also dilate the capillaries in the skin and induce sweating, cooling the body.

Muscle Aches and Arthritic Joints: The wax of the bayberries contains pain-relieving agents. Combined with the healing benefits of the powdered root, it makes an excellent salve for aching joints and muscles.

Harvesting: Collect the root bark in the late autumn or early winter and dry it for future use. Store the pieces in sections, then chop it or powder it when needed to keep it fresh. Store the bark in a tightly sealed container in a cool, dark place. Harvest the bayberries when they are at the peak of ripeness and extract the wax as soon as possible. Retain both the wax and the water for medicinal use.

Recipes. Bayberry Tea: 1 tablespoon dried bayberry leaves or crushed root, 1 cup water. Bring the water to a boil and pour it over the leaves or root. Allow leaves to steep for 10 to 15 minutes and root bark to steep for 20 to 30 minutes. Strain the tea. Use hot or cold.

Bayberry Fruit Extract and Wax Extraction: Around five pounds of berries are needed to yield about one pound of wax. Gather bayberries in the mid-fall when the fruit is fully ripe. Wash the berries in cold water and place them in an old pot, preferably one reserved for wax making, and cover them with at least 2 inches (5 cm) of water. Bring the pot to a simmer, but do not boil. Simmer for at least one hour. Turn off the heat and cool overnight. In the morning, remove the solid wax from the water and keep it for other uses. Put the water back over low heat and simmer it again to reduce the volume greatly, leaving a few cups of water only. This concentrates the medicinal qualities so that only a few drops are needed per dose. Store the extract for up to 3 days in the refrigerator or divide it into smaller containers and freeze it for future use. The dosage depends on how concentrated the extract is made. Try using a few drops of a concentrated solution in tea. Use the saved wax below to make salve.

Bayberry Salve – for external use only. 1/4 to 1/2 cup extracted bayberry wax, 1 cup organic olive oil or another carrier oil, more if needed, 1 tablespoon powdered bayberry root. Add the powdered bayberry root to the organic olive oil and place over low heat. Warm the oil and powdered root together for 30 minutes. Add the bayberry wax, stirring, until it is melted and the wax and oil are thoroughly combined. Cool the mixture and test the consistency. Add more wax if the salve is too runny or more oil if it is too hard. The consistency will depend on your extracted wax and may vary between batches.

Bilberry, Vaccinium myrtillus

Bilberry is sometimes called whortleberry, dyeberry, and European blueberry. It is often confused with true blueberries. This plant is a powerhouse of nutrition and medicine. There is no better reason to eat jam and jelly every morning than the medicinal benefits found in this little berry. Watch closely for them to ripen, as the birds also love them. It is in the Ericaceae (Heath) Family. The bilberry plant is found in meadows and moist northern coniferous forests, and is a common arctic and subarctic shrub. It likes acidic soil. It is a European plant but is commonly found in North America today. The plant is a close relative to blueberries, huckleberries, and cranberries.

Identification: This deciduous shrub grows low to the ground, usually less than 2 feet (0.6 meters) tall. Flowers are pink and urn-shaped. The fruit are small, blue-black in color, and contain many seeds. The flesh is dark red or blue, versus the pale-green inner fruit of blueberries. Bright green leaves are alternate with finely-toothed margins.

Edible Use: Bilberry is a relative of blueberry, but has a slightly tart bitter flavor, so it is mostly used cooked with sugar, though I quite like them raw. They are often used for pies and jams. The leaves are used for tea.

Medical Use: Bilberry is a strong anti-oxidant, anti-inflammatory, anti-bacterial, and anti-fungal that has many beneficial properties. It is also a natural antihistamine. The berries are very high in anthocyanins, which give it its blue-black color, and are a strong anti-oxidant and heavy metal chelator. Berries and leaves are used for medicine. Medicinally, you can eat the berries raw, in jams or jellies, or eat them dried and powdered in capsule form.

Powerful Anti-Inflammatory: Bilberries are rich in antioxidants and help reduce free radical damage. They also fight inflammation in the body. By reducing inflammation, they protect against many the many chronic diseases that are caused or aggravated by inflammation, including many autoimmune diseases.

Diabetes: Compounds in both bilberry berries and leaves help reduce blood glucose levels and insulin resistance. Reducing blood sugar levels helps protect the kidneys, eyes, nerves, and blood vessels. Bilberries may also help combat obesity by decreasing fat absorption and have been shown to both treat and prevent Type 2 diabetes.

Improves Vision: Bilberries are remarkable for their ability to improve the health and function of the eyes. It can help treat night blindness, cataracts, macular degeneration, poor vision, and chronic eye strain. Bilberry protects the cells of the eye, reduces inflammation, and helps prevent damage to the ocular nerves in diabetics. Use it internally; it is not used topically in the eyes.

Anti-Cancer: The anti-inflammatory and antioxidant properties of bilberries help lower the risk of cancer. Bilberries help reduce inflammation and reduce free radical damage in the body. They also inhibit the growth of cancerous cells as well as help kill off cancerous cells.

Liver and Kidneys and Detox Heavy Metals: Bilberry berry compounds help the body remove toxins and help improve function of the liver and kidneys. It helps balance chemicals in the kidneys and the anthocyanins help organs chelate heavy metals like arsenic, lead, cadmium, and iron from the blood.

Heart Health: Bilberries have many benefits for the heart and circulatory system. It supports the blood vessels, lowers blood pressure, and helps regulate cholesterol levels and the plaque that causes atherosclerosis. It also contributes to the formation of healthy blood platelets and reduces the chances of a heart attack or stroke. Bilberry compounds help strengthen blood vessel walls, improving varicose veins and hemorrhoids.

Gastrointestinal Problems, Irritable Bowel Syndrome, and Ulcers: Bilberries help soothe the gastro-intestinal system. Tannins and anti-inflammatory compounds reduce inflammation and irritation in the intestinal tract. It helps relieve symptoms such as nausea, indigestion, diarrhea, and IBS. Internally, the leaves are both preventative and curative of ulcers. A leaf extraction can be applied topically to ulcers in the mouth.

Alzheimer's Disease and Dementia: Antioxidants in bilberries help slow cognitive decline and reduce the effects of existing symptoms. It may also improve overall mental focus and clarity.

Promotes Healthy Gums: Bilberries are anti-inflammatory and help reduce inflammation and swelling in the mouth and gums. The anti-inflammatory astringent, and antibacterial compounds help fight gingivitis.

Harvesting: Harvest green bilberry leaves at any time before winter. Pick the berries when they are fully mature and blue-black in color. Cut or prick each berry and dry them on a dehydrator for future use.

Warning: Bilberries are safe, with no known side effects, and are often eaten as a fruit. However, they can interfere with some medications. Consult your health care professional before eating bilberries if you have problems related to blood clotting or if you take bloodthinning medications or aspirin. Consult your doctor if you are pregnant or breastfeeding. Diabetics should also discuss bilberry prior to use. Leaves should only be utilized short-term.

Birch, Betula spp.

Birch trees are members of the Betulaceae (Birch) Family and are related to alders and hazelnuts. They are found throughout most of the Northern Hemisphere. There are over 60 species worldwide.

Identification: Birch trees are deciduous and grow quickly, but they don't reach the towering heights of many trees. Most grow to about 30 feet (9.1 meters) tall or less, though yellow birch and paper birches reach about 80 feet (24 meters). They often grow in stands (groupings).

Birch trees often have several main stems or trunks, giving the tree an irregular shape. Some look bushy, others have a rounded crown. Birch bark can be quite varied. The paper birch has a thin, white bark that peels into paper-like strips. Yellow birch bark curls into small strips of bronze-colored bark. Mature river birch trees have a scaly blackish-gray bark. Birch leaves are alternate, toothed, and pinnately veined.

Leaves are oval or triangular, broad at the top and pointed at the end. Birch trees have male and female flowers on the same tree. The male flowers appear in late summer and remain on the tree. The female flowers are smaller green catkins that form on the end of the branch. Once pollinated, they become conelike, open, and fall apart.

Edible and Other Use: The sap of the birch tree can be tapped and made into a syrup. The sap can also be consumed as is. It is nutritious, containing vitamins, minerals, and amino acids. The inner bark of birch contains xylitol, a sweetener that also kills unwanted bacteria in the mouth when used orally (like in gum). The bark is used for making baskets and containers and birch bark is an excellent firestarter.

Medicinal Use: The leaves, twigs, catkins, bark, buds, and sap are all used medicinally. They have antiinflammatory, astringent, and diuretic properties. Birch contains salicin, which helps with pain and is an anti-coagulant. Inner birch bark also contains betulin, which is a triterpene and is best extracted in oil, vinegar, or alcohol as it does not extract well in water. We best utilize it as betulinic acid. Chaga mushroom, which grows on birch trees, is a good source of betulinic acid, which is antiviral, anticancer, and antibacterial.

Anti-Inflammatory, Arthritis, Eczema, and Sore Muscles: Birch leaves, buds, bark, and twigs have anti-inflammatory properties that are easily accessed by boiling the twigs, buds, and leaves. A medicinal tea or decoction can be used internally or as a wash on the skin. It is used to treat arthritis, painful joints, eczema, and sore muscles. You ca make a salve using infused birch oil made from the buds.

Diuretic, Edema, Heart and Kidney Problems: The diuretic properties of birch trees help the body release excess fluids, which helps lower blood pressure and helps the kidneys. Birch also helps lower cholesterol and break up kidney stones.

Urinary Tract and Kidney Infections: Birch Bark is useful in treating urinary tract infections and cystitis. It helps first by removing excess water from the body, increasing the urine and flushing out infections. It has anti-inflammatory and anti-bacterial properties that help treat the underlying disease.

Stimulates the Digestive System: Birch tree extracts stimulate the digestive system and aid digestion. Its anti-inflammatory properties are beneficial in calming the digestive system and relieving cramping, abdominal pain, bloating, and diarrhea. Try the recipe below for Birch Leaf Vinegar Extract.

Coughs and Congestion: Birch Leaf Vinegar Extract, recipe below, is effective in treating coughs. Add leaves to a water steam and inhale to help relieve congestion. Burns and Frostbite: The inner bark of the birch tree is useful in treating frostbite and burns. It soothes the damaged skin, reduces pain and inflammation, and helps the skin heal. Remove the bark from the tree and mash it to a pulp adding sap from the tree if necessary, to form a wet pulp. Apply the pulp to the damaged skin and cover with a clean cloth. If the area is infected, use a poultice of leaves and leaf buds in the same way.

Supports the Immune System: Birch Leaf Tea is excellent at supporting the immune system. It is anti-inflammatory, anti-bacterial and contains many vitamins, minerals, saponins, flavonoids, tannins, and other compounds that are excellent for the immune system. It helps cleanse and heal the body.

Cancer: Betulinic acid from birch is being actively researched as an anti-cancer drug. Note that the Chaga mushroom, which grows on birch trees, effectively converts the betulin found in birch into betulinic acid.

Harvesting: Harvest sap in early spring, and buds and branches in late spring, before the buds open. Harvest inner bark in spring or autumn. Collect birch leaves in the summer when the leaves are fresh and bright green, and harvest in the morning before the heat dissipates their oil. Use them fresh (best) or dry for future use. Strip the bark in shallow thin strips using a sharp knife.

Warning: Birch leaf is considered safe for external and internal use. However, pregnant or nursing mothers should not use it.

Some people are allergic to birch and should not use it. Birch leaves can increase salt retention in the body and may increase blood pressure in sensitive individuals. Avoid birch if you have high blood pressure. Do not use if you are taking diuretics or water pills. Drink plenty of water when using birch.

Recipes: Birch Leaf Vinegar Extract. Birch tree leaves, crushed, Apple cider vinegar. Crush birch leaves and stuff into a jar, about 3-quarters full. Cover the leaves with apple cider vinegar and stir to release air bubbles. Add more vinegar until the jar is full. Cap tightly. Let the leaves soak for 4 to 6 weeks, shaking the jar every day or two. Strain out the leaves and label the vinegar. Use the vinegar with meals, in salad dressings, or drink in water with meals. Good for 1 year.

Birch Leaf Oil or Inner Bark Extract: Pack a jar about 3-quarters full with fresh birch leaves and/or inner bark. Cover the leaves with organic olive oil or almond oil and fill to the top. Cover the jar and place it in a sunny spot on a windowsill and allow it to steep for 6 to 8 weeks, shaking the jar every day or two. Strain the oil into a glass jar with a tight fitting lid and label it. Store in a cool, dark place.

Black Crowberry, Empetrum nigrum

Black crowberry, crowberry, or mossberry, is a low evergreen shrub that is usually 4 to 10 inches (10 cm to 25 cm) high and forms a dense mat on the ground. It is in the Ericaceae (Heath) Family and is found throughout North America, Europe, and Asia.

Identification: The light green needle-like leaves are simple and narrow, with side margins that are strongly curled under. It likes to grow in rocky areas. The leaves have glands that produce toxic substances and leaves are shed every 2 to 4 years. Black crowberry produces small, individual pink-purple flowers during the summer and a sour blue-black fruit.

Edible Use: The berries are the only edible part of the plant, but the twigs can be used for tea. Crowberries have an acrid bitter taste, which is why they are rarely eaten fresh. They are usually used for pies, jams, juice, and wine. Berries ripen in autumn and remain throughout much of the winter, making them a good Vitamin C source in wintertime. The berries are very high in anthocyanins and are an excellent antioxidant.

Medicinal Use: The fruit, branches/twigs/stems, and roots are used for medicine.

Diarrhea, Dysentery, and Gastroenteritis: Diarrhea and other stomach illnesses respond well to a Crowberry Leaf Infusion made from the leaves and stems. The infusion stimulates mucous, calms the digestive tract, and reduces inflammation. The cooked berries are used for gastroenteritis.

Antibacterial and Antifungal: Crowberry branches are both antibacterial and antifungal.

Eye Wash: A tea made from the roots of crowberry can be used as an eye wash for sore eyes.

Antihistamine, Anti-inflammatory, and Pain Relief: The berries contain the antihistamine and anti-inflammatory quercetin. This anti-inflammatory also helps with pain relief and can be used for any disease resulting from inflammation.

Harvesting: The fruits of black crowberries are ripe and ready to harvest between August and September. They can be harvested until the onset of winter or they can be allowed to winter on the plant for harvesting in the spring.

Recipes. Crowberry Leaf Infusion: 1 ounce of the leaves and stems of the crowberry plant, 1 cup boiling water. Chop the leaves and stems into fine pieces and cover them with boiling water. Cover the container tightly. Let the herbs steep until the liquid has cooled to room temperature. Strain out the herbs.

Black Walnut, Eastern, Juglans nigra

The eastern black walnut is a deciduous tree in the Juglandaceae (Walnut) Family. It is widespread in Eastern North America.

Identification: Black walnut trees grow to 100 feet (30 meters) tall and have a tall, straight trunk with an oval crown. The bark is grey-black with deep, thin ridges that appear to give the bark a diamond-shaped pattern. It usually doesn't have lower branching – just the top crown. Buds are pale colored and covered in hairs.

Terminal buds are 1/4 inch (0.75 cm) long and oval shaped. Lateral buds are smaller. Its large (1 to 2 foot) pinnately compound leaves are alternately arranged with 13 to 23 leaflets, each 3 to 4 inches (7.5 cm to 10 cm) long. Leaflets have a rounded base, pointed tip, and a serrated margin. Leaves are dark green, smooth on top and hairy on the bottom.

The black walnut has both male and female flowers. Male flowers appear first on drooping catkins, approximately 3 to 4 inches (7.5 cm to 10 cm) long, on the previous year's growth. Female flowers appear on new growth in clusters of two to five flowers.

The fruit (nuts) ripen in the fall. A brownish-green husk covers the brown nut. The nut, including the husk, falls to the ground in October or November and is harvested from the ground. The seed is small and hard. While the nut lacks odor, most parts of the tree have a characteristic pungent or spicy odor.

Edible Use and Other Use: The seed is edible, either raw or cooked. The flavor is rich and sweet. The sap of the tree can be tapped and drunk or concentrated into syrup or sugar. Black walnut hulls work well as a dye.

Medicinal Use: Black walnut is an anti-inflammatory, anti-fungal, antiviral, astringent, emetic, laxative, painkiller, and vermifuge. The green hulls are more potent than the mature black hulls, and are what I use for medicine.

To Treat and Prevent Parasites: Black walnut hull, used along with garlic, cloves, Oregon grape root, and wormwood, is an excellent remedy for parasite and worm infections. I have used this herbal blend for many types of parasitic infections. This remedy will kill the eggs, larva, and adult worms and parasites.

Skin Care: For preventing and treating blemishes, acne, psoriasis, eczema, warts, poison ivy, and other skin conditions, use a poultice from ground black walnut husks and water. For sensitive skin, try mixing a little of the powdered husk with a carrier oil.

Antifungal: Black walnut hull is an excellent choice for treating fungal infections. Black walnut contains juglone and tannins that are very effective for treating yeast infections, including Candida, in the gut and on the skin. Externally, black walnut is effective against athlete's foot, ringworm, jock itch, and other common fungal infections. Use the juice from the fruit husk externally as a treatment for ringworm or make a poultice or salve from powdered husks when fresh hulls aren't available. Apply the absorbent powdered hulls into the folds of the skin for surface yeast infections and heat rashes.

Digestion and Laxative: The anti-inflammatory activity of black walnut is useful in treating upset stomach, inflamed colon or gut, and normalizing the digestive process. Black walnut hull also treats constipation, diarrhea, and is a laxative.

Heart Health: Black walnuts contain beneficial omega-3 fatty acids and other heart healthy compounds

Anti-Viral, HPV, HIV: People have long been using black walnut to prevent and treat viral infections. Black walnuts and black walnut hulls inhibit the reproduction of viruses, including herpes. A study published in Phytotherapy Research found that juglone in black walnut hulls inhibits replication of the HIV virus. While there are no therapeutic recommendations yet, it would be advisable for those exposed or infected by HIV to take Black Walnut Hull Tincture. In addition to the hulls, the roots and buds also contain juglone. Juglone is not soluble in water so best to use an alcohol extract/tincture.

Harvesting: Wear gloves when collecting black walnuts since the husk will stain your hands. Collect nuts that have fallen to the ground, nuts that remain on the tree are not yet mature. Remove the green to yellowish hull from the nut. Eat the nuts and dry and save the husk for use in poultices, tinctures, and to powder when needed.

To store black walnuts inside their shell, lay them out and allow them to dry for a few days after harvesting. Store them in a dry, squirrel-proof area. To crack nuts, use a hammer, nut cracker, or a vise to crack the shell. Remove the meat inside. Black walnut leaves can be picked for use throughout the season.

Warning: Side effects associated with black walnut use are not common. However, it is important to note that nut allergies are very common. Black walnuts or any of their products should not be given to anyone allergic to tree nuts. Risk during pregnancy is deemed low, but it is best to avoid black walnut internally if you are pregnant or nursing.

Recipes. Black Walnut Hull Tincture: Ground walnut hulls, vodka or another 80 proof or higher alcohol. Place the ground hulls in a clean, dry jar with a tight-fitting lid. Fill the jar 1/3rd full. Pour 80 proof or higher vodka or other alcohol over the hulls to within ½ inch (1.25 cm) of the top. Cover tightly and place the jar in a cool, dark place. Shake the jar every few days. Watch the alcohol level and add more if needed. Soak the hulls for 6 to 8 weeks. Strain the mixture through a fine sieve or cheesecloth. Squeeze out all liquid.

Discard the hulls. Place the alcohol extract in a cool place, undisturbed overnight. Strain again through a coffee filter or decant to remove any remaining hull residue. Store the tincture in a tightly capped glass bottle in a cool, dark place.

Blue & Black Elderberry, Sambucus nigra ssp. caerulea (blue) and Sambucus nigra ssp. canadensis (black)

Sambucus nigra tincture is with me 24/7 as an antiviral. I dose with it when traveling or at the first sign of illness. It is in the Adoxacaeae (Moschatel) Family and is one of my family's most important herbal medicines.

Identification: Elderberry grows as a wide woody shrub to about 12 feet (3.1 meters) tall. The segmented stems have a soft white pith. The bark is smooth and green when young. As the wood ages, the bark becomes smooth and brown, and you will notice round lumps on the bark. As the shrub continues to age, the bark develops vertical furrows.

Opposite compound leaves have 5 to 11 toothed lance-like leaflets per stem. Veins in the leaves may disappear after leaving the midrib, or they may continue to the tip of the teeth. The elderberry blossom is a dense head of white to cream-colored flowers. Flowers are radially symmetrical with five flat white petals and five protruding stamens. The flower head is 6 to 12 inches (15 cm to 30 cm) across. Elderberries are black or purplish-blue when ripe and occur in clusters.

Important Differentiation: Some people confuse elderberry with the deadly poisonous water hemlock. Water hemlock is an herbaceous plant, not woody, and it does not have bark. The main stem of water hemlock is hollow, while elderberry is filled with a soft pith. Water hemlock stems often have purple streaks/splotches and purple nodes. Older plants may be entirely purple.

Edible Use: The Sambucus nigra variety of elderberry is considered non-toxic when used fresh, but I always cook all varieties, and some people become ill from fresh berries. Other varieties of elderberry's fruit pulp and skin are edible when picked fully ripe and then cooked.

However, uncooked berries and other parts of the plant are poisonous. The flowers are edible when they are completely dried; do not use them fresh. I use cooked fresh berries to make elderberry syrup, elderberry wine, and cordials.

Medicinal Use: The flowers, leaves, and cooked berries are all useful. I use elderberry berry tincture once a day as a preventative during flu season or during travel, and 3x per day if feeling a cold or flu coming on. I extract the berries in glycerin or alcohol.

Colds and Flu, Anti-Viral: Taken early blue elderberry reduces the chance of catching the flu. Taken after a flu infection, it reduces the spread of the disease throughout the body and lessens the severity and duration of the virus. Blue elderberry is one of the best anti-virals out there and there has been much research supporting its effectiveness. It is deemed safe for children and my kids take it in the form of a tincture or syrup. The flowers also reduce inflammation, help drain mucous, and promote perspiration. They have anti-viral, anti-inflammatory, and anti-cancer properties. Elderberry is most effective in combination with yarrow to bring down fever.

Bruises, Sprains, and Hemorrhoids: For bruised tissue, muscle sprains, and hemorrhoids, use chopped elderberry leaves applied as a poultice to the affected area or infuse the leaves in oil to apply (my preference). Leaves are only for external use.

Eye Irritation and Conjunctivitis: Elderberry Flower Tea makes a gentle eyewash for eye irritations and conjunctivitis.

Strengthens the Immune System: Elderberries have long been recognized as a therapy for a variety of illnesses. It is thought that their beneficial effects are due to their ability to strengthen the immune system.

Harvesting: Harvest the berries during the early autumn when they are fully ripe. I like to harvest and then put the berries in the freezer. Once frozen it is easy to remove the berries from their stems. Remove all stems before using!

Warning: All parts of the fresh plant are mildly toxic. Dry or boil berries before use and dry the flowers. Do not use the fresh plant without cooking or drying. The bark and root are emetic, causing vomiting, and should not be used internally. The leaves and unripe berries are toxic.

Recipes: Elderberry Syrup. Use 1 to 2 teaspoons for adults and ½ to 1 teaspoon for kids. Take once a day as a flu preventative and 3 to 4 times daily if infected. 1 cup of elderberries, water, 1 cup of raw honey, and ½ tsp of ground cinnamon. Place fresh elderberries, with all stems removed, in a pot and add a small amount of water to cover. Heat the berries over low heat for 2 hours. Mash the berries to release the juice or puree the berries in a blender. When all the juice is released, strain the juice through several layers of cheesecloth. Squeeze the cloth to extract all the juice.

Measure the juice and mix in an equal amount of raw honey. Add cinnamon if desired. Put the syrup in clean pint canning jars and seal.

Place the jars in a boiling water bath, completely covered with water and boil for 15 minutes at sea level to 1000 feet (300 meters) in elevation, 20 minutes at higher elevations. Remove the jars from the water and place on a towel to cool. Allow the jars to cool undisturbed. When cool, check the jar seals. Re-process any jar that did not seal or refrigerate it for immediate use. Label.

Burning Bush, Western, Euonymus occidentalis

Western burning bush grows in Western North America. It is also called spindle tree, western wahoo and strawberry bush. It is found in shaded streambanks, moist woods, canyons, and high in the mountains. It is in the Celastraceae (Bittersweet) Family. E. alatus is used in Asia.

Identification: Western burning bush is a deciduous straggly shrub, growing to 6 to 15 feet (1.8 m to 4.5 meters) when mature. It has slender branches, often climbing, and twigs are usually 4-angled. It has opposite finely-toothed leaves that are 2 to 4 inches 5 cm to 10 cm) long, sometimes with rolled edges, with pointed tips and rounded or tapered bases. The flowers form on the end of a long peduncle with one to five flowers.

Each flower has five rounded brownish purple petals, sometimes dotted. Flowers bloom April to June. The fruit is a rounded capsule with three lobes. Each of the three lobes opens to reveal a brown seed surrounded by red pulp.

Medicinal Use: The root bark and the leaves are used for medicine.

Stomach Tonic and Liver: Root bark infusions, syrup, and tinctures are all useful as a stomach tonic for indigestion and constipation. It also stimulates the flow of bile and improves the appetite.

Irregular Menstruation: For suppressed or irregular menstruation, the leaves of burning bush were traditionally used. Do not use if pregnant as it may induce miscarriage.

Warning: Do not use during pregnancy. Do not ingest the fruits of burning bush.

Cascara Sagrada, Rhamnus or Frangula purshiana

Also called sacred bark and chittam stick, cascara sagrada is well known for its use as a laxative. It is very effective, but carries risks when used long-term, especially if a person's health is already compromised. Cascara is native to the Pacific Northwest, but it is cultivated in other parts of North America. It prefers moist, acidic soils and is usually found on the edges of clearings and forests. It is in the Rhamnaceae (Buckthorn) Family.

Identification: Cascara grows up to 30 feet (9.1 meters) tall. It has finely toothed ovate leaves, each 3 to 5 inches (7.5 cm to 12.5 cm) long, with prominent parallel veins leading off the central vein. Leaves are shiny green on top and a lighter, dull green on the bottom. The smooth bark is reddish-brown to silver-grey. In early to mid-spring, the tree produces tiny flowers with five greenish-yellow petals that grow in umbel-shaped clusters. Red berries appear and ripen to dark purple or black. The berries have yellow pulp and two to three seeds each.

Edible Use: The fruit is sometimes eaten raw or cooked, but is reported to be slightly toxic and also has a laxative effect. Tea is made from the bark after drying or aging. It has a bitter taste. Do not use fresh bark.

Medicinal Use: Cascara is usually prescribed as tea, however many people cannot tolerate the intense bitterness. The bark can be powdered and taken in a capsule as a more palatable alternative.

Its medicinal effects are usually felt within 6 to 8 hours. Cascara is recommended only for short-term use, no more than 2 weeks. Always use the smallest effective dose. Only used aged cascara bark.

Natural Laxative: Cascara bark is a natural laxative for the treatment of constipation. The herb acts as a stimulant on the large intestine, stimulating contractions and moving food through the digestive system.

Gallbladder, Liver, Stomach, and Pancreas Stimulation: Cascara stimulates the gallbladder to produce more bile. This action aids digestion and prevents and breaks up gallstones. It improves secretions from the stomach, liver, and pancreas, treating issues such as enlarged liver and poor digestion.

Lowers Cholesterol: Cascara is said to have a beneficial effect on cholesterol levels. However, it is not recommended for this purpose because of its longterm side effects and potential risks.

Hemorrhoids: Because of cascara's laxative properties, it is helpful, temporarily, in the treatment of hemorrhoids. It reduces the need to bear down, which eases the condition.

Antimicrobial Properties: Cascara has antibacterial and anti-fungal properties. It is effective against Helicobacter pylori, which causes ulcers, E. coli, Staphylococcus aureus, and others. It is also effective against Candida yeast.

Central Nervous System: Cascara sagrada improves anxiety, emotional well-being, and other central nervous system problems in some people

Anti-Inflammatory Effects: The herb is an antiinflammatory, however, there are more effective antiinflammatories with fewer risks available.

Cancer: Cascara has been used to inhibit the growth and spread of cancer. It can be used in addition to traditional cancer treatments with medical supervision.

Harvesting: Harvest cascara in the spring, at least a year before using it medicinally. Aging is necessary to reduce gastrointestinal irritation. Fresh cascara causes nausea, vomiting, diarrhea, and intense intestinal spasms. Dry the bark or bake at low heat until completely dry.

Warning: Cascara sagrada is a stimulant and should be used for the short-term only, less than 2 weeks. Cascara should never be used during pregnancy or lactation. It can stimulate menstruation and miscarriage. Cascara should not be given to children. Long term use can result in chronic diarrhea, electrolyte imbalances, dehydration, and severe intestinal pain. It can also cause toxic hepatitis. Cascara can interact with some prescription medications and should not be combined with other medications except under the advice of a medical professional.

Recipes. Cascara Tea: For this tea, you need bark that has been aged for at least 1 year. Do not use fresh bark. Ingredients: 1 teaspoon aged cascara sagrada bark, 1 cup spring water or distilled water. Bring the water and bark to a boil and reduce the heat to a simmer. Simmer for 30 minutes, then strain and allow to cool. Sweeten the tea with raw honey or fennel to mask the bitterness.

Chaparral or Creosote Bush, Larrea tridentata

Larrea tridentata belongs to the Zygophyllaceae (Caltrops) Family. It is also known as creosote bush and greasewood. It has a strong creosote smell. This plant is a prominent species in southwestern North America.

Identification: Chaparral bush is an evergreen shrub that grows from 3 to 10 feet (0.9 meters to 3 meters) tall. The stems of this plant bear resinous, small, dark green, compound, opposite leaves. Each leaf has 2 leaflets, which join at the base. The flowers have five yellow petals. The fruit is covered in dense white hairs.

Edible Use: Not generally considered edible. I do add some leaves to my water bottle when this plant is around. It helps keep my water bottle clean and microbe-free.

Medicinal Use: The leaves are used for medicine. They are antimicrobial, antibacterial, antioxidant, and active against protozoa.

Treating Toothaches: For sensitive teeth and toothaches due to cavities, heat the young shoot tips of the plant to produce sap, then drip the sap resin into the tooth cavity. This seals the tooth temporarily and stops the pain.

Wounds, Burns, Bruises, Rashes: Antibacterial and Antimicrobial: A salve made from chaparral leaves is a good choice for wounds, burns, bruises, and rashes. An external tincture is also a good choice if the skin is not broken. Chaparral has antimicrobial and antibacterial benefits on the skin's surface. I primarily extract it in oil for external use but you can also make a poultice from the ground leaves, apply it to the skin, and cover it with a clean cloth.

Acne, Psoriasis, Eczema, Dandruff: AntiFungal: Chaparral Tincture or Oil can be used externally on acne, eczema, psoriasis, and dandruff. The antibiotic and anti-inflammatory properties are beneficial as well as its tannins. It is a very good external antifungal. Arthritis: Chaparral Tincture made with alcohol or oil works as a rub to relieve the pain of arthritis.

Pulmonary and Respiratory Problems, Venereal Diseases, and Urinary Tract Infections: In the past, Chaparral Tea and Chaparral Tincture were used as an expectorant for respiratory problems and as a pulmonary antiseptic, as well as a treatment for VD, rheumatism, and UTIs. In recent years (since the 1960s), there has been some concern over possible toxic effects on the liver, so I strongly suggest limiting its internal use.

Harvesting: I prefer to harvest chaparral in dryweather before the plant has flowered so that the highest concentration of the active ingredients is in the leaves. Collection is best undertaken at midday when the chemical activity of the plant is the highest. It can be dried in a warm, shady place, or in the artificial heat at temperatures less than 130 degrees Fahrenheit. One of the simplest methods of drying the herb is to collect the leaves, put them into a large paper sack and then put the sack in a warm, dry place for a few days. Store in an airtight glass jar in a cool, dark place.

Recipes. Chaparral Salve: Carrier oil such as organic olive oil or liquid coconut oil, dried chaparral leaves, beeswax. Fill the jar half-full with dried chaparral. Cover the herbs with organic olive oil, filling the jar to near the top. Cover the jar with a tight-fitting lid and label. Place the jar in a sunny location for 6 to 8 weeks, shaking every few days. Strain out the herbs. Measure the oil and add 1/4 the amount of beeswax (if you have 1 cup of oil, add ¼ cup of beeswax). Heat the two together gently until the wax melts using a double boiler. Mix the wax and oil, and pour into your containers to harden. Use within two years.

Chokecherry, Prunus virginiana

Chokecherry is edible but rarely eaten these days because of its acidity and astringency. It is a North American native that grows across the northern US and Canada and as far south as North Carolina. It is in the Rosaceae (Rose) Family.

Identification: Prunus virginiana is a small tree or a deciduous shrub that grows as tall as 30 feet (9.1 meters). It has simple large elliptical leaves that are 4 inches (10 cm) long by 2.5 inches (6.4 cm) wide. They are dark green, have a glossy upper side and paler underside, and have toothed margins. They turn yellow in the autumn.

Between the clusters of leaves are white showy flowers that are approximately 3 to 6 inches (7.5 cm to 15 cm) long. The flowers bloom in May and June, and the fruit appears in August. Chokecherry bark ranges in color from brown or gray, to purple and red, and the texture of the bark is smooth and thin in appearance when young. Bark becomes more uneven and creased with age.

Edible Use: The edible parts of chokecherry are the fruits and seeds. The raw berry is edible and has a good flavor, but is highly astringent. In cooking they are used in pies and jellies where sugar counters their sour flavor. The berries contain high amounts of pectin, so they are often combined with lower pectin fruits when making syrups, jams, and jellies. The fruit is also used to make wine and syrups. Dried berries are used to make pemmican, and the twigs and bark make a good tea. Do not eat the seeds if they are bitter-tasting.

Medicinal Use: In addition to the uses below the inner bark is used as a flavoring agent for cough syrups and other bitter medicines. It is not used often used in other ways these days.

Stomach Illness: Dried chokecherry fruits and bark are used for diarrhea, bloating, heartburn, and stomach ulcers.

Wet Coughs and Bronchitis: Chokecherry bark is used as a base for cough medicine and also directly treats wet coughs and bronchitis. Best paired with other, more potent, herbs.

Warning: The seeds are said to have a high concentration of hydrogen cyanide, which is a poison that gives almonds their characteristic flavor. This toxin can be easily detected by the bitter taste. It is usually present in small quantity. In large amounts, it can be deadly; however, in small quantities, hydrogen cyanide has been shown to stimulate respiration, improve digestion, and suppress cancer growth. Use it carefully.

Cottonwood, Populus trichocarpa and P. deltoides

Some consider the cottonwood a sacred tree; at the least it is an important plant for medicinal purposes. Its roots run deep and are said to find water while the tree absorbs the energy of experiences happening nearby. "Balm of Gilead" is made from cottonwood buds and smells wonderful!

Cottonwoods grow along streams, rivers, and flood plains. It loves water, but also grows in dry sites. Black cottonwood grows in the Northwest from Alaska to the Rocky Mountains. Other species are found throughout the United States and Canada. All varieties can be used for medicinal purposes. It is in the Salicaceae (Willow) Family.

Identification: The cottonwood is a large tree, growing 150 to 200 feet (45 meters to 60 meters) tall when mature. It has deeply furrowed grey bark and shiny, dark green, triangular leaves with course teeth along the margin. The leaves turn yellow in the fall before falling. In winter and early spring, the tree produces large buds that are long and pointed. The buds are filled with fragrant resin, yellow-orange to red in color, and are greatly revered for medicine.

Each tree is either male or female. Male flowers are reddish, drooping into a catkin shape. Female flowers form 4-inch (10 cm) catkins followed by light green seed capsules. Ripe capsules open into three parts, releasing white, fluffy down covered seeds that float on the wind. When the seeds are released the tree is covered in cottony fluff. Many people think they are allergic to cottonwood but usually it is the grasses releasing pollen at the same time that are the culprit.

Edible Use: Cottonwood leaves are edible and very nutritious and are rich in protein – they have a higher amino acid content that of barley, wheat or rice. However, the taste is very bitter. Boiling the leaves and discarding the water relieves some of the bitterness as well as adding seasoning. It can be used in soups or eaten as a green. The inner bark is harvested in the spring. Dried and powdered it is used as a thickener for soups. The catkins, which are high in Vitamin C, can be eaten raw like Alder catkins (they have a nutty flavor) or added to a soup, steamed, or sautéed.

Medicinal Use: Cottonwood buds and bark are rich in salicylic acids, known for pain relief and treating fevers. The resinous leaf buds are used to create oils and salves for topical treatment of muscles, joints, tendons, and inflammation or pain. The recipe below is a very cooling and soothing ointment for inflamed tissues. Extracts also can be made with oil or alcohol to make pain relievers similar to aspirin. The inner bark is also used as a tea to being down a fever and as an expectorant.

Joint Pain, Sore Muscles and Arthritis: Cottonwood bud oil is very effective for relieving pain and inflammation in swollen joints, carpal tunnel, arthritis, and muscles. Massage the oil or salve into the affected area 3x/day. A poultice made from crushed fresh leaves is also effective in the treatment of arthritis and other joint issues. Cottonwood bark decoction can be used to relieve menstrual cramping.

Skin Injuries: The anti-bacterial, anti-microbial, anti-fungal, and antioxidant properties of cottonwood bud oil or salve make it useful in treating skin injuries including rashes, irritations, chapped lips, cracked skin, sunburn, and other burns. It helps the skin heal and prevents infection. For boils, sores, and infected skin, make a poultice from crushed leaves. Washing the skin with cottonwood decoction is also effective. Cottonwood buds also helps regenerate cells for healing and I use it along with Calendula Oil as an anti-aging face and neck cream.

Pneumonia, Flu, and Other Respiratory Ailments: Cottonwood Bark Infusion or Tincture is useful in the treatment of whooping cough, tuberculosis, colds, flu and Pneumonia. It kills and inhibits both bacteria and the influenza virus when used early in the disease and helps alleviate pain, reduce fever, and works as an expectorant.

Sore Throats: An infusion of cottonwood inner bark is used as a gargle for sore throats and mouth sores.

Intestinal Worms: Cottonwood Bark Decoction is effective in ridding the body of intestinal worms.

Harvesting: Harvest cottonwood leaf buds in late winter to early spring. The buds are ready to harvest when you can pinch the bud and see resin inside. The largest buds are at the top of the tree and difficult to harvest but after a windstorm you can easily find newly downed branches on the ground. Like willow they root easily, so I plant back small limbs when I gather so that new trees can grow. It's always a good idea to tend the wild when you harvest! Snap the buds off the branches (I leave the terminal buds on the tree) and place them in a container. Sticky resin will adhere to your hands and the container. You can wear gloves for this, coat your hands with salve or oil before harvesting, or remove the resin with rubbing alcohol.

Warning: Some people may be allergic to cottonwood sap. Cottonwood should not be used by people allergic to aspirin or bees.

Recipes. Cottonwood Bud Oil and Salve: Use this salve externally to treat skin ailments and to relieve inflammation and pain in arthritic joints. Ingredients: 1 cup cottonwood buds, 3 cups carrier oil: organic olive oil, coconut oil, or other skin friendly oil, beeswax. Infuse the oil with cottonwood buds. Place the oil in an old double-boiler over very low heat. Add the cottonwood buds and allow the oil to infuse. You should be able to smell the resinous odor and the oil should change color. I like to do this step in a small crockpot or double boiler that I use for this purpose or in a mason jar placed in water. Note that the resin will stick to the pot or jar and will be forever resinous (you can actually clean it with alcohol). I often kick-start my buds with heat and then cold-infuse them in a cupboard for another 6 to 8 weeks. You can also keep it on low for a few days.

When the oil is infused, let it cool and strain out the buds. Heat the oil again and add your beeswax. It will take approximately one-half to one cup of beeswax to reach the desired stiffness (ratio of 4:1 oil to beeswax). Once the beeswax is melted, test the salve by placing a spoonful in the freezer for a minute. It will thicken and indicate the consistency of the salve. If you want it thicker, add more beeswax. If you want it thinner, add more oil. How thick or thin you make it is up to you and how you plan to use it. A good rule-of thumb is 4 parts oil to1 part beeswax for a salve. Place the salve in a shallow glass jar or a tin with a wide mouth. Tighten the lid and leave it to cool and harden.

Cottonwood Decoction. Ingredients: ¾ ounce of cottonwood leaf buds and/or bark, 2 cups water. Bring the leaf buds and water to a boil and turn the heat down to a simmer. Simmer the decoction for 10 to 15 minutes. Strain out the herbs and allow the decoction to cool. Make a compress by soaking a washcloth in the decoction, wring it out and place on the affected skin. Allow it to sit for 20 minutes, repeating as necessary to relieve the pain and inflammation. You can also use the decoction directly on the skin.

Cranberry, Vaccinium macrocarpon

The cranberry shrub is a member of the Ericaceae (Heath) family. It grows in acidic bogs, swamps, wetlands, and poorly drained meadows throughout the colder climates of Northern North America.

Identification: These low growing, creeping shrubs rarely top 8 inches (20 cm) in height. They have long wiry stems, or vines, that stretch to 7 feet (2.1 meters) long. The plant has small, oblong, evergreen leaves that are speckled with tiny dots on the underside.

The leathery leaves are 1/4 to 1/2-inch (0.75 cm to 1.25 cm) long. Dark pink flowers with distinct reflexed petals appear June through August. The style and stamens are exposed and point forward. The cranberry fruit is a small berry that is larger than the leaves. The berry is white when immature, usually turning dark red when ripe.

Edible Use: The berries are edible, but they are very acidic. The addition of sugar makes them more palatable, as does drying them.

Medicinal Use: Cranberries are an effective preventative and remedy for early stage urinary tract infections. They work by preventing the adhesion of bacteria to the lining of the bladder and gut, thereby preventing infection. If the infection is too well entrenched, other remedies may be required, such as Usnea, Bearberry/Uva Ursi, and Oregon Grape Root. Cranberries have high levels of antioxidants, vitamin C, and salicylic acid, which help relieve pain and heal.

To get all of the benefits of cranberries for medicinal purposes, simply consume the fruit or its unsweetened juice daily for as long as needed. Cranberry juice is sour, but more palatable when diluted in water.

Urinary Tract Infections: Consumption of cranberries, their juice, or a concentrated cranberry pill prevents the bacteria in the urinary tract from multiplying and clinging to the walls of the bladder, allowing them to be easily flushed out of the system. Regular consumption of unsweetened cranberry juice prevents urinary tract diseases and can keep you from needing antibiotics. Cranberries are not as effective in treating established UTIs. The juice does not kill the bacteria, and reinfection can occur if cranberry is discontinued while bacteria are still in the system. You may need to add in an herbal antibiotic blend.

Cardiovascular Health: The flavonoids in cranberries are high in antioxidant and anti-inflammatory properties and decrease the risk of atherosclerosis. They also boost HDL ("good") cholesterol levels.

Respiratory Bacterial Infections: Cranberry juice inhibits Haemophilus influenza, which is a common cause of childhood respiratory and ear infections. The juice prevents these bacteria from adhering to the skin's surface.

Treats and Prevents Peptic Ulcers: Cranberries help reduce the risk of peptic ulcers caused by Helicobacter pylori. Along with preventing the adhesion of bacteria to the stomach lining, the high flavonoid content of cranberries suppresses infection and helps the body heal.

Antitumor and Anticancer Effects: Cranberry is a powerful anti-tumor agent and is also a cancer preventative. Medicinal compounds within the fruit inhibit the growth and spread of many types of cancers.

Warning: Patients who take Coumadin (Warfarin) need to be careful when taking cranberry. The additional anti-clotting effects of cranberry compound the Coumadin. Cranberries contain salicylic acid, a component of aspirin. People who are allergic to aspirin should not consume cranberries.

Recipes. Fresh Cranberry Juice. 4 cups cranberries, 4 cups water, 1/4 cup lemon juice, 1/4 cup orange juice, sugar to taste. Bring the cranberries and water to a boil, turn down the heat and simmer the berries for 25 minutes or until all the berries have popped and the berries are cooked. Pass the cranberry mixture through a food mill on the smallest setting. Pass the mixture through a fine-mesh sieve. Mash the pulp slightly to increase draining, but not hard enough to push the pulp through. Mix in the orange juice and lemon juice. Add sugar to sweeten the juice, if desired.

Fungi and Algae

A note on extracting mushrooms and lichens:

Many lichens and mushrooms need to be double/dual-extracted both in water and in alcohol in order to access all of the necessary medicinal compounds. For example, in Reishi (Ganoderma lucidum), the main components with pharmacological activity are polysaccharides and triterpenoids. The polysaccharides (including betaglucans) extract in water while the triterpenoids, like ganoderic acid, extract in alcohol. Below is a recipe for a double-extraction.

Double/Dual Extraction Method:

Feel free to scale down this recipe for at-home use.

You'll need: 8 ounces (225g) or more of dried mushroom or lichen, 24 ounces (650g) of 80 to 100 proof alcohol (40 to 50 % alcohol), and 16 ounces (500ml) of distilled water.

1. Fill a quart-sized (32 oz – 900g) canning jar half-full with diced dried mushrooms, then fill it to ½ inch (1.25cm) of the top with alcohol. Stir and cap it, shaking it every few days for 2 months. Then strain out the alcohol and set it aside to keep.
2. Make the decoction. Put 16 ounces (0.5L) of water into a ceramic or glass pot with a lid and put the mushrooms into it. Cover and simmer the mixture on low until half of the water has simmered off. This will take a few hours. If the water level drops too quickly, add more so that you can continue simmering your mushrooms. The end result should be 8 ounces (250ml) of your decoction. Do not boil.
3. Allow the water to cool, and then strain out the mushrooms, pressing them to remove all of the liquid. Mix this water (8 oz –250 ml) and the alcoholic tincture you have set aside (you should have about 24 oz – 0.75L of alcohol tincture) together to create the finished double-extraction. It has a high enough alcohol content (30%) that it should be shelf-stable for many years, as long as it is stored in a sealed container. The ratio of the alcoholic tincture to the decoction is 3:1.

Chaga Mushroom, Inonotus obliquus

Chaga mushroom, also known as cancer polypore and tinder conk, grows on live birch trees in temperate zones throughout the Northern Hemisphere. It looks like charcoal bursting from the tree. It grows in the form of a woody conk. The fungus grows slowly; only harvest from large growths and leave plenty on the tree. It is a valuable mushroom for use in treating can-cer and for immune system problems. It is also an excellent firestarter.

Identification: Chaga grows almost exclusively on live birch trees. Tree burls are often mistaken for chaga mushrooms. The burl is an outgrowth of the tree, while the chaga mushroom grows inside the tree then bursts forth from it. There is a distinct difference between the mushroom and the tree.

The outside surface of the fungus is black, brittle, and has a cracked appearance. The interior is gold-orange, and woody. The gold-orange interior is sometimes visible where the mushroom attaches to the tree. It feels like cork when freshly cut.

Medicinal Use: Chaga must be collected from birch trees, as the relationship between the birch and the parasitic chaga helps form some of the medicinal compounds found in chaga, like the terpenes betulin and betulinic acid. Chaga is best taken as a double-extracted tincture to access all of its medicinal compounds.

Cancer Treatment: Chaga mushrooms treat cancers of all types, including Hodgkin's Disease. Chaga helps prevent and treat cancer through increased antioxidant activity, by slowing or stopping the growth of the cancerous tissue and metastasis to other parts of the body, by killing off existing cancerous cells and reducing tumors, through boosting the immune system, and by helping eliminate cancer cells from the body.

Powerful Adaptogen: Adaptogens help the body adapt to changing conditions, increased work, and stress in general. Chaga is a powerful adaptogen that helps reduce the effects of these stressors on the body and improves overall body health. Chaga also has anti-oxidant, anti-inflammatory, and anti-viral properties.

Boosts the Immune System and Anti-in-flammatory: Chaga mushroom stimulates the immune system and helps the body heal itself. It has anti-inflammatory and antioxidant properties that reduce chronic inflammation in the body and help prevent further damage. It is valuable for patients with immune system dysfunction and weak immune systems, but it is still unclear if people with autoimmune disorders should use it due to the way it boosts the immune system. Until more research is done, best to use the adaptogenic Reishi mushroom instead.

Anti-Viral, HIV, Herpes, and Flu: Chaga is an excellent anti-viral. It has demonstrated efficacy against Influenza A and B, HSV (Herpes Simplex Virus), and inhibits HIV protease.

Reduces the Blood Sugar: Chaga helps lower blood sugar levels significantly and quickly. This can be helpful for people with diabetes, but it can also cause problems. Monitor blood sugars carefully when taking chaga, especially if you have had problems with blood sugars in the past or if you are taking medications to control blood sugar levels.

Ulcers, Ulcerative Coli-tis, and the Gastrointestinal Tract: Chaga protects the gastrointestinal tract and stops the formation of ulcers. Its anti-inflammatory effects work well for people with ulcerative colitis.

Protects the Liver and Hepatitis C: Because of its anti-inflammatory and anti-oxidant properties, chaga is beneficial for most body organs, however it is especially protective of the liver. It helps the body get rid of toxins, prevents hardening and scarring in the liver, and inhibits the production of chemicals that cause inflammation in the liver.

It is also effective against Hepatitis C. One of the ways chaga boosts the immune system is by protecting the liver and activating the white blood cells to destroy foreign substances in the body.

Reduces Fatigue and Increases Physical Endurance: Chaga helps reduce fatigue in people who have low energy levels. It may also boost endurance by lowering lactic acid levels and boosting glycogen stores.

Harvesting: The chaga mushroom takes a long time to grow to maturity, so only harvest large mushrooms (it grows up to 16 inches (40 cm) in size). Do not harvest any mushroom that is less than 6 inches (15 cm) across and always leave enough of the mushroom on the tree to cover the opening on the tree where the chaga is growing.

Take care not to damage the birch tree when collecting chaga and only harvest from living trees in a very environmentally clean area. It may be collected year-round, but it is more potent in the autumn. Using a saw or hatchet, remove the mushroom from the tree and break it into small pieces to dry.

Make sure that there are no tree parts still attached to the mushroom. If you find tree bark or wood, cut it away before drying. Use a dehydrator on its lowest set-ting, or dry them in a warm, dry place in your house. Store in a sealed container placed in a cool, dry place.

Chaga mushrooms must be taken with care for long term use. They are high in oxalates, which can cause kidney stones or other kidney problems when they accumulate. They can also inhibit absorption of some nutrients. Very high doses may be toxic but it is generally considered a very safe herb.

Lion's Mane Mushroom, Hericium erinaceus

Lion's Mane is a popular food and medicine throughout Asia. It is also called bearded tooth mushroom, bearded hedgehog mushroom, bearded tooth fungus, and pom pom mushroom. Its strengths lie in healing the brain and nervous system, but it has many other useful benefits. It is a powerful antioxidant and anti-inflammatory.

Identification: Look for lion's mane mushrooms around the middle of August through the autumn. They grow on dead and wounded hardwood trees of all kinds, but they prefer beech, oak, and maple trees. These fungi look like a clump of white icicles flowing downward to a point. Each spine is about ½ inch to 2 inches (1.25 cm to 5 cm) long and is soft and pliable. The spines and spores are white, with the spines turning yellowish to light pink as they mature. There are a few mushrooms that are similar to lion's mane in looks. They are all related and considered edible. One identifying characteristic of the lion's mane mushroom is the downward growing spines. Coral fungi is similar, but its teeth point upward. You should be careful of your identification when harvesting any wild mushrooms. Always consult a mushroom expert when you are unsure.

Edible Use: Lion's mane mushrooms are edible and tasty. The flavor and texture is like crab or lobster. The mushrooms can be eaten cooked, or dried and steeped into a tea.

Medicinal Use: I use Lion's mane daily as a double-extracted tincture. It can also be taken as a tea or in powdered form. It seems to work best with regular use.

Enhances Brain Function and Memory, Dementia, Alzheimer's, MS: Lion's mane mushrooms are known for their ability to enhance memory, stimulate cognitive function, prevent and treat neurodegenerative diseases, and encourage regrowth and recovery of nerve function. It slows down and is said to even reverse cell degeneration in the brain, which is important in diseases like Alzheimer's, Dementia, Parkinson's, Multiple Sclerosis and Diabetes, where nerve damage is a primary or secondary symptom of the disease. It also increases acetylcholine and choline acetyltransferase, which are severely depleted in Alzheimer's patients and necessary for nerve cell communication.

Heals the Nervous System, Stimulates Nerve Growth Factor: The nervous system is important to every bodily function and causes major problems when damaged. Lion's mane mushrooms can speed recovery to damaged nervous system tissue in the brain and spinal cord, and stimulate the repair of damaged nerve cells.

Lion's mane has been shown to stimulate Nerve Growth Factor (NGF), which is important in the repair of the myelin sheath. Studies show great potential for myelination and regeneration of nerves. I feel so strongly about the regenerative properties of lion's mane on the nervous systems that I use it every day for Multiple Sclerosis.

Protects Against Cancer: Lion's mane has had good results in treating lung cancer, stomach cancer, esophageal cancer, liver cancer, leukemia, cervical cancer, stomach cancer, skin cancer, colon cancer, and breast cancer. I imagine it will be proven to be effective in treating other cancers as well. It stimulates the immune system and helps kill off cancer cells, controls tumor growth, and prevents cancer from spreading to other parts of the body.

Supports a Healthy Heart and Improved Circulation: Lion's mane mushrooms support the heart and circulatory system in many ways. It has been shown to lower LDL (bad) cholesterol and blood tri-glycerides, improve fat metabolism, and prevent blood clots, reducing the of risk heart attack or stroke. It also increases blood oxygenation and circulation.

Improves Digestive Health, Ulcers, and Leaky Gut: Lion's mane mushrooms are beneficial to the function of the digestive tract and aid leaky gut repair. It is used it to treat gastric ulcers, gastritis, inflammatory bowel disease, Crohn's disease, and colitis. Its anti-inflammatory effects provide most of the benefits, but the mushroom also soothes the gut and encourages a healthy gut environment. It also reduces intestinal bleeding and protects against H. pylori.

Reduces Inflammation and Oxidation, Autoimmune Diseases: Lion's mane is a powerful anti-inflammatory, which is useful in the prevention of most chronic disease, including heart disease, diabetes, autoimmune diseases, and cancer. It is also an antioxidant, reducing or preventing oxidative stress on the body. Chronic inflammation and oxidation are the cause of most symptoms of aging and the root cause of many diseases.

Anxiety, Stress, Depression, and Mental Health Issues: Lion's mane mushrooms are useful in improving a number of mental health issues, including insomnia, anxiety, depression, and slowing the progression of dementia. The mushrooms help regenerate brain cells and improve brain function. It is excellent for stress and anxiety, and helps with their symptoms, such as heart palpitations, irritation, and concentration.

Enhances the Intestinal Immune System: Lion's mane mushrooms enhance the function of the intestinal immune system, helping the body fight infection from bacteria, viruses, yeast, and fungi. It is especially beneficial in helping prevent infections.

Diabetes and Neuropathy: Lion's mane mush-rooms have a variety of effects that are beneficial to diabetics. With consistent use, it lowers blood glucose levels and improves insulin sensitivity in type 2 diabetics. In lowering blood sugar levels, it helps prevent complications from kidney disease, eye damage, and nerve damage in the hands and feet. It also helps relieve the pain of diabetic neuropathy.

Strokes, Concussions, and Brain Injuries: Lion's mane is used to prevent strokes and after a stroke-related injury. Due to its neuroprotective effects it can help the nervous system deal with lack of oxygen, blood clots, memory issues, and more. Using it post-concussion makes sense since it is such an excellent healer for the brain and is a powerful anti-inflammatory.

Increases Energy, Relieves Fatigue, and Enhances Athletic Performance: Lion's mane mushrooms are a rich source of antioxidants. They re-duce lactic acid buildup in the blood, increase blood oxygen levels and reduce muscle fatigue. They also in-crease glycogen in tissues, providing a source of ready and sustainable energy for the body.

Harvesting: Harvest in late summer and autumn. Look for large mushrooms with multiple white spines hanging downward. If they have begun to turn pink, they are too mature and will not have good flavor if you are eating them. Cut the mushroom from the tree with a sharp knife, avoiding cutting into the wood of the tree. Leave some behind to establish a new crop for next year. Handle them gently.

Warning: Some people are allergic to mushrooms and thus should avoid lion's mane mushrooms as well. Symptoms of allergies can include skin rashes and difficulty breathing or even anaphylactic shock. If you have any burning, itching, swollen lips, or breathing difficulties, consult a doctor immediately.

Recipes. Lion's Mane Tea: Ingredients: ½ to 1 teaspoon Lion's mane powder, 1 cup water. Bring the water to a boil and turn off the heat. Put the lion's mane powder into an infuser or directly into the mug. Pour the hot water over the mushroom and allow the tea to steep for 10 minutes.

Lungwort Lichen, Lobaria pulmonaria

Lungwort lichen is a lobed lichen with leaf-like structures that resemble the human lung. It is known for its use in lung diseases but has many other uses. Lungwort lichen grows in old growth humid forests on conifers and hardwood trees. In its habitat, it is quite com-mon to find the lichen hanging from trees and rocks. All lichens are organisms that were formed via symbiosis. Lungwort is actually a mutualistic relationship between three different organisms. It consists of an ascomycete fungus, a green alga, and a cyanobacterium. (Note this is different that the Common Lungwort plant, also in this book).

Identification: Lungwort lichen is large lichen with leaf-like lobed structures that measure 2 to 6 inches (5 cm to 7.5 cm) in length. The top of the lichen is bright green, while the underside is pale with dark pockets. It is leathery in texture with a pattern of ridges and creases on the surface. Its thallus is loosely attached to the growing surface. Lungwort turns brown when dried.

Medicinal Use: The leaf-like thallus is harvested and dried for medicine. I use it in its double-extracted, tinctured form.

Respiratory Conditions, Asthma, Bronchi-tis, Whooping Cough, Tuberculosis, and Laryngitis: Lungwort lichen is mostly used to treat respiratory issues such as asthma, bronchitis, whooping cough, and tuberculosis. It is a natural antibiotic, and is ideal for treating bronchial and chest infections. It is excellent at clearing mucous from the bronchial passages. It reduces inflammation in the airways.

Lungwort lichen has high mucilage content and it is soothing on a sore throat or for laryngitis.

Antioxidant, Anti-Inflammatory, and Anti-Ulcer: Lungwort lichen contains high levels of anti-oxidants and anti-inflammatory compounds that work together to protect and heal the body. Antioxidants protect the body from free radicals that cause serious diseases like heart disease and cancer. Free radicals are also responsible for most of the symptoms of aging. Re-search on lungwort lichens as an anti-inflammatory show that, unlike many pharmaceutical anti-inflammatories (NSAIDs) it does not cause gastric distress. It even showed an anti-ulcer effect and may be useful for ulcerative colitis.

Degradation of Prions – Creutzfeldt-Jakob Disease: Creutzfeldt-Jakob Disease (CJD) is caused by prions. Prions also cause Mad Cow Disease in cattle and chronic wasting disease (CWD) in deer and elk (note that these are different diseases that CJD). The fungal part of the lungwort lichen has been shown to degrade prion proteins using a serine protease enzyme. This is a great find as prions are very hard to kill.

Anti-Bacterial: *Staphylococcus*, Pneumonia, TB, and *Salmonella*. Lungwort lichen contains powerful antibacterial agents. It is useful for treating staph infections and the bacteria that cause bacterial pneumonia and tuberculosis. It is also effective against *Salmo-nella* bacteria.

Digestive Health: Lungwort lichen is an effective remedy for digestive problems like constipation, stomach pain, indigestion, diarrhea, and bloating. It has mild diuretic properties that help remove excess fluid from the body. Best used as a tea for digestion.

Harvesting: Note: lungwort lichen is protected in some areas. Check your local laws before harvesting. Lungwort lichen grows very slowly and will not grow in heavily polluted areas, so it is becoming threatened in many environments. Harvest it carefully and do not take the whole plant. Only harvest in environmentally clean areas. The upper tissue edge must remain on the tree to regrow the lichen. Use a knife to slice off the outer lobes of the lichen, leaving the upper tissue attached to the tree. You do not need a large amount. Dry the lichen and store it in a sealed glass jar with a tight lid. Place the jar in a cool, dry place. Gathering after a windstorm is a great way to get fresh lungwort lichen that has blown down.

Warning: Do not use lungwort lichen if you are pregnant or breastfeeding, as safety is unknown.

Recipes. Lungwort Lichen Tea. Ingredients: 1 tablespoon dried lungwort lichen, 1 cup boiling water, 1 teaspoon raw honey, optional for sweetness.

Pour the boiling water over the herb and let it steep for 15 minutes. Strain and add raw honey, if desired.

Lungwort Tincture: Please follow our guide for a double-extraction like the one on page 39 or page 268. For most of the ailments above I use a dual-extracted tincture of Lungwort Lichen.

Reishi Mushroom, Ganoderma lucidum

The reishi mushroom is found on dead or dying trees, old stumps, and logs. They are quite easy to distinguish if you know your mushrooms well. They are also called *ling zhi,* the mushroom of immortality, and varnish cork, as they look like they have been painted with a clear coat of varnish or clear nail polish. Many places cultivate reishi for commercial use.

Identification: Always consult with an expert be-fore using any mushrooms you find growing wild, though reishi mushrooms don't have any poisonous look-alikes. The cap of this polypore mushroom is fan or kidney-shaped, red to reddish-brown, and has a wet, varnished look when young. This shiny, reddish, bright yellow or white cap is the first identifying feature of reishi mushrooms. As they age, they become tougher, turn more of a reddish-brown, and the spores drop. These spores can end up on the top surface of the mushroom, making the cap lose its shiny luster. The pore surface on the underside of the mushroom bruises brown. The cap can grow to be a foot across and up to 2-inches (5 cm) thick. It may be attached to a stem, but not always. New growth appears along a whitish edge.

The underside of the cap does not have gills. Instead, tiny brown spores come out of tiny pores on the under-side. When stems are present, they are 1 to 6 inches (2.5 cm to 7.5 cm) long and almost 2 inches (5 cm) thick. They can be twisted or irregular, angling to one side of the cap. Like the cap, they are varnished and colored.

Edible Use: While reishi mushrooms are technically edible when cooked, they have a bitter taste and are very tough, so they are rarely eaten. They can be used to season soups and are then strained out.

Medicinal Use and Adaptogenic Herb: I primarily use reishi mushrooms in their double-extracted tinctured form (page 39/268) to make available both the water-soluble and alcohol-soluble components. If you are only consuming reishi as a tea or a tea/coffee/hot chocolate-mixture you are missing out on a lot of the medicinal compounds. I take my reishi tincture every day. It is an excellent adaptogenic herb. Adaptogens help our bodies deal with the negative aspects of stress, such as inflammation, hormonal imbalances, increased cortisol levels, fatigue, and low energy levels. They help with quality of sleep, adrenal fatigue, and with immune function.

Anti-Inflammatory Properties, Autoim-mune Diseases, and Leaky Gut: Reishi mush-rooms are a powerful anti-inflammatory both internally and externally. When applied topically, it relieves inflammation better than over the counter and many prescription steroid treatments. Because many auto-immune diseases are inflammatory in nature, reishi mushrooms are being used to slow or reverse the dis-ease process. It also has immune modulating effects. I take it daily, along with Turkey Tail and Lion's Mane Mushroom Tinctures, for Multiple Sclerosis and believe that it greatly helps my condition. It is also indicated for Lupus, Myasthenia Gravis, Hashimoto's Thyroiditis, Crohn's, Inflammatory Bowel, Ulcerative Colitis, Guillain-Barre, Rheumatoid Arthritis, Psoriasis, Vasculitis, and Celiac Disease. It has been shown to have neuroprotective effects and is also good for treating Leaky Gut, a common cause of inflammation and immune response. Note that the anti-inflammatory properties in reishi (triterpenoids) are not water-solu-ble.

Anti-Aging and Anti-Oxidants: Reishi mushrooms are rich in antioxidants, which relieve oxidative stress in tissues and prevent age-related stress in the liver and body. It also has neuroprotective effects and is recommended for people with Alzheimer's and other nervous system diseases.

Cancer: Reishi mushrooms are used traditionally to prolong life in cancer patients and are currently used with modern cancer treatments to improve strength and stamina in patients. Reishi enhances immune system function and allows the body to better fight cancer. It has demonstrated significant anti-tumor and anti-cancer activity. They are also effective at alleviating nausea and kidney damage caused by cancer drugs and in reversing chemotherapy resistance. It can be used in tandem with traditional chemotherapy and radiation treatments in the same manner as Turkey Tail mushrooms are used.

Fatigue, Depression, Insomnia, Anxiety, and Adrenal Fatigue: People who regularly take reishi mushrooms report improvement in depression, fatigue, insomnia, anxiety, sense of wellbeing, and quality of life. Reishi is an adaptogenic herb and helps with adrenal fatigue.

Anti-Microbial, Anti-Fungal, Anti-Bacte-rial, and Anti-Viral: Reishi has anti-microbial, anti-fungal, anti-bacterial, and anti-viral effects. It reg-ulates immune system activity and helps the body heal. These properties work together to help the body heal from wounds, infections, and diseases. It has been shown to be antiviral for HIV, HPV, herpes simplex 1 and 2, and influenza. It demonstrates antibacterial ac-tivity against *Streptococcus*, *Staphylococcus*, *Salmo-nella*, *Bacillus* (one of which causes anthrax), *E. coli*, and *Micrococcus*. It also works well for Urinary Tract Infections.

Liver Function, Hepatitis, Hormone Bal-ance, Acne, PCOS, and Prostate: Reishi mush-rooms have healing effects on the liver and help it re-lease toxins that reduce its function. The mushrooms also speed up regeneration of healthy liver cells and promote overall liver health and whole-body vitality. It has shown great efficacy in the treatment of hepatitis. Through its help with liver function, hormones are better broken down and metabolized and hormonal balance is restored. It may be helpful for acne treatment, prostate health for men, and for women with PCOS due to its anti-androgenic effect.

Seizures, Convulsions, and Restless Legs Syndrome: Reishi mushrooms have been successfully used to relieve stress on the nervous system and reduce seizures and convulsions. Anticonvulsive and anti-inflammatory properties work together to calm the nervous system and help with recovery. It also helps people suffering from Restless Legs Syndrome (RLS).

Bronchitis, Allergies, and Asthma: Reishi is used to treat chronic bronchitis, allergies, and asthma. It helps prevent the release of histamines and reduces inflammation.

Blood Sugar Regulation: Reishi mushroom is known to improve symptoms of type II diabetes and to lower elevated blood sugar levels.

Heart Benefits, Blood Pressure, Blood Flow, and Cholesterol: Reishi mushrooms bene-fit the heart in several ways. They increase oxygenation of the blood, increase blood flow, lower cholesterol and fatty acids in the blood, and help lower blood pressure. People report improvement in symptoms of cardiovascular disease and improvement in heart function when taking reishi mushrooms regularly. It also seems to regulate irregular heartbeats. People also notice a drop in "Bad" LDL cholesterol and an increase in "Good" HDL cholesterol.

Altitude Sickness: Reishi mushroom's ability to increase blood flow and oxygenation of the blood is useful in treating altitude sickness. Breathing improves and dizziness is reduced. It is best to start taking reishi mushrooms before the trip and to continue use throughout.

Warning: Reishi mushrooms are safe, however it is possible to ingest too much. Use reishi mushrooms from a reputable source or consult an expert. Think about avoiding reishi mushrooms if you are pregnant or breastfeeding, since there is no information on their safety. Consult a doctor before using reishi mushrooms if you have a bleeding disorder. Do not use before sur-gery, as reishi is a vasodilator.

Recipes. Reishi Mushroom Tincture Dou-ble-Extraction: Use the double-extraction method found on page 39 or page 268 to make your tincture so that you extract all of the medicinal compounds from your mushrooms. If you have a cloudy solution in your finished product that is a good thing – it is the water-soluble polysaccharides coming out of solution as they are mixed back with the alcoholic part of the tincture. Just shake before using. The alcoholic portion has the triterpenoids, which lend the reishi its bitter taste, as well as other compounds. Note that you can also do the alcoholic extraction first and follow up with the water extraction.

Turkey Tail Mushroom, Trametes versicolor or Coriolus versicolor

Turkey Tail Mushrooms have been in use for many years in Japanese and Chinese Medicine; they are called *Yun Zhi* in China. They are commonly used as an adjunct cancer therapy as they complement both radi-ation and chemotherapy. This polypore mushroom is found around the globe.

Identification: Turkey tail mushrooms grow in col-onies on tree stumps or fallen logs. The caps are multi-colored with concentric circles of alternating colors. Bands may be black, brown, tan, gray, blue, red, or-ange, or white. The edges of the cap form wavy ripples like the outside edge of a turkey's tail and they can grow up to 4 inches (10 cm) wide, though I usually find them around 1.5 to 2 inches (3.75 cm to 5 cm) wide. They are stemless. The cap of the turkey tail mushroom is velvety or fuzzy, thin, and flexible. It has pores on the underside that are evenly spread out (3 to 5 pores per mm). They do not have gills. The wavy growing edges are white or nearly white.

Gathering wild mushrooms without expert knowledge can make you violently ill, or worse. Always consult with an expert before eating any wild mushroom. Look for these identifying characteristics and have an expert verify the mushroom's identity before using it.

Edible Use: Turkey tail mushrooms are very nutritious and full of vitamins and minerals. However, they do not digest well, so they are rarely eaten.

Medicinal Use: I use turkey tail in tincture form and take this daily as part of my daily health routine. They are also taken in dry, powdered form or as Turkey Tail Tea. I use a double-extraction method to access all of its medicinal properties.

Regulates the Immune System, Prevents and Treats the Cold and Flu: The nutrients, antioxidants, and anti-inflammatory components in turkey tail mushrooms regulate the immune system and help fight off diseases. It is a very good anti-viral.

Fights Cancer and Supports Cancer Patients: Turkey tail mushrooms are often used for cancer patients to kill cancer cells and tumors and to support the immune system while undergoing chemo-therapy. It strengthens the immune system, helping your body fight the disease and also protects the body from additional infections. Its anti-cancer properties help prevent the spread of the cancer and have been shown to augment the effects of Western cancer therapies. The two primary compounds in it for cancer are Polysaccharide - K (PSK) or Krestin and Polysaccharo-peptide (PSP). PSK has been in common clinical use in Japan since the 1970s. The research on turkey tail mushrooms and cancer is too extensive to outline here but it is very effective for treating many types of cancers, and in greatly reducing relapse rates.

Treats HPV, Cervical Dysplasia, Herpes, and Shingles: Turkey tail mushrooms fight infections of bacteria and viruses. It is effective in treating the human papillomavirus (HPV) and fighting the cancers that HPV sometimes triggers. Use turkey tail along with reishi mushrooms to treat viral infections like HPV, herpes, and shingles.

Improves Digestion and Leaky Gut: Digestive disorders respond well to treatment with turkey tail mushrooms. Turkey tail increases the levels of vitamins and minerals in the diet and supports healthy gut flora. Turkey tail helps Leaky Gut due to its prebiotic effects on the gut's microbiome (they feed the beneficial gut bacteria).

Helps Prevent and Treat HIV/AIDS and Kaposi's Sarcoma: There has been much research done on HIV and AIDS and turkey tail mushrooms have shown a remarkable ability to strengthen the immune system of these patients and help them fight the disease. It has been successfully used to treat Kaposi's Sarcoma, a skin cancer that affects AIDS patients. It stimulates interferon production and the probable mechanism of turkey tail for HIV is via the inhibition of the binding of HIV to lymphocytes. Lymphocyte depletion is the cause of the "acquired immunodeficiency" in AIDS.

Diabetes: Turkey tail mushrooms help lower the levels of glucose in the bloodstream and can be helpful in managing blood sugar levels in diabetics.

Reducing Inflammation, Autoimmune Diseases, and Chronic Inflammatory Diseases: Many modern diseases are caused by out of control inflammation in the body. These diseases are usually chronic and can become severe. Turkey tail mushrooms are high in anti-inflammatory properties and help reduce internal inflammation. It is also effective when applied to the skin to reduce rashes, swellings, and other external inflammations. Immune modulation coupled with its anti-inflammatory effects is most likely responsible.

***Candida* Overgrowth:** Turkey Tail helps with overgrowth of *Candida* as well as other bacterial flora in the small intestine.

Malaria: Turkey tail has been shown to be effective against malaria, including the chloroquine-resistant strain of Plasmodium.

Chronic Fatigue: Turkey tail has shown great efficacy in treating chronic fatigue syndrome.

Heart Health, Lowers Cholesterol and Blood Pressure: Turkey tail mushrooms are helpful in lowering LDL cholesterol levels in the body. It also reduces blood pressure in patients with hypertension. The mushrooms should be taken daily for full ef-fects. By lowering cholesterol and reducing hypertension, it also reduces the risks of heart disease.

Harvesting: Choose mushrooms with clean white pore surfaces. Snip off the rough tissue where the mushroom was attached with a pair of clean scissors. Gather in environmentally clean areas.

Warning: Turkey Tail mushrooms are considered to be very safe. There are no known negative side effects but it is always a good idea to consult with a medical professional.

Usnea Lichen

Also known as Old Man's Beard, Usnea lichen grows in a similar fashion as Spanish Moss. Once you get to know this lichen, you will not mistake it for anything else. Usnea has a distinguishing characteristic of a white, rubber-band-like core, so always look for this. Usnea is an indicator of a healthy ecosystem with clean air. The lichen will not grow in heavily polluted areas and is now considered endangered in many areas. If I had to pick only one medicine to have available to me this would be the one. All Usnea species are medicinal.

Identification: Usnea can be found hanging from the bark of trees like long strands of an old man's beard. It can be distinguished from other lichens by its stretchy inner fibers and its exclusive white core. It is gray-green in color and can take many different forms. It prefers to grow in areas with a lot of rainfall.

Edible Use: Usnea is considered edible when leached a few times, but it is not very palatable. It can cause great stomach upset and I don't eat it. It is, how-ever, one of my favorites go to medicinal plants.

Medicinal Use: Usnea lichen is a powerful antibiotic, antifungal, antimicrobial, and antiviral. I always carry Usnea and Blue Elderberry tinctures when I travel on airplanes and when I am around people who may be ill, as they both prevent and cure illness. I often put Usnea in a spray bottle for this use. I find that a spray of Usnea Tincture in the back of the throat helps prevent illnesses from taking hold. It is also a handy delivery mechanism to spray on to a wound or skin condition. Usnea extracts well in oil and as a double extracted tincture in alcohol and water.

Antibiotic Use: Strep, Staph, MRSA, Tuberculosis: The outer portion of the Usnea lichen contains antibiotic compounds that rival penicillin. For gram-positive bacteria like *Streptococcus*, *Pneumo-coccus*, MRSA, and tuberculosis, it works extremely well. I use it topically as well as internally. It doesn't seem to work as well for gram-negative bacteria like *E. coli*.

A Powerful Antiviral: Epstein-Barr, Herpes, HPV: Usnea lichen is effective in treating viral infections such as herpes simplex and the Epstein Barr virus that is implicated in so many modern diseases. Douching with Usnea can help with cervical dysplasia.

Respiratory System, Urinary Tract, Bladder, and Kidney Infections: Usnea helps heal respiratory problems such as bronchitis, pneumonia, sinus infections, strep throat, colds, flus, and other respiratory complaints. It is very effective in healing uri-nary tract, bladder, and kidney infections. Its antibiotic and antiviral properties help eliminate the infections while the immune system helps the body heal. I primarily use it in the form of a double-extracted Usnea tincture.

Skin Problems, Wounds, and Infections: Usnea's antibiotic and healing properties work on wounds and skin problems when it is applied as a poultice, salve, or tincture di-rectly on the affected skin. This lichen also has analgesic and anti-inflammatory properties that help relieve pain.

Yeast Infections, Thrush, Athlete's Foot, Jock Itch, Ringworm, Dandruff, and Other Fungal Infections: Usnea is a powerful antifungal and treats yeast infections in women. It is also effective against the fungi causing athlete's foot, jock itch, ringworm, dandruff, and other common fungal infections. For vaginal use, dilute the tincture in boiled water and use as a douche. For thrush, put your tincture in a spray bottle and spray on the affected area. This is such a relief to cancer patients experiencing thrush.

Conjunctivitis: Usnea can be used in a cooled down tea as an eyewash along with other herbs (Yarrow, Chamomile, Plantain, raw honey) for conjunctivitis.

Stops Bleeding: When applied to wounds, this lichen quickly facilitates clotting and controls bleeding. Apply the lichen directly to the wound and bind in place with a gauze bandage for best results.

Harvesting: I like to harvest Usnea just after a storm has just passed. At this time, tree branches have broken and are lying on the ground, just waiting for me to collect Usnea. In this way, I do not have to struggle to reach high branches or harvest from live trees. Usnea, like other lichens, grows slowly, so only collect from downed branches. Lichens are used as pollution indicators so make sure you collect from very environmentally clean areas.

Pull on the lichen strands to find its white core. In this way, you'll have confirmation that you have the right lichen and good medicine. Use fresh or dry and store in a cool, dark place for future use.

Warning: Usnea lichen is a highly concentrated medicine and should not be taken continuously in large doses. Take it as needed for specific problems. I personally use a spray in my throat often as a preventative for illness but that is a very low dose (versus taking a large amount of internal tincture daily) and I have had no ill effects or abnormal liver enzyme readings. Do not use Usnea internally during pregnancy or breastfeeding, as safety is unknown. Usnea lichen absorbs pollutants and toxins from the environment. Do not harvest the lichen in areas exposed to heavy metals, roadway exhaust, industrial areas, or waste areas.

Recipes: Tea is ineffective as a delivery method to access all of the medicinally active compounds of Usnea. Personally, I use a tincture double-extracted in water and alcohol to access all of the medicinal compounds (p. 38). I do this for most lichen and mushroom extractions and also add a little heat. You can either extract it with water first as in the recipe below or else extract it in alcohol and then extract the Usnea in water afterwards, pouring the alcoholic tincture back in to your medicinal water in a ratio of 3 parts alcohol: 1-part water. If you have a cloudy solution in your finished product that is OK – it is the water-soluble polysaccharides coming out of solution as they are mixed back with the alcoholic part of the tincture. Simply shake before use. Usnea is also very soluble in oil for internal and external use – follow our recipe for oil infusions (page 38 or page 268) and grind the Usnea well before infusing in oil.

Usnea Lichen Tincture (Recipe can be scaled up or down as desired). *Note: I like to use a small crockpot for this recipe. You may also place the herbs and water into a jar, which is then covered and placed into the crockpot of water or a pot of water on low on the stove.

Double-extraction: You'll need: 8 ounces (230g) or more of dried Usnea Lichen, 24 ounces (710ml) of 80 to 100 proof alcohol, 8 ounces (250ml) distilled water.

Cut up the Usnea into very small pieces so that the core is also exposed to your solvent. Place the distilled water and the dried herbs into the crockpot and stir well. Cover and cook on the lowest possible setting for 3 days. Allow the herb and water mixture to cool and pour it into a glass jar. Add the alcohol while the mixture is still quite warm, but not hot. Cap the jar tightly, label and date the jar and allow it to macerate for 8 weeks, shaking the jar daily. Strain out the herb (cheesecloth works well for this). Store it in a tightly capped glass jar. Label and date. Note: If you are using this tincture internally, your alcohol must be drinking quality.

Aquatic Vegetation

Cattails, Typha spp.

Traveling through wetlands, I am always happy to see cattail spikes growing near the water's edge. Practically the whole plant is edible, depending on the time of year. It is in the Typhaceae (Bulrush) Family.

Identification: Cattails are common in and near marshes, ponds, and other wetland areas throughout the world. The sword-like leaves are similar to many grasses, but the plant is readily identifiable by its brown corndog-like flowerheads.

Cattails are perennials and grow 5 to 8 feet (1.5m to 2.4 meters) tall. The alternate leaves are spear-shaped and grow from a simple stem that terminates in a large number of male flowers forming a spike at the end of the stem. The flowers wither once the pollen is shed.

Cattails flower from May through July. Tiny female flowers form a dense, sausage-shaped structure just below the male spike. This structure can be up to a foot long and is 1 to 2 inches (2.5 cm to 5 cm) in diameter. Tiny seeds grow on fine hairs. When ripe, the cottony fluff blows away to disperse the seeds.

Edible and Other Use: Cattail rhizomes are edible and nutritious. They are made into a flour by scraping the starch from the fibers, drying, and pounding. They can also be boiled, steamed, or mashed and eaten like a potato. The small shoots on the rhizomes in early spring are good peeled and sliced. The flavor is mildly sweet.

In the spring, the outer part of the young plant can be peeled and eaten raw or cooked. In the summer, harvest the green flower spike and remove the outer sheath like you would shuck corn. Boil the flower spike and eat it like corn on the cob. The flavor is delicious.

In late summer, an abundance of pollen forms and can be harvested for edible and medicinal use. It is easy to collect quickly in a thick patch. Simply bend the pollen-laden stalk over and shake it into a bag or other container. This pollen makes an excellent thickener or lour extender for baking and for making cattail pancakes. The leaves are used for weaving mats and baskets.

Medicinal Use. Treating Skin Conditions: Every part of the cattail is useful for this purpose. The starchy root makes a healing poultice for burns, boils, sores, cuts, insect bites, and bruises. Pound the roots and use the pulp or split the root and bruise the fibers inside, then apply the exposed pulp to the wound. The fuzz from the flowers treats small burns and skin irritations. Apply it directly to the wound and cover with a clean cloth.

Treating Small Wounds, Insect Bites, Toothaches, and Relieving Pain: The jelly-like sap that seeps from the lower stems has antiseptic and analgesic properties. I can usually find it between young leaves and scrape it up with the back of a knife.

Use it for treating small wounds, especially when worried about infection. It also acts as a powerful pain killer when applied topically and can be ingested with-out harm. It is an ideal pain reliever for toothaches, teething pain, and sore gums, and it can also be used on insect bites and other skin irritations. Just rub a little on the sore spot for fast pain relief and to reduce inflammation.

Abscesses and Infections: Clean abscesses with an antiseptic skin wash made by boiling the leaves. When the abscess is clean, combine cattail pollen with a small amount of raw honey and spread over the wound. Cover with a clean cloth and leave in place. Wash and replace the honeypollen two to three times a day as needed.

Well Baby Care: Apply the fuzz from the flowers into skin folds to prevent chafing and diaper rash in babies. The jelly-like sap found between the lower stems numbs the gums and relieves teething pain when rubbed sparingly onto a baby's gums.

Cancer Prevention: Cattails are currently being researched as a cancer preventative. Cattail's anti-inflammatory and antioxidant properties may slow the growth and spread of cancer.

Antiseptic and Styptic Properties: Burned cattail leaf ash is an excellent styptic and antiseptic for wounds. To make the ash, build a small fire using cat-tail leaves. Allow the fire to burn completely, then scoop up the ash. Use when cool or store it in a dry place for future use. Cattail pollen, dusted on externally, is also good for bleeding. It speeds clotting and helps prevent infection. Once bleeding is no longer an issue, mix the pollen with raw honey and use it to pre-vent infection and speed healing.

Menstrual and Postpartum Bleeding: Cattail pollen, taken orally, lessens the severity of heavy menstrual bleeding and postpartum bleeding and pain. 5 to 10 grams is the usual dose.

Internal Bleeding: Both the pollen and the flower are useful for internal bleeding. It helps with bruising, vomiting blood, bloody stools, bloody urine, and uterine bleeding. It doesn't treat the cause of the bleeding but helps stop the bleeding.

Warning: Its coagulant properties could be problematic for people with poor circulation, as it may slow down the blood even more and stimulate clotting in the skin. Pregnant women should not use cattail.

Cocoplum, Chrysobalanus icaco

The cocoplum is also called paradise plum and Icaco. It grows along beaches in tropical and subtropical areas. In North America it is found in Southern Florida, Mexico, and the Caribbean. It is in the Chrysobalanaceae Family.

Identification: Along the shoreline and in cultivated situations, the cocoplum forms a shrub that is 4 to 8 feet (1.2m to 1.8m) tall, but inland the plant forms a bushy tree that grows to 20 to 30(6m to 9.1m) feet tall. There are three main types of Cocoplum. "Red Tip" and "Green Tip" varieties that grow inland, and a "Horizontal" type that grows along the coast and is salt tolerant.

While all three varieties have a similar medicinal use, I am most familiar with the coastal-horizontal type. It sends down roots from branches that creep along the soil or sand. The leaves are alternate and egg-shaped with a small indentation at the tip. Each is about 1 1/2 inch to 3 inches (3.75 to 7.5 cm) long and has a tough, leathery texture and glossy appearance.

New leaves can be yellow-green to reddish; mature leaves are light green in color. Small white flowers appear in clusters at the end of the stems. The thick-skinned fruit can be white, yellow, red, or purple. They usually bear crops in the spring and another in later fall. The fruits are oval shaped and about 1-inch (2.5 cm) long. The bark is grey to reddish brown with white flecks.

Edible and Other Use: The cocoplum fruit is of-ten eaten raw or made into jams and syrups. The seed is also edible raw or cooked after the hard shell is re-moved. The seeds can be pressed and used like almond oil. The leaves are used to make a black dye that is de-cay resistant, and are used to treat cloth and fishing nets. The seeds within the fruit are very oily and can be used as a light or heat source.

Medicinal Use. Eye Health: Cocoplums fruits are an excellent source of beta-carotene and vitamin A, useful for treating night blindness and macular degeneration. It also helps protect the eyes from harmful UV rays. Eat the fruits either raw or cooked.

Heart Health and Weight Loss: Cocoplums help treat atherosclerosis and reduce the risk of heart attack and strokes. It prevents fat accumulation and may help prevent weight gain.

Healthy Immune System: In addition to its vitamin A content, cocoplums also contain high levels of vitamin C, K, and the building blocks that your body uses to make vitamin D. They are also rich in minerals and antioxidants. Eating cocoplum fruits strengthens the immune system and helps prevent degenerative diseases.

Duckweed, Lemna minor

Duckweed, also called water lens and bayroot, is a fast-growing perennial aquatic plant that floats on or just below the surface of still or slow-moving water. It is in the Lemnaceae (Duckweed) Family. It is found throughout the world.

Identification: Duckweed is a small floating plant. Each plant is actually only one small flat floating modified stem, which looks like a leaf, and is 1/16 to 1/2 inch (1.25 cm) across, A single root hair protrudes down from each floating frond. They usually grow in large fresh water colonies.

The entire plant is less than 1/2 inch (1.25 cm) from the root tip to the top of the floating frond. While the plant does produce flowers, reproduction is mostly by asexual budding, which occurs at the base of the frond.

Miniscule flowers occasionally appear, in groups of three, in summer.

Edible Use: It is eaten in some parts of the world as a vegetable. It is an excellent protein source, and contains more protein than soybeans. It is a good food source as it grows very quickly. Be careful to harvest from clean water.

Medicinal Use: The entire plant is used and can be dried or used fresh. Both water and alcohol extractions work well, as does fresh consumption or juicing.

Anti-Bacterial and Anti-Fungal: Duckweed helps cure bacterial and yeast infections. It works for many different bacterial infections including *Staphy-lococcus*, *Streptococcus*, *Bacillus*, *Citrobacter*, and *Neisseria*, and also against *Candida* with great suc-cess.

Jaundice and Detox: Duckweed juice is said to absorb toxins and help detox the blood and liver.

Headaches, Swelling, and Body Aches: Duckweed juice treats aches and pains including head-aches and body aches. Its anti-inflammatory proper-ties help relieve swelling and inflammation in the muscles and joints, and help with arthritis and gout. For muscle and joint pain, make a poultice of crushed plants and apply it to the painful area.

Harvesting: Avoid harvesting duckweed from road-sides and polluted waters. It is known to accumulate heavy metals and other toxins. It is fairly easy to grow your own supply in clean water.

To grow duckweed, take a few plants from a clean water supply and move them into a pool or other container with a non-chlorinated clean water supply. They reproduce and grow quickly. To harvest, scoop the plant from the water and use it fresh or dry for later use.

Warning: Duckweed contains high levels of calcium oxalate, which can contribute to the formation of kidney stones.

Watercress, Nasturtium officinale

Watercress is an aquatic plant in the Brassicaceae (Mustard) Family. It is related to mustard and horseradish. Even though it bears the name Nasturtium, do not confuse it with the garden plant with the common name of nasturtium, which is in the genus Tropaeolum. It is a fast growing, aquatic or semiaquatic, perennial plant that grows in clumps. Watercress was introduced to North America from Europe and is now found in almost every state and province. It is especially prevalent in the Pacific Northwest.

Identification: Watercress leaves are compound with 3 to 7 wavy-edged, oval leaflets that grow from a central stalk. The spicy leaves have a strong taste of pepper. Leaves are 2 to 5 inches (5 cm to 12.5 cm) long. Its flowers are at the top of these stems and are less than 1/5-inch-(0.5 cm) long with four white petals. Watercress fruits are thin, slightly curved, and measure less than 1 inch (2.5 cm) long and about 1/10 of an inch (0.25 cm) wide. They are borne on short stalks and contain 4 rows of small, round seeds.

Edible Use: The peppery leaves and seeds are edible and are used mainly as a condiment or a garnish in salads.

Medicinal Use: The leaves are used for arthritis, as a diuretic, a purgative, an expectorant, and have stimulant properties. It is very rich in vitamins and minerals. It is an effective cleansing herb, and is high in Vitamin C. It can be eaten fresh or taken as an infusion. It is best used fresh, but can also be dried for future use.

Immune Booster: The high nutrition and medicinal properties of watercress make it an excellent treatment for restoring immune function and health to the body. Eat watercress raw, drink the juice or the infusion, or cook. All provide the necessary nutrients and healing benefits.

Treating Tuberculosis: The freshly pressed juice of watercress is used to treat tuberculosis. Healers who use it report that they have patients drink one cup of watercress juice daily, in divided doses. Large doses taken all at once can cause stomach upset.

Swellings of the Lymphatic Systems: Make a poultice by crushing fresh watercress leaves to help drain swollen glands.

Headaches and Anxiety: Use Watercress Tincture made with vinegar to treat headaches and anxiety.

Saturate a handkerchief or a piece of cotton cloth in the tincture and wring it out. Place the cloth on your fore-head and relax.

Mouth Sores, Swollen Gums, Bad Breath, and Hot Flashes: Watercress Soup is used for many mouth and gum issues as well as to cure hot flashes caused by menopause. Soup recipe below.

Dermatitis, Eczema, and Chronic Skin Dis-eases: For chronic skin conditions, watercress juice or Watercress Infusion is very effective. It is not an immediate fix. You will get a boost to the immune system, added nutrition, and gradual healing. Drink one cup of the infusion daily and use it to wash the affected areas twice a day.

Gout, Kidney Stones, Water Retention, and Expelling Mucous: Watercress is a diuretic. An infusion treats swelling in the body and helps expel mucous. Watercress Infusion also encourages the dissolution of kidney stones so that they can be flushed from the body.

Harvesting: The leaves of watercress can be harvested most of the year and are used fresh. Snip the tops of stems when they are about 6 inches (15 cm) long. Never take more than a third of the plant at any one time to protect the future supply. Do not pull on the stems of the plant directly as you may uproot the entire plant. This plant wilts quickly, so it is best harvested for immediate use. It can stay in the fridge for up to 3 days in a plastic bag or submerged in water. Harvest watercress only from known clean water supplies.

Warning: Collect your watercress from clean water sources. Fouled water can contaminate the herb. Excessive use of this plant can lead to stomach upset.

Recipes. Watercress Tincture: Rinse freshly picked watercress thoroughly and pack it into a clean and sterile glass jar with a tight lid. Bring some apple cider vinegar to a low boil and pour it over the water-cress to fill the jar. Let the watercress steep for 6 to 8 hours, then strain it through a coffee filter. Pour it back into the glass jar and cap it tightly for long-term storage.

Watercress Soup: 1/2 cup loosely packed water-cress, washed thoroughly, 1/2 cup sliced carrots, 1-quart (1 Liter) of water, salt and pepper to taste. Simmer the watercress and carrots in the water slowly over low heat for about 45 minutes or until the water is reduced by half. You may put it in a blender or eat as is (I prefer it blended). Consume it all. Makes one serving (it is easy to scale up this recipe).

Watercress Infusion: Gather a saucepan full of watercress and clean. Place the watercress in a ceramic or stainless-steel pot. Add enough cold water to barely cover the watercress. Bring the herbs to a boil and lower the heat. Simmer the herbs until they are soft. Filter the herbs out and store the infusion in the refrigerator for up to 3 days. The flavor can be enhanced if needed by mixing it with tomato juice or other vegetable juices.

Water Plantain, Alisma subcordatum

Southern water plantain grows in swamps, wetlands, lakes, marshes, and coastal areas. It is also known as *Alisma lantago-aquatica var. parviflorum*. It is in the Alismataceae (Water Plantain) Family. It grows in eastern North America.

Identification: Water plantain grows from 1 to 3 feet (0.3m to 0.9m). The broad leaves may float on the water surface but are often submerged. The leaves are widest at or near the middle and taper at the ends. Underwater leaves are often long, and ribbon-like.

The flowers are highly branched with whorls of white or pink to pink-purple flowers. Flowers have three petals and six stamens, and many carpels. Each carpel has one ovule and style. Flowers bloom all summer and seeds ripen from July to September.

Edible Use: Boil the leaves and petioles of water plantain to eat. The leaves and root are toxic raw, but the poisons are destroyed by heat and drying. Cook them for a long time to make sure all toxins are destroyed. The cooked roots are salty and rich in starch. They are a good starch source in the winter when wild food supplies are low.

Medicinal Use: Most of water plantain is used medicinally, including the fresh and dried roots, leaves, and seeds. The easiest way to use it is to eat it as part of a daily diet. Make sure it is thoroughly cooked before use.

Diuretic, Kidney Stones, and Cystitis: Dried water plantain root is a diuretic and helps the body get rid of excess water (edema). The leaves treat cystitis (bladder infection) and kidney stones.

Powdered Water Plantain Seed for Bleeding: Dried and powdered water plantain seed is a good astringent and helps control bleeding. Apply it directly to the wound to disinfect the area and stop bleeding.

Digestive Ailments: Water plantain is a good source of dietary fiber (cook it well!). It also treats digestive issues such as cramps, stomach flu, bloating, and heartburn.

Lowers Cholesterol and Blood Pressure: Water plantain lowers blood pressure and cholesterol levels. It is heart healthy.

Poultice for Bruising and Swelling: Water plantain contains anti-inflammatories that work to re-duce swelling and bruising. It is also a rubefacient. Crush the fresh leaves and use them as a poultice. Cover it with a clean cloth and replace as needed.

Harvesting: Harvest the roots in winter and boil for immediate use, or dry them for the future. Harvest leaves in spring and summer.

Warning: Water plantain can cause skin irritation in some people. While water plantain is considered safe, it can irritate the digestive tract with longterm use.

Western Skunk Cabbage, Lysichiton americanus

This plant is aptly named skunk cabbage because of its odor when crushed. It is very easy to identify by its physical characteristics, like its bright yellow spathe (leaf-like bract) surrounding a dense flower spike. This member of the Araceae (Arum) Family is also known as Swamp Lantern and Meadow Cabbage.

Identification: One of the first plants to bloom in the spring, it grows low to the ground in wet and swampy areas. The bright yellow spathe appears around the flower spike from February to May. Shiny large waxy green leaves appear after the flowers and can have a putrid smell. Skunk cabbage attracts flies, which facilitates pollination. The leaves are large, and can grow up to a few feet in length.

Edible Use: Do not consume raw due to calcium oxalate crystals. When boiled for long periods, traditionally 3 days or longer, the roots are edible. Boiling with multiple changes of water is necessary to remove the toxic substances, so routine use is not recommended. They are mostly known as a starvation food. The young leaves, thoroughly cooked with at least one change of water, are edible and have a pleasant peppery flavor. I use the large leaves as a wax paper for pit roasts or to wrap my fish in prior to cooking over a fire. It does not impart a skunky smell or flavor and it holds in moisture nicely.

Medicinal Use: The root is toxic raw and must be thoroughly cooked or dried and aged to remove the toxin.

I dry my roots in a dehydrator and store them in a cool, dry, and dark place for at least 6 to 8 weeks before use. Use aged skunk cabbage root dried and powdered or apply the leaves directly to the skin as a poultice, compress, or wash.

Skin Infections, Wounds, Rashes, Burns, Bruises, and Insect Bites: Skunk cabbage is an anti-inflammatory and anti-infective. Use it in a poultice to draw out infection or treat an insect bite, and as a wash to treat burns, bruises, rashes, poison ivy, and psoriasis.

Carpal Tunnel, Arthritis, Sore Muscles and Joints: A skunk cabbage poultice or compress made with Skunk Cabbage Tea placed on the joint or aching muscle helps reduce inflammation and pain.

Bronchitis, Asthma, Tuberculosis, and Anti-Spasmodic: Skunk cabbage root is an expectorant and antispasmodic, making it useful in treating bronchitis and asthma as it calms inflammation and bronchial spasms, while also helping to expel mucus. It also treats the underlying infection.

Nervous System: Aged skunk cabbage root is slightly narcotic. It calms the nervous system and treats headaches, vertigo, and some nervous conditions. It has been used to treat epilepsy and convulsions with mixed success.

Pregnancy and Labor: Skunk cabbage is beneficial during pregnancy and labor, promoting normal function of the nervous system and reproductive sys-tem. It soothes irritation and promotes efficient muscle contractions. Consult a medical professional before using during pregnancy or breastfeeding.

Harvesting: Skunk cabbage contains crystals of calcium oxalate, which can be irritating on the skin. Wear gloves to handle the plant. Harvest the leaves and dig up the roots. Bring a good shovel as the roots are hard to dig up. Boil for several days, changing the water of-ten, or dry the herb and age for at least 6 to 8 weeks before using. Boiling or drying destroys the calcium oxalate crystals.

Warning: Skunk cabbage contains large amounts of calcium oxalate, a toxin that is very irritating if ingested. Calcium oxalate is destroyed by cooking or by drying and aging the plant. Excess doses of skunk cabbage can cause side effects such as nausea, vomiting, dizziness, impaired vision, headaches, and vertigo. Some people may have allergic reactions to skunk cabbage. The fresh plant is extremely irritating and can cause itching, blistering of the skin, and redness when touched. If not treated properly the plant can irritate the mouth and throat. Never eat it raw, cook it as directed above.

Recipes. Skunk Cabbage Tincture: You'll need: dried and aged skunk cabbage root, 80 proof or higher vodka and a clean, sterile glass jar

Chop or grind the dried and aged root into small pieces and place it into a sterile jar, filling 1/3rd of it. Cover the root with vodka and fill to within ½ inch (1.25 cm) of the top of the jar. Cap the jar tightly, label and date it. Shake the jar to mix well and store the jar in a cool, dark place. Shake every few days for 6 to 8 weeks. Strain the herb out and store the tincture in a clean, labeled jar for up to 5 years.

Home Remedies

Activated Charcoal

Activated charcoal is very fine and porous. It is an effective way to remove toxins and poisons from the body. It reduces bloating, traps toxins and gases so they don't get absorbed by the body, and acts as an antidote to some poisons.

Medicinal Use. Detoxify the Body: Activated charcoal has tiny pores throughout that attract and traps toxins in the body. The toxins bind to the activated charcoal and pass through the body. To use activated charcoal to detoxify the body, take 10 grams of activated charcoal approximately 1 to 2 hours before each meal. Do this for two to three days. Drink 12 to 15 glasses of water per day during your cleanse. If you be-come constipated, drink a glass of warm water with lemon and raw honey every half hour until the constipation is gone.

Poisoning: Activated charcoal is useful for removing chemical poisons that have been ingested. Organic poi-sons such as pesticides, fertilizer, bleach, and mercury bind to the surface of the charcoal, preventing absorption in the body. It is also used it to prevent the absorption of an accidental or intentional overdose of drugs. It is effective against the ingestion of overdoses of aspirin, acetaminophen, opium, cocaine, and morphine. Charcoal must be administered quickly, within an hour of ingestion, and in quantity. The sooner the better and get medical help immediately. For adults, a large dose of 50 to 100 grams is required and 10 to 25 grams for children. Charcoal must be taken with a large quantity of water.

Food Poisoning: Many people do not realize that activated charcoal is useful for the treatment of nausea and diarrhea in cases of food poisoning. Adults take 25 grams of activated charcoal and children need 10 grams. Take the charcoal with large quantities of water immediately upon suspicion of food poisoning. Larger doses may be needed.

Snake Bites, Poisonous Spider Bites, and Insect Stings: For snake and poisonous spider bites, including bites from the black widow spider and the brown recluse, use a mixture of equal parts activated charcoal and coconut oil. Mix them together and cover the bite and a wide surrounding area with the mixture. Cover with a bandage to prevent staining clothes. The poison from the bites moves into the tis-sue surrounding the bites, so a wide area around the bite needs to be covered with the activated charcoal. After two to three hours, rinse the area well and reap-ply. Repeat the application until the inflammation is gone and the wound is healing. For insect bites, apply a small dab of the mixture, repeating every hour until the sting is gone. If it's a serious poisonous bite be sure to seek medical attention.

Acne: Treat acne with activated charcoal mixed with aloe vera gel. Smooth the mixture over the affected areas and let dry. Then rinse off completely. I prefer to treat the entire area, but it can also be used for spot treatments. Activated charcoal can also be mixed into soap and body wash for use in affected areas.

When to Avoid Activated Charcoal: Do not use activated charcoal in cases of poisoning by petroleum, alcohol, lye, acids and other corrosive chemicals. Do not take activated charcoal if you are taking prescription medications. It can interfere with some medications. Consult your doctor for more information on your medication.

Warning: Activated charcoal is not the same as barbecue charcoal. Barbecue charcoal should never be consumed. Drink 12 to 15 glasses of water daily when taking activated charcoal. The water prevents dehydration and constipation caused by the activated charcoal.

Bleach

Bleach is a good disinfectant for most household sur-faces. It kills most bacteria, viruses, and fungi. Use it to sanitize surfaces in treatment areas, disinfect laundry, decontaminate blood spills, and disinfect equipment. In addition, it has medicinal uses for treating skin.

Medicinal Use. Bed Sores, Diabetic Ulcers, Eczema, and Inflammatory Skin Conditions: Soaking skin in a very dilute bleach solution is effective to treat bed sores, diabetic ulcers, eczema, and other inflammatory skin conditions. Use one tablespoon of regular strength bleach per gallon (per 4 liters) of water. The bleach solution is dilute enough not to harm the skin while calming inflammation and killing bacteria on the skin. Do not use undiluted bleach or bleach in higher concentrations. I prefer herbal medicine to bleach but it is a good remedy to know. You can also follow up a bleach treatment with soothing herbal oils specific to your condition and needs.

For a full 40-gallon (151 Liters) tub, use ½ cup of household bleach in warm water. Soak in the water for five to ten minutes, then rinse the skin completely with fresh water. Pat dry. Apply lotions, emollients, or medications after a bath. Repeat two to three times weekly, or as needed.

Sanitizing Water for Drinking: Unscented bleach is suitable for sanitizing water for drinking purposes. Add five drops of bleach per quart (liter) of water or 1/4 teaspoon of bleach per gallon (1 Liter) of water. Stir thoroughly and allow it to sit for at least one hour before drinking. If the water is cloudy, filter it be-fore adding the chlorine. This treatment kills most bacteria and viruses found in water, but may not kill all. It does not remove chemicals or other toxins from water.

Using Bleach for Disinfecting: For disinfecting surfaces, use a higher concentration of bleach: 1/4 to 3/4 cup of bleach added to 1 gallon (4 liters) of water (1 to 3 tablespoons per quart (liter) of water). Let the bleach water stand on the surface for at least 2 minutes, then wipe dry or allow to air dry. This solution needs to be made fresh daily.

Warning: Do not use undiluted bleach or high concentrations of bleach directly on the skin. Bleach can cause dryness of skin irritations. Do not use with patients who have an allergy to chlorine.

Boric Acid

Boric acid is useful for a number of different purposes. It is especially effective for treating fungal infections of all kinds. Boric acid is not the same as borax. For medicinal use, always use therapeutic grade or pharmaceutical grade boric acid. Boric acid is a white crystalline acid (H_3BO_3) containing boron. It is sometimes called hydrogen borate or orthoboric acid. It is usually used as a dry powder, although it can be mixed with water to make a dilute acid for sanitizing purposes. Boric acid should never be taken orally.

Medicinal Use. Treating Yeast Infections:
Boric acid suppositories are an excellent treatment for vaginal yeast infections. They are particularly useful for treating people who have had multiple yeast infections that keep returning because the boric acid can be used regularly as a preventative once the infection is cured.

Usual dose is 600mg of boric acid per suppository. Stuff the boric acid into a size "00" gelatin capsule and place the cap on it securely. Insert one suppository into the vagina every night just before bed. Patients should be warned that they may experience irritation or a burning sensation, but it will quickly pass. There will also be a discharge. Use one suppository each night for one week if this is an isolated yeast infection. If a person has been having problems with recurring infections, use the suppository every night for two weeks and then continue using one suppository twice a week for a year. This long-term use kills off the roots of the infection before it can re-infect the person.

As an Eyewash: Boric acid makes an easy eye-wash for treating even serious and contagious eye infections. It can also be used for minor eye irritations and common childhood infections such as pink eye and conjunctivitis. It kills the bacterial infection and reduces inflammation. Before using the eyewash, make sure all of your materials are sterile including they eyedropper or eyecup. Sterilize before every use. Follow the recipe below to make the eyewash. Use an eyedropper or eye cup to wash the eye with the sterile eyewash. Blink several times and roll the eyes to be sure the eyewash gets into all the corners of the eye. Repeat three times a day until the infection is cleared.

Athlete's Foot, Nail Fungus: Boric acid is an excellent remedy for athlete's foot and toenail fungus. Dust the boric acid powder onto the foot or nail and put a few sprinkles into your socks each morning. At night, use the Boric Acid Foot Cure (recipe below.) The boric acid kills the infection, neutralizes the odor, and eases the associated itching. Continue to use daily until the infection is completely gone.

Jock Itch: Jock itch also responds well to a dusting of boric acid over the affected area. Apply boric acid in a light dusting, but make sure the entire area is covered. Repeat the application morning and night until the infection is completely cured.

Swimmer's Ear, Ear Infections: To treat swimmer's ear, mix two tablespoons of rubbing alcohol with ¼ teaspoon of boric acid. Mix thoroughly until all the boric acid is dissolved, then drop into the ear. Fill the ear canal, then drain it completely. Treat both ears, even if only one is infected. Do not use for a punctured eardrum.

Recipes. Boric Acid Foot Cure: 1 cup rubbing alcohol, 2 teaspoons of boric acid. Mix the ingredients in a sterile jar with a tight-fitting lid. Apply to the feet with a cotton ball or swab every night. No double dipping. Allow the alcohol to dry on the feet and leave on until morning.

Boric Acid Eye Wash: 1/8 teaspoon pharmaceutical grade boric acid powder. One cup distilled water, boiling. Sterilized jar, lid, and spoon sterilize in a pressure cooker (best), or by boiling for 10 minutes. Place the boiling water into the sterile jar and allow it to cool. Mix the boric acid into the sterilized water and stir it with the sterilized spoon until it is completely dissolved. Use the eyewash up to three times a day, as needed. Always use sterile tools with each use.

Cayenne Pepper

Cayenne is used sparingly as a seasoning agent because of its spicy heat. It is a spice found in most home spice cabinets and has significant medical benefits.

Medicinal Use: Cayenne is a warming herb, heart tonic, and digestive aid. It also releases hormones that improve the mood. It is rich in vitamins and minerals that support the immune system. Use cayenne as a powder, in capsules, added to water for soaking, in rubs, and in salves.

Cayenne is a powerful stimulant and consuming too much can cause stomach problems. A small amount goes a long way with this herb.

Stops Bleeding: Cayenne is a powerful styptic. It helps blood to clot both internally and externally. For small cuts put a thick layer of cayenne directly onto the cut. Large wounds benefit from both external administration and internal use. As soon as the wound is covered in cayenne, drink a glass of water containing one teaspoon of cayenne pepper. It helps the blood clot quickly.

Sore Throats: At the first sign of throat irritation, gargle several times a day with 10 to 20 drops of Cayenne Infusion mixed into a glass of water. It works if you can stand the heat.

Colds and Flu: Cayenne is an excellent supportive preventative and remedy for colds and the flu. I help bring down fevers and expel mucus. It works best in combination with other herbs such as Echinacea, goldenseal, and marshmallow.

Poor Circulation, Warming the Hands and Feet: Cayenne is an effective herb for increasing circulation and for warming cold hands and feet.
Sprinkle a powder made from equal parts cayenne and dried ginger powder into your shoes or socks. Cayenne can be used alone, but it is often too irritating. Use only a pinch, approximately 1/8 teaspoon at most.

Another remedy is to add five drops of Cayenne Infusion to a foot bath of warm water. You can also rub Cayenne Oil or Salve on the hands and feet, taking care not to touch your eyes.

Achy Joints, Arthritis, and Muscle Strains:
Cayenne salve works well for achy muscles and joints. The pepper increases blood circulation to the area and warms it naturally. It soothes and relaxes the muscles and helps relieve pain. Rub a small amount of Cayenne Salve over ache muscles and painful joints regularly for relief.

General Tonic and Immune Booster: Take Cayenne Infusion added to a cup of vegetable juice or water as a general tonic. It improves whole body blood circulation and gives the immune system a boost. Take the infusion once or twice a day, as needed.

Diabetes and Blood Sugar Control: Cayenne has a significant effect on blood sugar levels and can help bring them down in diabetic patients. Take one capsule of cayenne powder with each meal. The cayenne must be taken regularly to give the best effects, which increase over time. Hypoglycemic patients should avoid the use of cayenne in foods and supplements.

Warning: Use gloves when preparing this herb. Do not touch your eyes after using it.

Recipes. Cayenne Infusion: 1 teaspoon dried cayenne powder, 1-pint (0.5 Liters) water. Mix the cayenne powder and water together in a small pot and bring to a boil. Turn off the heat and let the infusion cool. This infusion should always be used diluted. For most uses, a few drops of Cayenne Infusion added to a cup of water is enough. It can also be used topically.

Cold and Flu Prevention Capsules: Mix together thoroughly. Not to be used by people with Autoimmune Issues due to the Echinacea and Goldenseal. 1/4 cup Echinacea root powder, 1/4 cup goldenseal root powder, 2 tablespoons marshmallow root powder, 1 to 2 tablespoons cayenne powder. Pack the powder into large gelatin or vegetable capsules. I use the "00" size. If you use smaller capsules, increase the dosage. Store the capsules in a glass jar with a tight lid. To Use: Take 2 capsules every 2 to 3 hours at the first sign of symptoms. Continue this dosage for the first two days, then reduce the dosage to 2 capsules, 3 times daily until all symptoms are gone.

Cayenne Salve: Use this salve with care. Wash your hands very well after applying it and do not touch your eyes! ½ cup olive oil, 1 tablespoon dried cayenne pep-per flakes, 2 tablespoons beeswax, 3 to 4 drops winter-green essential oil. Place the olive oil and cayenne flakes into the top of a double boiler. Bring the water in the bottom of the double boiler to a simmer.

Simmer the pepper and oil mixture for 60 minutes, keeping an eye on the water levels in the bottom of the double boiler. Remove the oil from the heat and allow it to cool slightly, strain the pepper flakes out and dis-card. Return the oil to the heat and add the beeswax. Stir until the beeswax is completely melted, then re-move from the heat. Add the wintergreen essential oil and stir well. Pour the salve into a suitable container with a tight-fitting lid.

Warming Ginger Cayenne Salve and Mas-sage Oil: This salve is a great choice for muscle pains, arthritis and achy joints, bruises, and other deep tissue pains.

Warming Ginger Cayenne Massage Oil: 1 cup of olive oil, coconut oil, or other carrier oil, 1 table-spoon cayenne pepper powder, 1 tablespoon ginger root, dried and powdered, 1 tablespoon arnica flowers. Add the cayenne, ginger root, and arnica to the oil in a jar with a tight-fitting lid. Shake well. Place the jar in a warm place like a sunny window for 4 to 6 weeks, shaking daily. Strain the oil through a coffee filter to remove the herbs.

Warming Ginger Cayenne Salve: 1 cup Warming Ginger Cayenne Massage Oil, ¼ cup beeswax, shaved, chopped, or shredded. Combine the beeswax and massage oil in the top of a double boiled. Warm gently until the beeswax is melted. Stir the salve to completely combine the wax and oil. Pour into wide-mouth jars or tins to cool. When hardened, cover and store in a cool, dark place.

Massage a small amount of salve into sore muscles and joints 2-3x/day. It can take a few weeks to get maxi-mum results. Do not use on face or mucous mem-branes or open cuts or wounds. Do not use with pregnant or nursing patients. Wash your hands thoroughly with soap after use.

Cinnamon

Cinnamon is a spice taken from the inner bark of various species of the Cinnamon tree (genus *Cin-namomum*). There are two different kinds of cinnamon: Cassia and Ceylon. Both are beneficial, but the type you should use is controversial. Cassia cinnamon contains coumarin in higher amounts, which can be harmful in high doses. For this reason, Ceylon is often preferred as a supplement.

In my research and experience, Ceylon cinnamon may have more antioxidants and is often touted as the best for medicinal use; however, Cassia has more benefits for treating diabetes and controlling blood sugar. For general use, I prefer Ceylon, but for diabetes control, I prefer Cassia.

Medicinal Use: For medicinal use and preventative care, the common suggested dose for "true cinnamon" (Ceylon) is 1-2 grams of cinnamon with each meal. You can add it to a smoothie or food, use it in tea, or put it in capsules for easy consumption. Each capsule will hold about 500 mg, tightly packed, so take 2-4 capsules with each meal if needed.

Diabetes and Blood Sugar Control: Cassia cinnamon dramatically lowers fasting blood sugar levels and improves insulin sensitivity with consistent use. Taking 1 to 6 grams of cinnamon daily is enough to show beneficial effects immediately and full effects over time (6 grams is approximately 2 teaspoons).

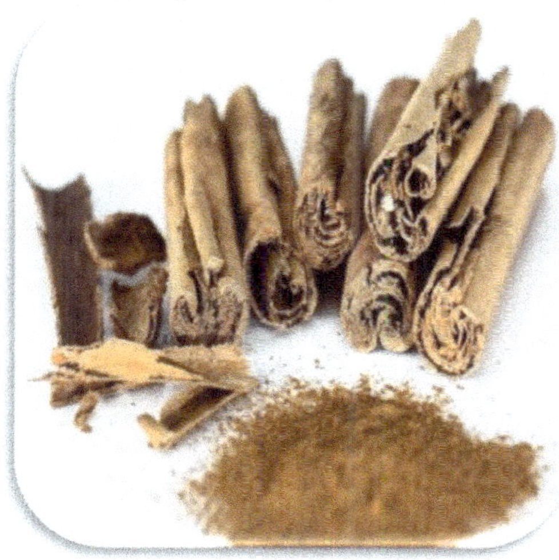

Cinnamon improves sensitivity to insulin, a key hormone in regulating metabolism and blood sugar. In some metabolic conditions, the body may become insulin resistant. By increasing insulin sensitivity, cinnamon lowers blood sugar levels and helps prevent or treat diabetes. Additionally, cinnamon decreases the amount of glucose that enters your bloodstream after a meal. It slows the breakdown of carbohydrates and prevents blood sugar spikes. Another compound in cinnamon acts like insulin to improve glucose uptake in the cells. Care is needed as cinnamon may cause blood sugar levels to drop too low.

Reduces Triglycerides and Cholesterol: 1 to 6 grams of cinnamon lowers triglycerides and "bad" LDL-cholesterol. The full effects are seen over time, but one to two months of use should bring triglyceride and cholesterol levels down significantly.

Neurodegenerative Diseases: Parkinson's and Alzheimer's: Cinnamon has been shown to protect the neurons in the brain. Animal studies have found that it helps normalize neurotransmitter levels, which could help improve motor function in Parkinson's patients. It also has two compounds (cinnamaldehyde and epicatechin) that inhibit the buildup of brain proteins (called "tau") that are found in Alzheimer's patients. We do not have human research on these processes yet; however, it is easy to add cinnamon, along with turmeric and other brain protecting herbs, to the daily diet.

Anti-Inflammatory: Cinnamon is loaded with antioxidants and anti-inflammatory compounds that fight free radicals and help lower your risk of disease.

Heart Disease: Because of its antioxidants and anti-inflammatory compounds, cinnamon can help re-duce the risk of heart disease. It reduces blood pressure, triglycerides, and cholesterol, which contribute to heart disease.

HIV: Cassia cinnamon helps the body's fight against HIV-1, the most common HIV form in humans.

Anti-Bacterial and Anti-Fungal: Evidence shows that cinnamon inhibits the growth of some bacteria, including Salmonella and Listeria on surfaces, especially when cinnamon oil is used. We have no data on whether cinnamon will treat internal infections.

Warning: Coumarin may increase cancer risk in animals. More research in needed for humans. Coumarin may also cause liver damage in large amounts. Some people have an allergy to cinnamaldehyde, a com-pound found in cinnamon. The reaction usually presents as mouth sores. As always, please check with your doctor for possible medication interactions.

Diatomaceous Earth

Diatomaceous earth (DE) is composed of fossils formed by tiny algae-like organisms called diatoms. It is a slightly abrasive powder that is safe for consumption by humans and animals. It has health and medicinal benefits to the body. Be sure that your DE is marked as food-grade. Non-food grade DE is not safe for human consumption.

How to Take Diatomaceous Earth: Mix one teaspoon full of diatomaceous earth in a glass of water. Drink it one hour before eating or two hours after eating. Repeat this dose for 10 days, then wait another 10 days before repeating the cycle. Do this for 5 full cycles of 10 days on and 10 days off. Diatomaceous earth can also remove medications from the body, so check with your doctor before use if you are taking medications.

Medicinal Use. Diatomaceous Earth Detoxifies the Body: Diatomaceous earth holds a negative ionic charge. This causes it to attract positively charged toxins and heavy metals, helping to flush them out of the bloodstream and the body.

Kills Parasites: Diatomaceous earth naturally kills parasites and viruses in the digestive tract. By using the 10 days on and 10 days off schedule, it kills parasites in all stages of the reproductive cycle, ending the infestation.

Improves Joint and Bone Health: DE is a natural source of silica and other trace minerals required by the body. Silica is essential for healthy joints, ligaments, and bones.

Encourages Heart Health: Diatomaceous Earth helps lower cholesterol and blood pressure, which encourages a healthy heart and circulatory system.

Clean Teeth: DE is an abrasive that is safe to use as a toothpaste.

Other Uses: Diatomaceous earth has many uses around the home. One of its most valuable household and garden uses is in killing fleas, bedbugs, cock-roaches, spiders and other insects. You only need to dust it in the areas where infestations exist. It is completely safe with kids and pets. It is also valuable as an abrasive cleanser, an absorbent, deodorizer, and in water filtration.

Warning: Diatomaceous earth is a fine abrasive powder. It can be harmful if inhaled or if it gets in the eyes. Wear proper protective clothing when using.

Recipes. DE Toothpaste: ½ cup of diatomaceous earth, ½ cup coconut oil, 1 to 2 drops peppermint essential oil, vegetable glycerin, as desired for texture. Mix together and use as toothpaste.

Epsom Salts

Epsom salts is a crystalline mineral salt with the chemcal formula MgSO4. When mixed with water, the salt breaks down into magnesium, sulfur, and oxygen.

All of these are beneficial for the body and can be absorbed through the skin, one of the reasons that Epsom salt baths and foot soaks are so popular. It is also a powerful anti-inflammatory used to treat muscle sore-ness and skin inflammations.

Medicinal Use. Epsom Salts Treat Magnesium Deficiency, Stress, and Benefits the Body Systems and Chronic Diseases: An Epsom salt bath is a good way to de-stress and treat a number of health issues at the same time. Magnesium is a mineral that is vital to health, yet many people are deficient. An Epsom salt bath allows the magnesium to be absorbed by the body and is beneficial for the heart, bones, muscles, and other organs.

Epsom salt baths are beneficial for treating any disease that might cause or result from a magnesium deficiency, especially chronic diseases like heart disease and arrhythmias, osteoporosis, chronic fatigue syndrome, arthritis, and some mental illness.

Detoxifying the Body: The dissolved sulfur in an Epsom salt bath helps the body flush out toxins. It pulls toxins and heavy metals out of the body.

Reduces Inflammation: A soak in Epsom salt also reduces inflammation and pain in sore muscles, swellings, and skin inflammations. A long soak has the ability to reduce swelling and pain almost immediately.

To Benefit from an Epsom Salt Soak: To receive all of these benefits, soak in an Epsom salt bath for at least 40 minutes to 1 hour. Use two cups or more of Epsom salt in a full bath tub of warm water. For a foot soak, add 2 tablespoons of Epsom salt per gallon (4 Liters) of warm water. To aid the detoxifying process, drink plenty of water before, during, and after the soak.

Listerine

Listerine is a combination of alcohol and essential oils that are good for killing bacteria and fungus on the body. In addition to sanitizing the mouth and sweetening the breath, it is useful for killing bacteria and fungus in wounds and on the skin.

Medicinal Use. Get Rid of Lice: Listerine can be used to kill lice in the hair. Apply Listerine to the scalp and hair, soaking it well. Cover it with a disposable shower cap and leave it on for 2 hours. Wash and rinse like usual. Use a lice comb to remove the nits.

Get Rid of Ticks: To get a tick to turn loose soak a cotton ball or pad with Listerine and use it to cover the tick for 10 to 15 seconds. The tick will usually let go quickly and can be removed with tweezers.

Treat Itchy Skin: Listerine treats pain and itchy skin caused by bug bites, bee stings, poison ivy, allergies, psoriasis, and acne. It sanitizes the area, reduces pain, and relieves the itch temporarily.

Clean Blisters and Wounds: Clean wounds and blisters with Listerine to keep them from getting infected. The Listerine kills bacteria on the skin surface. Repeat several times daily to keep the wound clean.

Toe and Nail Fungus: Add a cup of Listerine to your foot soak to treat nail fungus. Soak daily until the fungus clears up completely.

Other Uses. Kills Mold and Mildew: Listerine also kills molds and mildew. Use it in a spray bottle to kill small spots of mold and mildew. Spray the area thoroughly and let it soak in.

Potassium Permanganate

Potassium permanganate is a chemical compound with medicinal use for the cleaning of wounds, treating skin conditions, and disinfecting water. It is a strong oxidizer, capable of starting fires when in con-tact with oxidizable materials.

Medicinal Use. Skin Infections: Potassium permanganate can irritate or even burn the skin when used in strong solutions. It must be carefully prepared into very dilute solutions before use. Only a small amount is needed to provide relief from skin infections including canker sores, ulcers, abscesses, acne, dermatitis, eczema, vaginal thrush, and vulvovaginitis.

Apply a small amount on small wounds and soak larger areas in a very dilute solution. If necessary, a dilute potassium permanganate water bath can be used. Compresses can also be used.

Wound Cleansing: Cleaning wounds with dilute concentrations of potassium permanganate kills bacteria, funguses, and viruses. This prevents wound infections.

Fungal Infections: Fungal infections such as athlete's foot is easily treated by soaking the foot in a di-lute solution of potassium permanganate for about 15 minutes, twice a day, for two or three weeks. These soaks kill or inhibit the growth of the fungus. The patient should be aware that the treatment will temporarily stain the foot brown, but normal color will re-turn when the soaks are finished.

Cholera Prevention: Potassium permanganate is an effective way to sanitize water for drinking.

Clean food and drinking water is necessary to prevent infective diseases such as cholera and dysentery. To

Dissolve one 400 mg tablet or granules in 1 gallon (4 liters) of water. Use the water to soak weeping skin wounds and infections for 1 hour, but no more. Use potassium permanganate as a short-term solution while treating the underlying conditions. Do not use potassium permanganate internally or in the eyes.

Other Uses: Water purification, as described above under preventing cholera. Potassium permanganate is also useful for starting fires. prepare water for drinking with potassium permanganate, add permanganate granules to 1 gallon (4 Liters) of water, one or two at a time, until the water turns pink. Allow the water to sit for 30 minutes before drinking or using. The water is safe to drink while the pink color remains. If the color is purple, you have added too much permanganate and the water is un-safe for drinking. Add more water to dilute it until the color is pink.

How to Prepare: Potassium permanganate must be dissolved and diluted by clean water before using.

Warning: Potassium permanganate is an aggressive oxidizer and will readily start fires when in con-tact with suitable materials. It must be stored in a non-reactive plastic bottle. Strong solutions can cause burns. Dilute the solutions as recommended. Potassium permanganate will stain almost everything it comes into contact with a nice shade of pink or purple.

Raw Honey

Honey is made by bees. It is made up of concentrated flower nectar that bees break down into simple sugars using an enzyme in their salivary glands (invertase). It is then deposited into honeycomb for long-term storage. Honey contains many medicinal qualities taken from the flower. Once the honey has been cooked or diluted, these properties may no longer exist in beneficial quantities. I prefer to use undiluted raw honey, as it contains pollen and parts of the waxen honeycomb in addition to the honey itself.

Honey has a rich medicinal history. It has been used since ancient times for the dressing of wounds and as a cough suppressant.

Medicinal Use. Burn and Wound Healing:
The antibacterial and anti-inflammatory properties of raw honey make it a natural for wound care. It kills germs and helps the wound heal. Use it applied directly to burns, infected wounds, diabetic foot ulcers and other skin conditions such as psoriasis and herpes. You can apply it in a layer directly on the skin or apply it to the bandage before use.

For especially difficult infections and ulcers, the use of Manuka honey is recommended, if available.

Antibacterial, Antimicrobial, and Anti-Inflammatory: Some kinds of honey have more in-tense antibacterial and anti-inflammatory properties than others. In particular, Manuka Honey from New Zealand is known to be very high in these active com-pounds. However, any natural raw honey has these properties in varying amounts.

Cough Suppressant: Honey is a natural cough suppressant. Take a spoonful of honey straight or use it to make a cough syrup infused with beneficial herbs.

Allergies: Local raw honey may help with seasonal allergies. I use it in conjunction with stinging nettle tincture.

Lowers Blood Pressure: When used moderately, in place of sugar, honey may help lower blood pressure. Because of its antioxidant compounds, modest blood pressure reductions can occur when reducing sugar use and replacing it with a small amount of honey. In-stead of sucrose, honey is made up of glucose and fructose, and has a lower glycemic index than sugar.

Lowers Cholesterol and Triglycerides: High LDL-cholesterol is a strong risk factor for heart disease and plays a major role in atherosclerosis. Honey can improve cholesterol levels, lowering the dangerous LDL-cholesterol and increasing the beneficial HDL-cholesterol ratio.

Additionally, replacing sugar with honey lowers tri-glyceride levels, which are associated with insulin resistance and type 2 diabetes.

Warning: Never give raw honey to an infant or child under 1 year old. Their immature immune systems cannot handle the botulism spores, where older children and adults have a natural immunity.

While honey is considered a "healthy" sugar, it is still a sugar and should be used in moderation. It will affect blood sugar and contains the same calories as sugar.

Choose high quality, raw honey. Lower quality brands may be mixed with syrup and may contain very little honey. Unless your honey is marked as "raw", assume that it has been pasteurized.

Turmeric/Curcumin

Turmeric is a spice used to give flavor and color to curry and other foods. It has many known medicinal uses, most derived from the curcuminoid compounds it contains. The main active ingredient in turmeric is curcumin and some brands list the curcumin content on the label, usually around 3% by weight. You can also buy curcumin extracts.

Turmeric, because of its curcumin and other curcuminoid compounds, is a powerful anti-inflammatory and a strong antioxidant. Unfortunately, the curcumin is not well absorbed into the bloodstream. Absorption is helped by the presence of piperine, a compound found in black pepper. Using turmeric with black pepper in-creases the absorption of curcumin by 2,000 percent.

Medicinal Use: Using turmeric in food is beneficial, but food consumption alone is not enough to get the amounts of curcumin needed. For this reason, I mix turmeric with finely ground black pepper when taking it as a supplement. I pack the mixture into capsules and take 1 to 4 grams (2 to 8 capsules) daily.

Anti-Inflammatory: Acute, short-term inflammation is beneficial and helps signal your body of an invading virus or bacterium. However, when inflammation becomes chronic, it is the root of many modern chronic illnesses. Calming chronic inflammation is vi-tally important.

Turmeric is strongly anti-inflammatory and is as effective as many anti-inflammatory drugs, without their side effects. It is my # 1 go to for internal inflammation.

Antioxidant: Oxidative damage is one of the mechanisms that promotes aging and many diseases. Cur-cumin fights free radicals that cause oxidative damage and protects the body. It also boosts the body's own antioxidant enzymes.

Improves Brain Function and Lowers Risk of Brain Diseases, Including Alzheimer's Disease & Depression.

Curcumin can increase the levels of brain-derived neurotrophic factor (BDNF), which is a growth hormone for the brain. Many brain diseases, including Alzheimer's Disease and depression, are linked to decreasing levels of the BDNF hormone. Increasing BDNF levels with curcumin can effectively delay or possibly reverse many age-related brain function diseases.

By increasing BDNF, curcumin may also improve memory and cognitive performance by increasing the growth of new neurons and fighting degenerative processes in the brain.

Alzheimer's disease is characterized by a buildup of amyloid plaques in the brain. Curcumin crosses the blood-brain barrier and helps clear these plaques. Long-term use is required.

Arthritis and Pain: Curcumin supplements are beneficial in reducing the inflammation in arthritis and slowing or stopping the progress of the disease. Patients report the improvement of symptoms and a reduction in joint inflammation, as well as a reduction in pain.

Cancer. Prevention and Treatment: Studies show that curcumin affects cancer growth, development, and spread at the molecular level. It promotes the death of cancerous cells and reduces the growth of new blood vessels that feed tumors. It also reduces the spread of cancer and inhibits its growth.

Lowers the Risk of Heart Disease: Because of its powerful anti-inflammatory properties, turmeric can lower your risk of heart disease. It improves the function of blood vessels, the regulation of blood pressure, and blood clotting. Studies show that taking 4 grams of curcumin per day decreases the risk of a heart attack.

Reduces Cholesterol Levels: Using turmeric, especially when eating fatty foods, helps reduce blood cholesterol levels, including the dangerous LDL cholesterol levels.

Promotes Wound Healing: Turmeric is effective as a disinfectant and reduces healing time in wounds. Apply turmeric as a powder, directly to the wounded area.

Warning: Turmeric may slow the clotting of the blood. People taking blood-thinners and pregnant women should be especially careful.

www.ingramcontent.com/pod-product-compliance
Ingram Content Group UK Ltd.
Pitfield, Milton Keynes, MK11 3LW, UK
UKHW060801021225
9322UKWH00021B/267

9 782844 738400